While America Sleeps

While America Sleeps

♦

How Islam, Immigration and Indoctrination Are Destroying America From Within

Wells Earl Draughon

iUniverse, Inc.
New York Lincoln Shanghai

While America Sleeps
How Islam, Immigration and Indoctrination Are Destroying America From Within

Copyright © 2007 by Wells Earl Draughon

All rights reserved. No part of this book may be used or reproduced by any means, graphic, electronic, or mechanical, including photocopying, recording, taping or by any information storage retrieval system without the written permission of the publisher except in the case of brief quotations embodied in critical articles and reviews.

iUniverse books may be ordered through booksellers or by contacting:

iUniverse
2021 Pine Lake Road, Suite 100
Lincoln, NE 68512
www.iuniverse.com
1-800-Authors (1-800-288-4677)

The views expressed in this work are solely those of the author and do not necessarily reflect the views of the publisher, and the publisher hereby disclaims any responsibility for them.

ISBN-13: 978-0-595-43524-1 (pbk)
ISBN-13: 978-0-595-87850-5 (ebk)
ISBN-10: 0-595-43524-6 (pbk)
ISBN-10: 0-595-87850-4 (ebk)

Printed in the United States of America

They thought, because I could see their point of view, that like them, I could not see any other.

—John Stuart Mill
Autobiography

Contents

Preface ix
A wolf in sheep's clothing 1
An Economy in Hock 26
La Reconquista 35
Abolishing Self-defense 60
Subordinating Ourselves 75
Subordinating Our Culture 91
Subordinating Our Country 99
An Ideology of Submission 105
Enforcing the Ideology 111
Disabling Americans 126
Spreading the Ideology 147
Can America Be Saved? 181
Reclaiming the Individual 193
Reclaiming the Economy 205
Reclaiming the Government 211
If All Else Fails 215
Endnotes 221

Preface

Nations on top are always in favor of peace. Nations on bottom are in favor of war. American politicians believe that every nation in the world wants what they want: world peace, a global economy, and a united federation of nations. Their own politicians say they do. American politicians believe them.

Our politicians believe that every nation values what we value: basic decency, individual freedom, and social justice for all. They do not realize that these other nations and the individuals in them usually have quite different values, and that these Western values are alien to them. These nations are trying to better their condition; and playing along with America, the top nation, is one of the realities of their situation. Why shouldn't they do this? And why shouldn't we expect them to do exactly this? Since America is where the goods are, the United States occupies a central place in their goals, schemes and envy. Different people and different nations are making use of America in different ways. Some are asking. Others are taking.

All the while, Americans look around, and everything appears as peaceful as ever. The houses across the street are still charming and cozy. The people on the sitcoms are still confronting their little annoyances with amusing consternation. There are multiple spectator sports to choose from. Who is going to believe "alarmist" cries that America is facing the most severe threats in its entire history and heading into a period in which everyday life will be worse than during the War Between the States or the Great Depression? It doesn't make sense.

But what if the pictures on TV, even on the news, are woefully incomplete? What if the scene across the street is not indicative of what is going on elsewhere all over the country? This book is a nonpartisan status report that gives the big picture of what the trends and threats are and how they are functioning to bring about the decline and fall of the United States of America.

A wolf in sheep's clothing

On Patriot's Day, April 19th, 1995, one-year-old Baylee Almon[1] was in a daycare center in Oklahoma City. At 9:02 A.M., the Murrah Building exploded. As hundreds of parents, passersby, policemen and firemen raced to dig through the rubble for survivors, the baby girl was scooped up by a police sergeant and handed, still breathing, to a fireman. As the fireman was carrying her to safety, Baylee Almon died. A photographer snapped a picture of the fireman cradling the naked infant in his arms. The photo appeared on the front pages of newspapers throughout the Western world. Something had changed in America, something fundamental.

On July 17, 1996, sixteen-year-old Cheryl Nibert[2] left her Pennsylvania home with fifteen of her fellow French Club members and their five chaperones and traveled three hours on a bus to JFK airport in New York. All were excited. They were actually going to Paris! They would see the Eiffel Tower and the Arc de Triomphe and the Louvre! At 8:30 P.M. Cheryl and her friends were comfortably seated aboard a 747 ready to take off on TWA Flight 800. But Cheryl and her friends would never see Paris. Nor would they ever see their mothers and fathers again. Somebody had a plan for a greater scheme of things, and Cheryl was not part of that plan.

Twenty-five year old Lynn Goodchild lived with her brother in Attleboro, Massachusetts. She and her boyfriend, Shawn, decided to take a vacation to Maui, Hawaii before starting to work on their MBA degrees. She had met him in college four years before and they had traveled together several times. She woke early on September 11, 2001, drove to Logan Airport in Boston, and together they boarded United Airlines Flight 175. The flight was to take Lynn to Los Angeles. Instead, the plane took her to New York to the World Trade Center.[3] A great and important movement had begun to roll in America, and Lynn was in the way.

Bob Stevens was a photo-editor for a newspaper in Florida and happened to be in the wrong place at the time a letter was delivered to the newspaper. The letter contained anthrax. On September 27, 2001, Bob began to feel feverish and had no appetite. On October 2, he woke up nauseated and confused. He was taken to a local emergency room, disoriented and sweating, and admitted to the hospital. He died after three more days of suffering.[4] Most Americans would say that Bob was an innocent victim of biological terrorism, but others would say that he wasn't innocent at all. He was guilty of not believing in the right religion.

Religion. Given their Western culture with its presuppositions about what a religion is, Americans do not believe what they read about Islam. Honest presentations strike them as a vicious lie or at best an expression of extreme bias. At the same time, Islamists in America present a Westernized version of their religion that is credible to Americans and much more acceptable.

Muslims on the other hand, untroubled by Western assumptions and values, do not find their religion shocking or outrageous at all.

This ethnocentrism on the part of Americans is very useful to Islamists.

TAQIYYA

Taqiyya is the doctrine of dissembling or duplicity or a "white lie," which is justified provided it advances the cause of Islam.[5] There is even lying regarding *taqiyya* itself: most Muslims in America claim that there is no such doctrine.

Since we are being asked not to believe the ancient Islamic documents advocating *taqiyya*, all we can conclude is that we do not know one way or the other whether Islamists practice dissembling and the telling of lies or not. That being the case, the question becomes: would it be safer to assume that every claim Islamists make about their doctrines, policies and goals is true or to conclude that we should proceed with caution when confronting those claims?

If we adopt the more cautious approach, then we must take claims by Muslims about what Islam really commands with a grain of salt, especially when they contradict the rather blunt statements in the Quran. The same applies to statements by Muslims condemning books expounding Islam's doctrines.

Some examples of *taqiyya* are:

Islam is a religion of peace. This is true, but only after all people have been converted to Islam.[6] Until then, war is not only permitted but required. It does not have to be constant war. Signing peace treaties is permissible to give the faithful time to gain in strength. Dissembling is likewise permissible to gain a foothold in the infidel's nation, to infiltrate the infidel's organizations or army or government.

Muslims are enjoined from killing innocents. This is true, but according to a literal reading of the Quran, unbelievers are not considered innocent. Even the killing of women and children is excused if it is a side-effect of holy war. Even killing faithful Muslims is excused as a side-effect of holy war: they will be rewarded as martyrs in the hereafter.

Jihad means merely inner struggle. This is true, but only after all people have been converted to Islam or killed and there is no more need of violent war. Until then, inner struggle is needed to gather courage to take up the sword for Allah or to blow oneself up for Islam.

No doctrine of Islam has been more strenuously denied that jihad. In the wake of 9/11, this display of *taqiyya* is understandable. "Islamists seeking to advance their agenda within Western, non-Muslim environments—for example, as lobbyists in Washington, DC—cannot frankly divulge their views and still remain players in the political game."[7] "Non-Muslim colleagues who play along with this deception may be seen as having effectively assumed the role of dhimmi, the Islamic term for a Christian or Jew living under Muslim rule who is tolerated so long as he bends the knee and accepts Islam's superiority."[8]

Is jihad peaceful? The millions of people who were and continue to be the victims of jihad have their own opinion about how peaceful jihad is.[9]

Terrorism has nothing to do with Islam. Another application of *taqiyya* is to separate terrorism from Islam. "After all, goes the dogma, terrorism isn't an Islamic problem. Islam is a supremely tolerant faith. No, terrorism is a problem of political grievances or socioeconomic imbalances."[10] And in a masterpiece of understatement, this observer comments: "If this dogma [that Islam is peaceful] is false [and people believe it anyway], its destructive power will be very great."[11]

Jihad is separate and apart from Islam. Jihad is commanded by Islam. Jihad makes no sense apart from Islam. It is Islam that makes the war holy, Islam that offers the rewards for holy war in an afterlife. Without Islam, there is no jihad.

Example. By way of illustrating the use of *taqiyya* by Islamists, the CAIR organization on its website after September 11, 2001, had a message inviting all who wanted to donate money to the victims to send it to the Holy Land Foundation. (The Holy Land Foundation was one of the Islamic organizations that financed the attacks of 9/11.)[12] Contrary to the official newsletters written in English for the consumption of journalists and U. S. government officials which called for an open, diverse society, the message delivered in Arabic in mosques is "Let us damn America."[13] "Islam isn't in America to be equal to any other faith, but to become dominant. The Koran … should be the highest authority in America, and Islam the only accepted religion on earth."[14]

The way to find out what people really believe is to look at their actions. In the wake of September 11, 2001, people in the Muslim world took to the streets shouting "God is great!" An Egyptian newspaper said, "Millions across the world shouted in joy." Another paper wrote, "I am happy about the American dead."[15] These are curious reactions for a people supposedly committed to peace. It is a commonplace in the Muslim world to refer to America as "the Great Satan." Does a good Muslim make peace with Satan?

The obsession of American and European politicians "with the Arab-Palestinian conflict has obscured the criminal ongoing persecution of Christians and other minorities in Muslim lands worldwide, as well as the sufferings and slavery of millions from jihad wars in Africa and Asia."[16]

KEY DIFFERENCES BETWEEN WESTERN THOUGHT AND ISLAM

Any exposition of Mohammedanism is immediately hampered by the fact that unless it is completely flattering of Islam or helps to further the spread of Islam, any statements about Islam are attacked as a misrepresentation or a mistranslation. Some of these denials resemble those by American politicians caught in the act of deceiving the people. Others resemble the "Big Lie" technique: telling a lie so brazen that people believe it because they don't think anyone would say such an improbable thing if it weren't true.

The doctrines of Islam are contained in the Quran, which contains alleged revelations of Allah to the prophet Mohammad, and the *Hadiths*, the sayings and doings of Mohammad. These sacred texts regulate personal, social, political and legal activities of the faithful. The law is called *Sharia*.

Islamic ethics is what ethicists call "deontological," meaning that certain acts are right in and of themselves, in this case, those acts commanded by Islam. All other acts are wrong. It is not a Utilitarian or a Consequentialist ethics. Hence, appeals to unfortunate consequences of actions have no effect. This also means that there is no basis for arguing or even discussing the rightness or wrongness of the acts commanded by Islam. Insofar as there *is* an end, it is the worldwide triumph of Islam, and it is a given and not open to discussion. Any and all actions that further this end are not only permissible but required. This end justifies all means.

Hence, notions of individual freedom are neither compatible with Islam nor comprehensible to it.

Reasoning about the Quran and Hadiths is forbidden. "Dispute about the Quran is infidelity."

No man-made law is legitimate. Only the laws of Islam are. Hence, the state must be a theocracy ruled by Allah's regent on earth. The notion of popular sovereignty therefore is heretical. Hence, democracy and Islam are incompatible *in principle*. (The new constitution of Iraq sanctioned by the U. S. explicitly makes Sharia the law of the land.) Owing allegiance to a secular non-Islamic state would be an act of apostasy. Apostasy is to be punished by death.

The statements below come straight out of the Islamic holy scriptures. Still, Muslims deny that these statements in the holy writ say what they say. The usual dodges are misinterpretation and mistranslation. But the statements are so bald-faced that there is little room for interpretation or for translator license.

Making friends with Jews and Christians is forbidden.[17]

War is mandatory until Islam is established throughout the world.[18]

Belief in and acceptance of Islam is enforced by a carrot and a stick. The stick consists of vivid pictures of torture in the life after death and in the threat of being beheaded, stoned or beaten in this life. The carrot is the promise to the faithful of paradise, including virgins, in the hereafter.[19] What women would do with the virgins is unclear, but men are promised the manliness of a hundred mortals to enjoy their virginal rewards.[20] Fighting in a holy war is a no-lose situation: either you win the war or you win paradise with all its sensual pleasures, including the virgins.[21] Muslims in America, of course, deny that the Arabic word for "virgin" means virgin.

Fatwa. The most prominent use of the fatwa is to place on a death list persons who disagree with the fundamentals of Islam or who disobey. This is different from a Mafia contract. A contract on a person means that some specific person or persons are detailed to kill someone. A *fatwa* means that every Muslim everywhere has a sacred duty to kill the particular person.

Blasphemy. "Blasphemy includes denigration of ... the Muslim faith ... by suggesting that it has a defect."[22]

What all of the above add up to is *not* an incompatibility between Western democracy and Islam *at the present time* which could be overcome or resolved by discussion, but an *absolute* incompatibility or incompatibility *in principle*. To "assimilate" to Western culture, a Muslim would have to apostatize from Islam. Apparent assimilations, therefore, are more likely to be applications of the principle of *taqiyya*.

On a psychological level, the above paints a picture of the authoritarian personality or closed-minded individual. (More about this mental phenomenon in a later chapter.)

The question of moderate Muslims. An attempt is made to distinguish militant Muslims from moderate Muslims or Fundamentalism from Islam proper. But "fundamentalism" means getting back to fundamentals, ridding a religion of additions and heresies. Just because a modified Islam might be more to *our* liking does not make it the real Islam. A former Muslim writes, "And I mean Islam, I do not accept some spurious distinction between Islam and 'Islamic fundamentalism' or 'Islamic terrorism.'"[23]

The work of a Christian Arab professor, Edward Said of Columbia, in 1978 was a stroke of genius. In this influential work, he established the now accepted practice of vilifying anyone who says Islam is not tolerant as a *racist*, a Western *imperialist*, and a prejudiced *ethnocentric*. No one seemed to notice that this move was itself a demonstration of intolerance.

Islamists themselves take a more direct approach: in emails and other communications they make it clear to those who question Islamic tolerance that "you must say that Islam is peaceful and tolerant, or we will kill you."[24]

It's all Israel's fault. One anthology contains numerous documents from the United Nations Commission on Human Rights which "reveal the stark realities of Islam's human rights record."[25] "The human rights records of Iran, Sudan, Pakistan, and elsewhere, and the enormous obstacles that Muslim freethinkers [moderates?] and apostates face ... illuminate a deeper problem of ingrained Islamic intolerance.... [They] show conclusively that the source of the conflict that the Islamic world has with the non-Muslim world is not Israel; Israel acts only as the canary in the mineshaft."[26]

Are there moderate Muslims? In a nation such as the United States, where Muslims are a minority, every Muslim claims to be moderate. Muslims suspected of terrorism, Muslims convicted of terrorism—all claim to be moderates. But think about it: Would a Muslim who is not moderate tell anyone that he is not moderate? So, how can we know? Individual cases certainly exist, such as Rushdie, but these individuals immediately get placed on a death list. These individual cases may be the exceptions that prove the rule.

What are the doctrines of moderate Islam? Nobody spells it out, although a lot of vague and flattering claims are made. If we don't know what the moderate Muslims believe and what commandments they follow, how do we know whether or not to rejoice that there are moderates? One Muslim was put on the death list for the sin of winning the Nobel Prize for Literature. He was stabbed on a street in Cairo. Apparently, it does not pay to be moderate.

On the Western side, it is possible that the government insistence that there are moderate Muslims might be a ploy to drive a wedge between terrorists and the rest of the Muslims, insinuating that most Muslims should distinguish themselves (distance themselves) from the terrorists. But the terrorists have scripture on their side, and scripture is a powerful force in the Islamic world. Even "moderates" want their share of the goodies in the hereafter.

To be fair, let's say what is certainly true, that we do not know whether or not there are moderate Muslims. Political statements by American politicians that there definitely *are* moderate Muslims are either wishful thinking or a strategic move designed to appeal to Muslims. Since we do not and cannot know, the question is: Would it be safer to act under the assumption that most Muslims are moderate or to act under the assumption that most Muslims are not moderate or somewhere in between?

Everyone agrees that moderates are a minority (one self-designated moderate Muslim put the figure at 20%) and their numbers are getting smaller.[27] One self-designated moderate Muslim says that Muslim schools are removing everything from their curricula except Islam.[28] In any case, in an Islamic takeover, which side would these alleged "moderates" be on?

AN IDEOLOGY OF DOMINANCE

"Islam is the religion of masters and rulers. Christianity is the religion of slaves."[29] During most of its thirteen centuries, Islam has been the dominant military power in the Western world. Up through the eighteenth century, coastal towns in Italy, France, Spain and even England and Ireland were attacked, and men, women and children abducted and sold as slaves in Tripoli, Tunis, Algiers, and other north African cities.[30] The enslavement of abducted Christian women still continues today "in Pakistan, Sudan, Indonesia and Egypt."[31]

"European Christian lands, Islamized by jihad, were liberated only after centuries of bloody struggle. The process of de-Islamization began in the Middle Ages, first in Spain, Portugal, and the Mediterranean Islands; it then continued in the eighteenth century and through the whole of the nineteenth century in the Balkans. In central Europe, Islamized territories had reached up to southern Poland and Hungary; in the nineteenth century they still encompassed Greece, Serbia, Montenegro, Bulgaria and the semiautonomous Romanian principalities. These wars of national liberation continued up to World War I."[32]

The shift in power gained momentum in the nineteenth century when France conquered Morocco and Algeria, England established control over Egypt, and the Greeks fought for and won their independence from the Turkish Empire. As we all know, in the late twentieth century, the predominance of power shifted back again to Islam. So, the "American imperialism" that we hear so much about, even if it exists, was only a brief interlude in the thirteen hundred years of Islamic imperialism.

Islam, as envisioned in the Quran, is a species of benevolent dictatorship complete with The Leader (in Italian "*Il Duce*", in German "*Der Fuhrer*"). The Leader is Mohammad, whose spokesmen are the *Imams* of each mosque throughout the world. The Quran and the Hadiths are the standing orders of this religious-social-political-military system. Disobeying orders is punishable by death. It is not only treason but a sin. The leader of Iran, for one, has made explicit his goal of a global nation of Islam, as commanded by the Quran.[33] Many others have said the same.

This is not to say that the Imams are like Hitler or Mussolini. The Imams, being spiritual as well as temporal leaders, have a degree of power that the Nazis and Fascists could only dream of having.

Most people, in spite of all the counterpropaganda and disinformation, hazard the guess that religionists who blow people up, chop people's heads off and the like in the name of their religion, probably do not belong to a religion of peace. Instead, they are inclined to believe that the Arabic word "jihad" really does mean what some passages in the Quran say it means: the sacred obligation to make holy war.

What is less widely known is that jihad comprises more methods and actions than what we in America normally think of as war. All of these methods are being used concurrently in America, Europe and throughout the world, and they reinforce each other.[34]

Terrorism. Acts of violence are not only permissible but obligatory provided the purpose is to spread Islam: to convert as many as possible, to subjugate and heavily tax others,[35] and to kill the rest. This obligation of domination is fulfilled only when all persons on the planet Earth have either been converted or killed or have submitted. Those who submit to Islam are called *Dhimma*.

"Terrorism is not a consequence of poverty. Many societies are poor, yet they do not produce an organized criminality of terror. To subsidize societies that nourish ideologies of hate will not suppress terrorism; rather, such pusillanimity will reinforce it."[36]

Economic jihad. Weakening the infidel by undermining his economy is a useful practice which can be and has been used in conjunction with violent jihad. When the infidel has been sufficiently weakened, then open warfare to subjugate him has a better chance of success.

The downing of TWA Flight 800 on July 17, 1996 is a case in point.[37] Had the strike become publicly known as a terrorist attack, it would have resulted in a substantial drop in air travel which would have had a severe economic impact on the airlines. As it was, the attack on the World Trade Center on September 11, 2001 had the desired economic result. Similarly, the mailing of letters containing anthrax did comparatively little physical damage, but the economic impact on the Postal Service was substantial.

And the result of both was the so-called "War on Terror," which is costing billions of dollars, not counting the invasion and occupation of Afghanistan and Iraq. The result has been a soaring national debt.

The use of oil as an economic and political weapon will be discussed in the next chapter.

Infiltration. Infiltration of the infidel to gain access to useful information and provide a means of influencing events is another method of jihad. To date, Islamists have infiltrated the FBI, the Department of Homeland Security, the White House, corporations (including those providing airport security), prisons, and the military.[38] They have been taken on tours of nuclear facilities, including those making nuclear weapons.[39]

Population expansion. A larger population means more people to carry out all of the various forms of Jihad. A majority in American districts, of course, means acquiring elective offices. Long before that, however, Muslims can acquire significant power over politicians, as has happened in a number of Congressional districts, since large minorities can sway elections.[40]

The birthrate of Muslims is five times as fast as that of American "white" people. This does not include the flood of Muslims coming into this country. Thus, the increase in power is inevitable unless immigration policies change—which is extremely unlikely. There is no guesswork about it. To illustrate: as recently as twenty years ago, people scoffed at demographers predicting Hispanic majorities in New Mexico and California. This has now come to pass. Muslims are well on the way to becoming majorities in various Congressional districts.

Public relations. "Islam has an image problem."[41] Influencing the beliefs, opinions and expectations of the infidels is "jihad of the pen,"[42] an important method of jihad. It has been given prominent attention by jihadists.

A number of organizations have been established to put out favorable propaganda about Muslims and to guard against and punish unfavorable media. The names of these organizations change frequently as one or another of them is caught engaging in terror-related activities and put out of business, while others spring up overnight. The Council on American-Islamic Relations or CAIR[43] is one of the most heavily financed and influential of these organizations. Some of the others are: The Islamic Society of North America, the Islamic Circle of North America, World Muslim League, International Islamic Relief Organization, World Assembly of Muslim Youth, International Institute of Islamic Thought, the Holy Land Foundation, The American Muslim Council, The Muslim Public Affairs Council, The American Muslim Alliance, The Muslim Arab Youth Association, The American Islamic Group, Islamic Cultural Workshop.[44]

Many of these "charities" also launder money for terrorist organizations. They are sometimes raided or shut down, but others spring up to take their places.

They also monitor the media, advertising and movies for unflattering portrayals of Muslims.[45] In two cases, CAIR was able to command sufficient force to compel the publisher of U.S. News and World Report to publicly apologize for printing a simple, historically accurate statement about Muhammad in its pages.[46] It was also able to muzzle a popular syndicated radio commentator.[47] And to force a major Hollywood star to change a movie to remove Islamic terrorists and substitute drug dealers.

People who have no compunction about saying that their holy book does not say what it says would have few qualms about saying whatever it takes to neutralize any book by a mere mortal that exposes Islam's agenda.

Political lobbying. Directly influencing infidel lawmakers is another important method of jihad. It has been called "jihad by way of buying hearts and minds (corrupting politicians, academics, and intellectuals)".[48]

CAIR is one of the big Muslim lobbying organizations with chapters in more than twenty major cities throughout the U.S. One journalist names the names of a number of Congressmen of both parties who, as a result, support Islam.[49] Muslims themselves occasionally run for Congress. *There is no background security checking for members of Congress.* If elected, these Muslims would have access to top secret security information! The American Muslim Alliance has also mapped out 532,000 elective offices, large and small, throughout the U. S. and targeted them as eventual potentials for Muslim politicians.[50]

At the United Nations, the Islamic nations have organized into the OIC, Organization of the Islamic Conference. They have attempted to get the Islamic prohibition against "blasphemy" accepted as a rule at the UN. This would make any criticism of Islam illegal at the UN. As it is, criticizing Islamic racism, genocide, etc. has been protested by OIC and has succeeded in getting any mention of Islam's attitude toward Jews, Christians and other "infidels" excised from UN documents and reports—in clear violation of the free speech proclaimed in the UN's own Declaration of Human Rights.[51]

"Jihad can also consist of dividing the enemy camp. For example, anti-Zionism and anti-Americanism in Europe is largely the result of political pressure exerted by the Arab-Islamic world on European political parties captivated by the oil mantra. Anti-Americanism divides two allied continents and weakens still further a Europe eroded by massive immigration."[52]

Legal harassment. Counterattacking infidels who would stand in the way of any of the methods of jihad is an important type of jihad in itself. Organizations which attempt to fire, demote, criticize or otherwise discipline Muslims are sued, sometimes by Muslim organizations and sometimes by the American government's own EEOC (Equal Employment Opportunity Commission). CAIR maintains a staff of lawyers to sue corporations for racial discrimination on any pretext. If no pretext exists, one will be created by having Muslims employees demand special treatment, such as separate rest rooms, time off for prayers twice a day, etc. Dismissing a Muslim is guaranteed to produce a lawsuit for discrimination. Some of these cases are so ridiculous they are mind-boggling.

American Airlines dismissed some of its Muslim employees from airline security after 9/11. These airlines were promptly sued for racial discrimination. The U.S. government EEOC fined American Airlines $1.5 million for discrimination.[53] The same thing happened with United Airlines.

Five of the 9/11 hijackers passed through airport screening at Dulles and set off metal-detector alarms. The airport security people were Middle-eastern and didn't even bother to check the men but waved them on through. All this was caught on surveillance video.[54]

STATUS AND PROSPECTS OF THE HOLY WAR IN AMERICA

Surely the "War on Terror" has had some effect. You'd never know it. It has been about as effective as Lyndon Johnson's "War on Poverty." It is even arguable whether we are gaining or losing ground.[55]

Population expansion. The Census Bureau does not collect data on religious affiliation, so the number of Muslims in the United States cannot be known. Surveys have estimated the number at between four million and six million. Since the birthrate of Muslims is five times that of "whites", both the number and the proportion of Muslims in America are increasing. This does not include the number of Muslim immigrants and the number entering the country illegally. It is acknowledged that not all Muslims are militant, but the proportions are not known. One figure has the militants at 80% and growing.[56] However, "we must not blind ourselves to the bitter reality that militant Islamic fundamentalism holds the far more powerful upper hand in the intra-religious debate within Islam."[57]

How do they get in? Many come as students, get in on a student visa and get lost. Others come in allegedly seeking asylum. Most come in as relatives, wives, etc. of Muslims already in. Others enter illegally. One terrorist, for instance, shipped himself to America inside a cargo container which he had fitted up as living quarters. Due to the tens of thousands of such containers unloaded from ships every day, it is not possible for customs to inspect more than a small fraction of them. It was only by chance that the container with this terrorist was inspected. This is one of the methods of smuggling people, guns and munitions into the United States. To inspect all the containers would bring shipping to a near standstill and would be an economic disaster. This method also demonstrates why "gun control" has and can have no effect on the number and types of weapons and munitions wielded by Islamic terrorists.

Mosques as hubs. The number of mosques, community centers and Islamic education centers is also increasing rapidly and is currently estimated at six thousand. The building of these mosques and education centers is financed by Saudi Arabia which is in turn financed by our gasoline dollars. Unlike Christian churches, mosques feature political speeches.[58] Some of these speeches were first captured on film by Steven Emerson and shown on PBS in 1994 in a documentary called "Jihad in America" which is now available on video. This documentary did not show the tortures and executions which Emerson found on Arabic training videos on sale at a store in Brooklyn.[59] More recent documentaries include "Obsession: Radical Islam's War Against the West" (2006) and "Islam: What the West Needs to Know—an Examination of Islam, Violence and the Fate of the Non-Muslim World" (2006) which is available at the website What TheWorldNeedsToKnow.com. It is one thing to read books claiming that such hate speech does or does not exist, and other thing to see and hear for yourself Islamists and their young children making such hate speeches. "Sermons are framed in terms of 'us' and 'them.' America and Americans are referred to as 'them,' even though many congregants ... are U. S. citizens."[60]

It is estimated that over a hundred Islamic day schools and more than a thousand weekend schools exist in the U. S.[61] According to a study of ninety-three textbooks published by the Saudi Ministry of Education and used in U. S. Muslim schools, the teachings include: "Islam is the only true religion. Saudi Arabia is the leader of the Muslim world. Christian and Jews are infidels. The West is a decaying society and the source of Muslim misfortunes. There can be no peace between Muslims and non-Muslims."[62] One Saudi Foreign Minister told *60 Minutes* that "85 percent of what was being taught in the schools was not hateful."[63] This, of course, implies that 15 percent of what is being taught *is* hateful.

The mosques are also used by terrorists for recruiting.

Terrorist groups. Known terrorist groups are located throughout the United States, everywhere except the northwest (excluding Seattle), the Deep South and the northwestern portions of the Northeast. Specifically, Ft. Lauderdale, Boca Raton, FL, Tampa, Orlando, Charlotte, NC, Raleigh, NC, Springfield, VA, Herndon, VA, Washington, Potomac, MD, Laurel, MD, Philadelphia, New York, Boston, Cleveland, Detroit, Chicago, Plainfield, IN, Columbia, MO, Kansas City, MO, Oklahoma City, Arlington, TX, Dallas, Denver, Tucson, San Diego, Los Angeles, Santa Clara, CA, San Francisco, and Seattle have known terrorist cells.[64] Other observers have included Falls Church, VA, El Cajon, CA, Bridgeview, IL, Lackawanna, NY, Jersey City, NJ, Dearborn, MI, and Hollywood, FL as home to known terrorists.[65] Another observer adds Miami, Indianapolis, Cincinnati, St. Louis, Houston, and New Orleans.[66]

Infiltration. One of the most distressing features of the status of jihad is the presence of Islamists in key positions in American society. This is no accident, but part of the plan, as captured terrorist documents indicate. Muslims are urged to "infiltrate the sensitive intelligence agencies in order to collect information and build close relationships with the people in charge."[67] "The Islamic terrorists have studied our system inside and out, and they know its weaknesses and how to exploit them."[68]

Years ago, the FBI recorded suspected terrorists saying that the U. S. provides an ideal base because the terrorists "can disguise their activities as religious activities protected by the Constitution and no one will question them."[69] Now, they have the additional protection of the "racist" lawsuit threat. A Muslim FBI agent, who was fired for having unauthorized contacts with Muslim targets, threatened to sue the FBI for discrimination. He was reinstated.[70] Another captured document called for "establishing charitable organizations in America that would front for jihadi operations."[71]

One Islamic organization with terrorist ties, CAIR, provides books *free* to public libraries throughout America. The Council on Islamic Education provides instructional materials free to U. S. public schools, and one of their members became an editor of a Houghton-Mifflin textbook used nationwide in public schools. It provides a "sugar-coated version of Islam" while denigrating Christianity.[72] One wonders if school children still read the story about the wolf in sheep's clothing.

Infiltrating the FBI. Initially, the FBI tried to enlist the help of those "moderate" Muslims we hear so much about, asking them to contact the FBI if they heard of any suspicious activity. Instead of being pleased at being asked, they "howled discrimination" and swung into action to get the media and friendly members of Congress to cry "racism."[73] As a result, FBI agents were forced to take "sensitivity" training sessions to develop the proper pro-Muslims attitudes.[74] It worked. When a sniper was randomly shooting passersby in Washington, DC, the FBI was busy searching for a lone white gun nut, even though numerous eyewitnesses had reported the sniper as dark-skinned. This increased "sensitivity" on the part of law enforcement resulted in many more people being shot and killed before reality overcame sensitivity and the police began looking for a dark-skinned sniper.

Meanwhile, Muslims have been hired as translators and given top secret clearance, even though a dozen have "major red flags" in their personnel security files.[75] How did this happen? The ethnically sensitive Director of the FBI went to militant Islamic organizations to ask for recruits! Yes, you read that right. In fact, one new employee who showed up for work a week after the 9/11 attacks found the Muslims working at the FBI still *celebrating* the attack![76] One translator started an Arab-rights group within the FBI to coordinate complaints of discrimination and racism.[77] Worse still, agents rely on the translators' judgment as to whether probable cause exists to conduct raids on suspected terrorists.[78] Some Muslims have even been hired as FBI agents, and some have openly refused to tape-record other Muslims.[79] Such obstructionist Muslims agents could not be fired, since that would constitute racism!

Infiltrating the U. S. nuclear facilities. Muslims, including visitors from Iran and other terrorist-sponsoring countries, are and have been permitted to tour U. S. nuclear weapons facilities and many have been hired to work at them.[80] "Between 1998 and 2003, federal investigators documented more than thirteen hundred disappearances of radioactive materials in the U. S."[81] However, as one observer points out, would-be terrorists wouldn't have to steal it. They can just detonate it at the facilities to create a mega-nuclear explosion.[82]

It is not known how many Muslims are employed at nuclear power plants, but more than twenty are located within five miles of an airport, and almost none were built to withstand attack from even a small plane.[83]

Infiltrating the U. S. government. Muslims make up such a large voting block in some Congressional districts and contribute so much money to campaigns that they have substantial influence over seven Democrat Congressmen and even four Republicans. Muslim strategists have also mapped out over 500,000 elective offices in the U. S. and plan to try to get their people elected to as many of them as possible. If they could elect even one person to Congress, that person would have unlimited access to top secret documents without undergoing any FBI check.

A Muslim, with no background in security or intelligence, has been appointed policy director for the Department of Homeland Security's intelligence division.[84] He has access to top-secret data concerning America's seaports, refineries, nuclear plants, etc.

The ultimate indicator of the mindset that is allowing terrorism to flourish in America is the fact that in 2004, the Attorney General agreed *not* to target Muslims in the War on Terror![85]

A man, who was a lobbyist for a Muslim later convicted of terrorist activity, was appointed chief of staff of the General Services Administration, which contracts to private firms the custodial and maintenance services for government buildings. None of these workers get FBI background checks and they do not have to be U. S. citizens![86] The GSA also contracts security guards for the government's buildings. The government's Equal Employment Opportunity Commission "protects guards of Middle Eastern origin from having to undergo extra background checks by their employers."[87]

With a government like this looking out for us, we have nothing to worry about.

Economic infiltration. Muslim organizations threaten a nationwide boycott of companies who do not give special treatment to Muslims. Even though every one of the suspects on the FBI's most-wanted terrorist list are Muslim, the government excludes national origin, ethnicity, and religion from criteria that may be used to decide which airline passengers should be given extra scrutiny. And airlines that removed Middle-Eastern passengers who appeared to pose a security threat from their airplanes were fined $1.5 million by the government. Some airlines, to their credit, elected to pay the fine rather than risk the lives of their passengers and crew[88] to such government insanity.

Public disinformation and non-information. The Islamic public relations organizations are not the only ones putting out misinformation. Besides the American mainstream news media, the U. S. government issues pro-Islamic propaganda.[89] U. S. academics also are among "the ideological mercenaries offering themselves up for service in the jihad,"[90] as we shall see in a later chapter.

And the mantra of all is the same: Muslims are moderate, Islam is tolerant, jihad is peaceful. The facts, however, are another matter. "The history of dhimmitude, so long repressed by our collective cowardice, is unfolding around us, before our very eyes. It is claiming victims in Algeria, Egypt, Palestine, Lebanon, Sudan, Nigeria, Iran, Pakistan, Kashmir, the Philippines, Indonesia, and elsewhere."[91]

NEWS MEDIA CONTRIBUTIONS TO THE PROBLEM

One of the frequently heard cries from people who are just breaking out of the media blackout and beginning to find out what is actually going on in

America is, "Why didn't I read about that in the papers?" The news media's unintentional role in keeping the problems going is one of the most serious aspects of the weakening of America, because it keeps the people from doing what needs to be done to deal with the situation.

American mainstream news media have been uniformly hostile to the government's anti-terrorist efforts, attacking wherever they can, omitting reports and facts where silence will best serve. For instance, the Washington Post reported heavily on the sensitivities of Arab-Americans in Dearborn, Michigan of feeling scrutinized, but made no mention of the fact that this "scrutiny" resulted in a federal indictment against a sleeper combat cell in Dearborn which was planning attacks in the United States, recruiting members, making false identification papers, and trying to obtain weapons.[92]

The news media have come down so hard against "ethnic profiling" that the FBI restrained its Phoenix office from investigating the unusually large number of Arab immigrants taking flight training in Phoenix and elsewhere. Had the FBI or the news media investigated, the attack of 9/11 might have been averted.[93]

But the news media did not learn from the experience. After a brief spurt of honesty following the attack, the media settled down to its previous prejudices and "has put less and less emphasis on the connection between 9/11-style terrorism and problems in the immigration process."[94]

Similarly, one of the D. C. snipers was an illegal immigrant who entered as a stowaway. Taken into custody and ordered deported immediately in accordance with federal law, the future sniper was released on bond by order of Immigration officials in Washington, D. C, in violation of that federal law. Instead of climbing all over the bureaucrats as in years past and on other types of issues, almost every major news organization, except FOX News, refused to delve into the matter.[95]

If it didn't happen on TV, it didn't happen. And if it isn't presented in the media news, it does not exist. Media silence on terrorism, immigration and other factors weakening America "has diluted our moral outrage, contributing to a drift back into the indifference and apathy that made us vulnerable in the first place."[96]

On the other hand, if it *did* happen on TV and in the New York Times, then it did happen. Following 9/11, the mainstream media were full of stories of "hate" crimes, harassment and discrimination against Arab-Americans. "Not a day passed" without "some kind of major story in the New York Times highlighting victimized Middle-Easterners" during this period of "anti-Muslim fervor." And the networks were in on it too. The truth is that the media did not investigate many of these claims by Arab-American "rights" organizations but simply accepted and printed the complaints (allegations) as reports.[97] Similarly, with the story of the alleged "erosion of constitutional protections" of detainees, people suspected of terrorist activity.

In addition, there continues to be "overly favorable coverage" of Muslim Americans and stories on the nature of Islam:[98] Islam is a religion of peace. Jihad means inner struggle, etc.

Some news organizations after the 9/11 attacks found evidence of questionable Muslim-American loyalty to the United States, yet most news media preferred not to see such evidence. Particularly, "the story of incendiary rhetoric" at Muslim mosques in America "has not been a reporting priority".[99] In more blunt terms, it doesn't happen.

When Muslim teenagers went on a violent rampage in France, American media reported that *"French"* youth were *"protesting"*.

The news media reported relentlessly on the "Chechen rebels" as freedom fighters fighting for their independence against big bad Russia. In fact, they were Islamic jihadists whose ranks were swelled by thousands of veteran jihadists from Osama's training camps in Afghanistan.

Major incidents of jihadists slaughtering non-Muslims in African nations are routinely reported merely as "factions" fighting each other.

After Islamic terrorists set off a bomb in Bali that killed many tourists, American news media ran stories about "sectarian violence", thus concealing the fact that it was jihadists who had acted. You probably also didn't know that half a million Christians have become internally displaced and more than five thousand killed in Indonesia in an ethnic or religious cleansing campaign by the jihadists. By the way, Indonesia's national motto is "Unity in Diversity."[100]

WHAT MUST BE DONE AND WHY IT IS NOT BEING DONE

A number of proposals have been made to reduce the risks.

Spy on Muslims.[101] Since the only way to know which Muslims are jihadists and which are not is to gather intelligence, surveillance methods provide the only means of identifying those threatening Americans and America. When it became known that the President had authorized such intelligence-gathering, the New York Times went into action and accused the Administration of eavesdropping on "Americans." It didn't bother to tell its readers *which* Americans were being spied on.

The CAIR and other Muslim organizations sprang into action too and cried "racism." And other elements of the mainstream press did not lose the opportunity to blast the Republican President. Newsweek accused him of "acting like a dictator."[102] An accusation of racism is equivalent to a conviction and is the kiss of death in American politics.

It's time such accusations were regarded with suspicion.

Rescind citizenship of all Islamic activists. Preaching antidemocratic ideas was considered grounds for legal action in the time when the Soviet Union was the major threat to America. It should be considered so now.

The oath of allegiance which every person must swear to in order to acquire U.S. citizenship would be for a Muslim an act of apostasy punishable by death under Sharia law.[103] Hence, swearing the oath of allegiance to the United States by Muslims can be viewed as an act of *taqiyya* or dissimulation.

All proposals to ban the preaching of sedition against the United States by Muslims, however, are condemned as racist by Muslims and by the dominant media.

Reintroduce profiling. All of the 9/11 hijackers were Muslims. Thus, it would make sense to screen Muslim passengers more carefully than other passengers. This is called "profiling." Profiling is the use of demographic data that indicate the *likelihood* of an individual committing a crime. The data include anything that past experience has indicated are good predictors of possible criminal activity. Profiling merely leads to surveillance or increased scrutiny. It is *not* an accusation and is *not* grounds for arrest.

In June 2003, the Republican Administration ordered an end to profiling.[104] This order hamstrung seventy government law enforcement agencies, including the FBI, DEA, Homeland Security Department, Bureau of Alcohol, Tobacco, Firearms and Explosives, the Coast Guard, etc.

The excuse for this insanity was racism. But surveillance of Islamists is not based on race or even religion. It has been claimed that most Arabs living in America are not Muslims, but are Catholic, Armenian, Coptic Christian, Lebanese Christian, etc.[105] A white or Black American convert to Islam needs to be watched as much as an Arab Muslim. Doing this, however, would be objected to as a violation of freedom of religion. The authors of the Constitution did not imagine a religion which advocates violence. Current politicians and news people are having the same mental block.

Islamists, thus, are protected by the legal rights and customs of the very country they are striving to undermine. Still, they have contempt for us for having such rights. It is a sign of weakness in their eyes.

Transfer Muslims out of jobs requiring Security Clearance. By the same reasoning, it would make sense not to hire Muslims for jobs requiring high-level security clearance and to transfer Muslims already holding such jobs to other positions which have no access to top secret documents. Such a transfer would not be an accusation; it would simply be taking precautions. If the Muslims in question really were loyal, they would understand the need for the precaution and would voluntarily agree to the transfer.

They do not. Instead, they accuse the government of racism. Hence, this problem is allowed to continue, and there is no way to stop it, short of disallowing the playing of the all-purpose racism card.

Reform immigration laws to exclude anti-Americans. This would include all persons actively supporting discrimination against women and minorities, discrimination against "infidels," practicing or sanctioning slavery, etc. What would constitute active support is, of course, the problem. No one seeking "asylum" in the U. S. would admit to favoring these things.

Even so, these reforms are not taking place because any Congressman voting in favor of such legislation would be accused on racism, being against freedom of religion, etc. The fact that these criteria for exclusion are actually *political* rather than racial or religious would get lost in the noise.

Another problem is that the behavior and attitudes of Muslims often change dramatically after they have been in the U. S. for awhile and acquire U. S. citizenship.[106] They may be genuinely peaceful on entering and remain so until they hear the incendiary rhetoric in American mosques.

Parity for Mosques and Islamic Centers. Apply the same criteria and rules to these centers that "apply to other cults prone to violence and to 'hate groups' such as the KKK or the Aryan Nation."[107] To make supervision for illegal content practicable, all sermons should be required to be in English.[108] Violation should result in the closing of the mosque or "education" center and confiscation of its property.

During the 1950s, long debates were held as to whether American Communists had the right under the First Amendment to advocate the overthrow of the United States. The same debate needs to be held regarding Islam, and cries of "racism" or whatever should not be allowed to stifle such a debate.

To create such a debate, an educational campaign is needed to inform the public and the members of Congress as to the *political* nature of Islam, and "that we are dealing with a new phenomenon even more dangerous than anarchism, fascism or communism."[109]

None of this is being done, of course, because Muslims immediately claim to be a religion, not a political movement, and claim immunity under the First Amendment. They also charge racism, Islamophobia, etc.

ISLAMIC TREATMENT OF NONMUSLIMS

"There was nothing dramatic about [the slide of non-Muslims into dhimmitude]: it was a gentle death, a phasing out."[110] This gentle death, this phasing out "applies perfectly to Europe today."[111] Since all indications are that the growth and spread of Islam in America will not be stopped, it behooves Americans to know what their lives will be like if the Islamists finally complete their takeover. The options are these:

Convert to Islam. Besides giving up all freedoms in the Bill of Rights and being required to follow the regimen of Islam, *converts* do not enjoy quite the same rights as people who are born Muslims, although their children might. Still, they are better off that the dhimmi.

Submit to dhimmitude. Bat Ye'or has written, "The civilization of dhimmitude does not develop all at once.... It is a long process that involves ... a specific mental conditioning. It happens when peoples replace history by myths, when they fight to uphold these destructive myths ... as if they were the only guarantee for their survival, when in fact they are the path to destruction."[112]

What is the condition of dhimmitude? "The law required from dhimmis a humble demeanor, eyes lowered, a hurried pace. They had to give way to Muslims in the street, remain standing in their presence and keep silent, only speaking to them when given permission. They were forbidden to defend themselves if attacked, or to raise a hand against a Muslim on pain of having it amputated. Any criticism of the Koran or Islamic law annulled the protection pact. In addition, the dhimmi was duty-bound to be grateful, since it was Islamic law that spared his life."[113] Also, dhimmis pay crippling taxes, the *kharaj* and the *jizya*. They are at "constant risk of jihad conditions being re-invoked—of massacre and dispossession—if the dhimmi community was considered to have failed to live up to the conditions of their pact."[114] Failure to pay the full *kharaj* is such a failure. In Europe today, Muslims steal the property of Europeans or destroy it, because Europeans are not paying the *jizya* to Muslims, even though the Muslims do receive huge welfare payments.[115] "I should emphasize that all these principles are not merely of historical interest but are indeed still applied against non-Muslims in modern Iran, Pakistan, and Saudi Arabia, to name but a few countries."[116]

Significantly, dhimmitude forbids the dhimmi from arming themselves.[117]

Muslims have been explicit about this one. "All Islamic human rights schemes, such as the 1981 Universal Islamic Declaration of Human

Rights, ..., and so on, severely restrict and qualify the rights of women as well as minorities such as non-Muslims and apostates, unbelievers, and heretics."[118]

The courtesy of being allowed to submit to dhimmitude applies only to Jews and Christians, according to some Muslim authorities. Communists, atheists and non-Muslim Arabs have only two choices: "accept Islam or be killed."[119]

Fight. If dhimmitude does not appeal to you, and if you're also not inclined to kneel down and put your head on the floor at five o'clock in the morning and at four other times throughout the day, your only remaining option under Muslim rule is to fight for your freedom. Today, Americans, with ample help from movies, TV and newspapers, are deeply opposed to doing this.

An Economy in Hock

That the American economy swings on a pendulum lubricated by oil is not news to anyone who has been awake since 1973.[120] At that time, OPEC imposed its first oil embargo against America and the price of gasoline shot up. Since then, prices of all commodities have continued to rise, all blamed on the cost of "energy." Even services such as medical insurance have blamed their skyrocketing prices on "the energy crisis." To stay in business, clever American business people have devised ways to make their products cheaper and cheaper, at the same time as they raised the prices of these products—everything from half-baked bread to using dried vegetables instead of fresh. And Americans have paid the price and eaten it.

How long these stop-gap measures can suffice is anyone's guess.

How did we get into this mess? Part of the reason and much of the excuse is U. S. support of Israel. Another is botched relations with Iran.[121] However, this oil dependency would probably have happened anyway eventually, because by the early 1970s, something fundamental had changed, and it was America's own doing. "President Dwight Eisenhower imposed mandatory quotas on foreign oil imports in 1959. Fourteen years later, when Richard Nixon removed the import quotas, the U. S. had exhausted its surplus and become a net importer of oil."[122] This, of course, was in 1973.

OIL SUPREMACY

Since then, for the oil-rich Islamists of the Middle-east, the rule has been: pump more oil and make more money, or alternatively pump *less* oil and make *even more* money. The American economy is like those prisoners of war during World War II who were kept strapped down to hospital tables and bled periodically to provide blood for wounded Nazi soldiers. Not too much blood was withdrawn, since it would cause the soldiers to die and deprive the enemy of a source of blood. The soldiers were allowed to retain only enough blood to keep them barely alive. The price of crude oil similarly regulates the American economy, keeping it barely alive, preventing it from going into a depression but also preventing it from becoming too prosperous.

In 2001, the National Energy Policy Development Group warned that in 20 years the U. S. will be importing nearly two-thirds of its oil.[123]

But the price of crude is not the only leverage the Islamists have. "Saudi Arabia keeps possibly as much as a trillion dollars on deposit in U. S. banks.... The Saudis hold another trillion dollars or so in the U. S. stock market.... Just to make sure no one is tempted to complain."[124] Imagine the economic effects if these deposits were transferred to banks in other nations, or if the stock were dumped. "On the ... scale of economic catastrophe, having the Saudis withdraw all their U. S. bank deposits and vacate the stock market is probably only a six, well below the Saudis turning off the oil spigot or having the spigot blown to bits."[125]

But these are not the only sources of Islamic power over the U. S. The huge and rapidly climbing national debt has to be paid for by someone, and that someone includes the oil-rich Islamists. "The idea was to get the Saudis to underwrite the U. S. budget deficit. Eager to become America's lender of last resort, with all the leverage that implied, the Saudis took the bait and happily swallowed it."[126]

Oil imperialism. The Saudis have done the same to Europe to force the E. U. to agree to the unlimited Islamic immigration that is now threatening democracy in all the European nations.[127] This policy of appeasement and collaboration is represented in an official pact called "the Euro-Arab Dialogue (EAD)."[128]

This same oil imperialism now threatens America.

SAUDI ARABIA AND AMERICAN DOMESTIC POLITICS

The power bestowed by oil does not stop with economic power. It also entails political power. "The White House put out its hand to fund pet projects that Congress wouldn't fund or couldn't afford, from a war in

Afghanistan to one in Nicaragua. Every Washington think tank ... took Saudi money."[129]

Bandar, the Saudi ambassador, can get in to see the President anytime he likes, while the directors of the FBI and the CIA can only talk to assistants. There is a joke around that if a plane crashes into the White House, it's the head of the FBI trying to get in to see the President.

But the handouts don't stop with the Presidents of both Parties and members of Congress. "Aware that government bureaucrats can't retire comfortably on a federal pension, the Saudis put out the message: You play the game ... and we'll take care of you."[130] As Saudi prince Bandar told an associate, "If the reputation then builds that the Saudis take care of friends when they leave office, you'd be surprised how much better friends you have who are just coming into office."[131] "Any Washington bureaucrat ... knows that if he stays on the right side of the kingdom," he'll be able to retire with "a consulting contract with Aramco, a chair at American University, a job with Lockheed," or whatever.[132]

There are also lucrative contracts with American corporations for construction, computers, military equipment, etc. "Washington likes to describe all this with an inoffensive, neutral economic term: recycling petrodollars. But it's plain old influence peddling."[133]

Acquiring these contracts is, naturally, much sought after. "Every deal with the Saudis involves rake-offs, commissions, theft, bribes, graft. Call it what you want."[134]

How has Saudi Arabia used its leverage? An ex-CIA man claims that so thick were the relations between the Washington politicians and the Saudis that the politicians did not want to hear anything bad about Saudi Arabia from the CIA. "[T]he CIA decided that the safest bet was to ignore Saudi Arabia by cleverly pretending it was a U. S. domestic problem, and thus by statute not in its jurisdiction."[135] "It's what I call ... deference."[136]

SAUDI ARABIA AND THE SPREAD OF ISLAM

"Beginning in the early 1970s," Saudi Arabia "used their vast reservoirs of petrodollars to build a network of mosques and religious schools, in the kingdom and abroad, where a fresh generation of Muslim teenagers could be indoctrinated into the most violent and radical interpretation of Islam."[137]

The Saudis set up Middle-eastern "studies" programs in over a hundred American universities. These Studies programs help to spread the message of Islam as a peaceful cultural phenomenon. The Saudis also help fund a bewildering variety of organizations in America from youth organizations to lobbying organizations to "charitable" organizations to research organizations to general Muslim organizations. These organizations maintain websites and blogs, publish newsletters and generally keep close tabs on everything said about Islam in print and on the web.

Every book that is critical of Islam is immediately deluged on Amazon.com and other web bookstores with one-star reviews designed to kill the sales of the book. These attacks, sad to say, are very effective, since many American readers are not knowledgeable enough to distinguish between a review and a politically motivated attack.

OIL AND TERROR

In trying to appease its Fundamentalist Muslim majority, Saudi Arabia has been pumping money to them as well as building mosques for them on every continent of the world. "In mid-2002, ... the semiofficial Defense Policy Board ... endorsed an assessment that Saudi Arabia wasn't our friend when it came to terrorism.... The Saudis are active at every level of the terror chain, from planners to financiers, from cadre to foot-solders, from ideologist to cheerleader."[138]

"The mosque schools were teaching jihad, just as the Saudi *madrasahs* do today. The mosque public-address systems blared out a message of hate and revenge, just as they do in Saudi Arabia today."[139] Today, Saudi Arabia's "secondary schools and universities have become the West Point of global terrorism."[140]

Nor have the Saudis been cooperating with America's attempts to contain terrorism. Saudi Arabia "basically hit the mute button beginning in the mid-1990s, and it hasn't let up since."[141] "So thorough has been the lockdown that the FBI has not been allowed to interview suspects, including the families of the fifteen Saudi hijackers [of 9/11]."[142]

This is an indication of how independent the United States of America already has become. But given the political leverage that Saudi Arabia exercises with U. S. government officials at all levels, it is not surprising that nothing is done about this outrageous security situation. In fact, citizens of Saudi Arabia are given special treatment in all ways and at all levels, for instance, when it comes to entering the U. S. "Right through September 11, 2001, Saudis were not even required to appear at the U. S. embassy ... for a visa interview." This makes it easy for terrorists to enter the U. S., not only in cargo containers or sneaking across the border, but on ordinary commercial air flights. "According to law, all fifteen Saudis who took part in the 9/11 attacks should have been turned down for visas."[143]

Nor has the situation improved. "Long after September 11, Saudi Arabia refused to provide advance manifests for flights coming into the U. S., a base and potentially fatal breach of security."[144]

Terrorist attacks are not, of course, limited to the United States but have been occurring all over the world. Terrorists move back and forth from one Middle-Eastern country to another. Nations allegedly friendly to America claim that they cannot find the terrorists the U. S. asks them to turn over. "In other words, there are no hard-and-fast borders to this terror network."[145]

At the same time, control of crime has become next to impossible due to the influx of Islamists who do not consider themselves obliged to obey any laws but *Sharia*. France, for instance, has some of the toughest gun control laws in the world. "Ten years ago an enterprising French criminal would have been lucky to put his hands on an unregistered handgun.... Today he could buy a Kalashnikov for five hundred dollars in one of Paris's ghetto suburbs, or a rocket launcher and grenade for three hundred."[146]

The war in the Russian province of Chechnya was reported in the American press as a valiant struggle for independence of a group of people in one of the southern provinces. Seldom was it mentioned that these people were Islamists, and never was it said that their numbers had been augmented by fighters trained in the Afghan training camps of Al Qaeda. The Chechen rebellion "seemed to go on forever. It had to be costing hundreds of millions of dollars."[147] Who was paying for all that? The Saudis were "giving money to Islamic groups in Chechnya to slaughter Russians, military and civilian alike."[148] In 1998, "Chechens were quietly brought to a secret military camp" in Saudi Arabia and "trained in explosives, hand-to-hand combat, and small weapons. A lot of time was set aside for indoctrination into Wahhabi Islam."[149]

A lot of media attention has been given to Central Asian oil and how it will solve the U. S. energy crisis. Seldom is it mentioned that the pipelines to carry that oil out of Central Asia would have to pass through the very nations that now control most of the earth's oil or through Russia itself, which charges a high premium on any oil flowing across its land. Worse still, the Saudis have been pumping millions into setting up mosques and schools to teach their fundamentalist or militant version of Islam. "The U. S. was closing its eyes while Muslim extremists set up shop in the very places we most needed to stop them—the oil-rich former Soviet states of Central Asia."[150]

Terrorism is not limited to suicide bombers and grenade and rocket attacks. "… beginning in the mid-1970s, Saudi Arabia poured over $1 billion into Pakistan to help it develop an "Islamic" nuclear bomb to counter the "Hindu" nuclear threat from neighboring India."[151] As we now know, the head of Pakistan's nuclear program has given out these atomic secrets to other nations like Iran and North Korea and to various terrorist groups. The *deployment* of a suitcase radiation or "dirty" bomb is now just a matter of time.

THE INSTABILITY OF SAUDI ARABIA

Is there danger that Saudi Arabia might fall into the hands of the vast majority of its people, most of whom are fanatical Islamists who don't care about keeping the American economy barely alive? "If Saudi Arabia tanks and takes along the other four dysfunctional families in the region who collectively own 60 percent of the world's proven oil reserves, the industrial economies are going down with it, including the economy of the United States of America."[152]

But is that really a serious possibility? One ex-CIA agent claims that the Saudi economy is in trouble. The Saudi welfare state, in which everything is paid for and dirty work is done by foreign workers or by the despised Shiites who work the oil fields, is costing huge sums and is enormously expensive, as is the building of mosques and schools around the globe. What happened to all the enormous sums of money that have accumulated from the sale of oil? "All changed when the Gulf War ate up Saudi Arabia's entire budget surplus. Since then the country has been living off credit."[153] "Helping to pay for the U. S. bases in Saudi Arabia was costing additional billions."[154]

Whether this is true or not, Saudi Arabia has other problems. "Over the next five years, Wahhabi militants continued to worm their way into military and intelligence jobs. By October 2002 the Saudi police were informing contacts in the American expat community that they could no longer count on the loyalty of junior military and intelligence officers."[155] By now, Islamic militants have become commonplace in the Saudi military.[156]

"Washington's answer for Saudi Arabia—apart from the mantra that nothing's wrong—is the same as its answer for the rest of the Middle East: Democracy will cure everything."[157] But no one seems to have thought it through. "There is no doubt ... that an Islamic government would succeed the Al Sa'ud if the Saudis [the people] were allowed to decide their own political destiny."[158] In other words, democracy—a vote by the people—could in this case make the situation much worse.

WHAT MUST BE DONE AND WHY IT WILL NOT BE DONE

In 1975, after the Saudis had flexed their oil muscles, Congress commissioned a study of what must be done. The study recommended seizing, securing, restoring and operating the Saudi oil installations.[159]

This was not done and will not be done because of American politicians' fear of international public opinion and because of politicians' fear of alienating a substantial minority of the electorate.

In 1933, Standard Oil of California signed a 60 year concession over a large area in Saudi Arabia's Gulf coast, paying in gold and future royalties if oil was discovered. After years of searching, Standard Oil struck oil in 1938, built the rigs, the pipelines, and all the other infrastructure.[160] In 1973, after only 40 years, Saudi Arabia simply grabbed the whole thing.[161] Nixon did nothing, weakened by the Vietnam War and popular opposition to it. He submitted to this outrage.

The U. S. government is afraid of public opinion if they took the oil fields back. Undoubtedly, Islamic nations would condemn the reacquisition, calling it theft, crusade, etc. Yet, they made no such accusations against the Saudis when they took the oil fields and equipment in the first place. This fits in with the teaching of the Quran that any action is justified if it advances the cause of Islam. Thus, stealing the oil is justified; taking it back is not.

Baer today also recommends taking the oil back. The Saudis have issued a statement since Baer's book came out claiming that they have rigged all their oil facilities with bombs—bombs laced with radiation. And in the event anyone tries to seize them, they will blow up all the facilities and the radiation will render the oil useless.

But wouldn't this be cutting their own throats? No. The Saudi royals would "flee the desert for their palaces strung out along the Riviera; their penthouses glowing against the night skies of Paris, London, and New York; their mountain aeries bathed by the cool evening breezes of Morocco."[162] They have been preparing such a backdoor escape for a long time anyway. They know the day will come when the Muslim extremists they have been trying to buy off will revolt and take over. If only U. S. politicians had this much sense!

What about alternative sources of energy? A lot of counter-cultural enthusiasts have been advocating this for years and are now more vociferous than ever; and a number of scientists are working on various sources, such as solar energy, wind energy, fuel cells, etc. The enthusiasts claim these solutions are feasible now or at least day after tomorrow. The scientists who are trying to develop these things are also optimistic, but their time estimates are stated in terms of decades or at least years, and then only a small percent of American's energy requirements would be provided.

Also, some corporate leaders would make less money if alternate energy sources were developed, and their lobby is influential with Congress.[163]

And still, all the real estate, stock, businesses, transportation, etc. that the Middle East oil barons have bought up will continue to be owned by them. And much of the political influence that comes with wealth will continue to be deployed.

What about oil exploration in U. S. held territory? Democrats oppose increased drilling for oil in the Gulf of Mexico (which would make the U. S. less dependent on Saudi Arabia) because it might harm coastal marshes, disturb wildlife, etc. Similarly, they oppose drilling in Alaska and other likely places.

La Reconquista

Before he moved to a small Arizona town twenty minutes from the Mexican border, John Petrello never believed the stories about an "invasion" of illegal immigrants. He found out. Among many other learning experiences, one morning, his pregnant wife was outside watching their young daughter when a pickup truck pulled up and dropped off twelve men. The men started toward his house. John got his gun and ordered them (in Spanish and in English) to stop, but they just kept walking toward him. He fired several shots directly at their feet in front of them, but that didn't even faze them, they just kept coming. He fired again. The men stopped and glared. They were pissed *at him*! Finally, they turned and went in another direction. John's wife, meanwhile, had called 911. They told her they couldn't help because it involved illegals and "was a civil matter."[164]

In another small Arizona town, a woman woke up at 7 A.M. to find a Hispanic man leaning over her bed reaching for her throat. She snatched her gun from her bedside table and ordered the man to leave her house. The man answered her in perfect English, "No, I just walked all the way from Mexico; get out of bed and cook me something." She told him her husband was a policeman (which was true). He just laughed at her and said, "They can't catch me and they don't even try." Finally, he left, and she called the Border Patrol. It took them an hour to get there.[165]

These cases are typical of life today near the border in New Mexico, Texas, Arizona and California. Women wake up to find men in their houses. Kitchens are trashed. Food and clothing are stolen. Ranchers along the border spend the first hour of every day repairing damage done the night before. They find fences knocked down, water spigots left on, their dogs poisoned, cattle killed, cars and pickup trucks stolen, trash (pill boxes, syringes, used needles, and piles of feces). People will not let their children play in the yard during the day unless they are with them and are armed. Certain roads are too dangerous to drive on after dark.[166]

One Indian Reservation reported that crossing illegals trash their land every day.[167] Drug enforcement officials seize about 1,000 pounds of marijuana *a day* on another Indian Reservation.[168] As for non-Mexican illegals, even if they are caught, they have an 80% chance of being released onto American streets because it takes months to arrange for deportation to their home countries and the U. S. authorities do not have enough beds to house them.[169]

THE ENEMY WITHIN

There are people in America who still do not know that some groups have publicly vowed to overthrow the United States, beginning in the southwestern parts of the nation.

MEChA, according to its website, has as its goal the "liberating" of the "occupied" state of Atzlan (in other words, California, Arizona, New Mexico, and perhaps Texas, Colorado and Nevada). La Raza Unida, one of the largest and most influential of Mexican-American organizations, claims that the southwestern United States rightfully belongs to Mexico. As its founder says, "Our devil has pale skin and blue eyes." "They are not making babies.... It's a matter of time.... The explosion is in our population."[170] Or, more explicitly, "We have got to eliminate the *gringo*, and what I mean by that is ... we have got to kill him."[171]

Also, a number of armed gangs of illegal Mexican immigrants are operating in the United States, among them "MS-13" with 10,000 members in 33 states, and "Los Zetas," which has committed home invasions, abductions, murders, extortions, and drug trafficking.[172] These gangs are financed by the drug trade and are heavily armed. And they are not the dumb punks that Hollywood portrays. They are well-organized, some with a constitution, and have branches in many cities throughout the nation. If one leader dies, the leadership elects a new leader, but the gang continues.

In Bosnia, it was Moslem gangs who won the early victories against the Yugoslav Army.[173] In Chechnya, it was Moslem gangs who won the early victories against the Russian Army.[174]

The U. S. Attorney General estimated that there were half-a-million gang members nationwide already in 1996.[175] "Some gangs have access to highly sophisticated personal weapons such as grenades, machine guns, rocket launchers and military explosives."[176] Gangs have infiltrated urban police forces and even the U. S. military itself, including the Army, Navy, Air Force and Marines.[177]

How did these people get *inside* the United States?

When Congress passed an act in 1986 giving amnesty to illegal aliens, the floodgates of immigration opened.[178] Most are Mexicans, but many are from Egypt, Lebanon, Syria, Iran, Iraq, Russia, Bulgaria, China and other Latin American countries. During the first nine months of 2004, 190,000 of these illegals disappeared into the American population.[179]

Immigration is a big business, with safe houses and buses to transport illegals to towns across the nation, coaching them on what to say if detained, legal aid societies to punish the legal system for trying to enforce the law, etc. Immigration affects more than just the border states. It has an impact on towns all across the nation. Danbury, Connecticut, for instance, is estimated to be 20% illegals.[180]

TURNING A PROBLEM INTO AN ISSUE

An important component of any political agenda these days is the creation of a verbal debate to forestall any action. For instance, some supporters of Jihad even tried to turn the atrocities of 9/11 into a debate, some arguing that it was America's fault, others even arguing that the whole thing was engineered by the U. S. government!

The same tactic has been used in support of La Reconquista. A number of arguments are used in the media and in Congress to turn the problem into an issue and delay any action to solve the problem.

Favoring illegal immigration. One of the giveaways that the debate is merely a forestalling action is turning even illegal immigration into an "issue." Presumably, illegal immigration by definition is immigration that the American people have decided against. So, what is the issue? Still more oddly, among those who favor illegal immigration, one would have to count most politicians, since they have voted to extend health care, schooling, driver's licenses and welfare payments even to illegal immigrants. It has been proven that rewarding behavior causes the behavior to be repeated. In California, the people voted to end such reinforcements, but a judge overruled the people!

Why these actions on the part of politicians and partisan judges are not considered a crime is puzzling. An ordinary citizen aiding or abetting a criminal would be arrested as a criminal himself.

In addition, one whistleblower in the Department of Homeland Security claims that the best agents are being hounded out of the Department and that the U. S. is less safe now than it was before 9/11.[181] A documentary called "Border War" has also been produced which contains interviews with border guards.

After 9/11, the feds became active for awhile and rounded up 1,000 illegals who were working in *secure* areas of domestic airports.[182]

A half-million illegals with deportation orders have gone missing. Of these, 84,000 were convicted criminals and 3,800 are from countries with a known terrorist presence.[183]

Safe havens. Some cities and two states have "sanctuary" policies. "These policies forbid police officers from arresting criminals based only on their immigration status and prohibit local law enforcement from cooperating with federal immigration authorities."[184] This explains why some illegals can be arrested an average of eight times and still be in the country. Besides the states of Maine and Oregon, some of the safe cities are Los Angeles, San Diego, San Francisco, Evanston, Illinois, Chicago, Cambridge, Massachusetts, Baltimore, Detroit, Minneapolis, Durham, North Carolina, Albuquerque, Santa Fe, Austin, Houston, and Madison, Wisconsin.[185]

Catch and release. Federal immigration officials are so understaffed and under-funded that they cannot respond to most cases in which local police catch an illegal. This has become so commonplace that local police often do not bother to call the feds because their calls are not returned or not responded to.[186]

A police chief in New Hampshire who arrested an illegal immigrant for committing a crime was called a "vigilante police chief" by the ACLU.[187] A California State Senator proposed to establish a California border police to enforce federal immigration law. A Latino Assemblyman in the California state legislature called the proposal "anti-immigrant bashing".[188]

Favoring unassimilated immigrants. Another indication that immigration is not an issue but a weapon is the fact that many proponents of immigration prefer that immigrants *not* assimilate to American society.

Past immigration to America was immigration for the purpose of becoming American. In other words, the immigrants assimilated. Present immigration to America is immigration with the intension of *not* assimilating and is usually accompanied by absence of assimilation, sometimes to the extent of not learning to speak English, not learning or obeying the laws, and not giving allegiance to the nation.

How does one recognize assimilation? Loyalty and acceptance of certain political assumptions as fundamental would seem to be the heart of it, but how can these things be measured? Certainly, seditious statements and threats to take over are an indicator of *absence* of assimilation, as are expressions of hatred for the majority of Americans or hatred for America itself. Many immigrants regard assimilation as a "racist concept."[189] One visible indicator of the actuality of assimilation is ability to speak English fluently.[190] Willingness to serve in the military to defend the country has always been a test of loyalty.

The best that those who *favor* immigrant *without* assimilation can do by way of a justification is to claim that this makes a cultural contribution. However, past immigrants who have assimilated, like the Italians and the Chinese, have managed to keep their cultures alive while becoming loyal Americans. So what is the advantage to Americans of having unassimilated immigrants?

What are the dangers? Do unassimilated immigrants increase the danger of the nation coming apart at the seams? Every citizen has a legal duty to defend the nation. Would unassimilated citizens do that? In the event of a conflict, which side would they be on? It seems commonsense to assume that unassimilated Mexicans would be more likely to favor Reconquista, in other words, sedition, while assimilated Mexicans would oppose it. And that unassimilated Muslims would be more likely to favor Jihad than assimilated Muslims (although, as we have seen above, the notion of an assimilated Muslim may be a contradiction in terms, since assimilation would be a sign of apostasy).

Biased immigration. At present, immigration is biased against Europeans and in favor of Third-World people. Is this kind of immigration beneficial to America? Other than cheap labor, no justifications for this discrimination have been offered.

The goal of exploiting cheap labor and dispossessing American workers is hardly an admirable goal. Yet, politicians are allowed to get away with it. They are not voted out of office. To paraphrase Edmund Burke, evil flourishes when the people do nothing.

The appeal to rights. More subtle are the arguments that try to turn the problem of immigration into an issue by appealing to the notion of rights to justify unrestricted legal and illegal immigration.

Right of ownership. Mexicans claim a right to the southwestern parts of the United States on the basis that they were there first and the U. S. took the land away from them. The principle implicitly appealed to by this argument is "First Come, First Served."

But if the principle is First Come, First Served, then the land belongs to the Comanche, the Navajo, and the Apache. If the Mexicans are not willing for the tribes to have the land, then they must give up their claim to the land based on the First-Come principle.

And what about Louisiana? Perhaps the Louisiana territory really belongs to France. Or the entire Ohio valley? That was "stolen" from France during the so-called "French and Indian War". Perhaps Illinois, Indiana, Michigan, Ohio, western Pennsylvania, and upstate New York all really belong to France and should be given back or should be annexed to Quebec. At the very least, as many French people as want to should be allowed to immigrate to the United States.

That is not going to happen. On the contrary, French are discriminated against in American immigration laws.

In short, claims of ownership based on "First Come" are dubious in principle and in practice are biased *in favor of* Mexicans. If the grounds for Mexican ownership of the land is not First Come, First Served, then what is it?

Right of location. The stance of some people on the immigrant issue seems to depend on an assumption of a right of any person to live anywhere on the planet they want.

But if everyone has a right to live anywhere they want, then everyone has a right not to be pushed off the land they want to live on. Otherwise, there is no *right* to live on the land, only a claim to the land. In other words, the alleged right to live anywhere is self-contradictory.

The alleged right could be amended to state that a person has a right to live anywhere, provided someone else is not already living on that land.

But what does "living on the land" include? Does it apply only to the house one is living in or does it apply to the land around the house that makes living in the house viable?

Only the latter makes sense. So, the question becomes, how much land is required to make living in the house viable? For a farmer, the land around the house is not "empty", it is necessary to grow food for survival and cash crops in order to buy other necessities. For Native Americans, the land they hunted and fished was not empty, it was required for their survival; and for some tribes that meant that they had to keep moving from place to place. In feudal times, living in a peasant's hut required all the land that the castle and its guards could defend. More recently, it includes the land occupied by a nation. Those who have failed to defend their borders have ceased to be nations and usually ceased to have any rights at all. And sometimes, they have ceased to exist: they have been exterminated.

When their communal land is encroached on, the viability of each person's life in his or her house is brought into serious question (as anyone who has lived through a war can testify from first-hand experience). It is therefore legitimate for a people to decide who else shares the land they depend on.

The burden of proof. Any argument which involves vested interests is likely to result in neither side being convinced. In such cases, it is important which side the burden of proof is taken to be on. In the immigration debate, oddly enough, the burden of proof is assumed to be on those who are *opposed* to immigration. But why should that be?

Right of self-determination. Members of a voluntary association, such as clubs, churches, political parties, labor unions, etc. are acknowledged to have a right to determine who can become a member of their organization. Why shouldn't members of a nation have the same right? If such a right of self-determination is admitted, then the question of immigration becomes one of *benefit*. What kinds of immigration are beneficial to the United States? How much of those kinds of immigration, if any, are beneficial?

Immigration is so small that it is not a problem. Another tactic to allow the problem to continue is the claim that so few people are entering the United States legally and illegally that the whole furor over immigration is just a tempest in a teapot.

Is this true? How much immigration *is* there in fact? Estimates and quotes of data vary according to whether the source of the data is a person or organization in favor of immigration or opposed to it. Paradoxically, those who are pro-immigration cite *lower* numbers, while those who are anti-immigration cite higher numbers. Why would people who are in favor of immigration put their figures low? People who are in favor of something usually give high estimates. Could it be that they are afraid that higher numbers might frighten away potential supporters of immigration?

The present administration in Washington is pro-immigration and the Census Bureau is among those providing low numbers. It claims that the present population of the United States (as of October, 2006) is 300 million and that it will reach 600 million in the year 2100. It also claims that there are 9 million illegal immigrants in the United States. If the people are illegal, it is unclear how the government can count them.

Anti-immigration sources put the number of illegal immigrants at 20 million and the current population of the United States at 330 million with a projected 1 billion people by 2076. Yes, one billion people.

It has also been estimated that 1–3 million immigrants cross the U. S.-Mexico border each year. However, the Border Patrol estimates that for each illegal apprehended, 3 to 5 more escape. Since 1.8 million a year are apprehended, that would make the number of illegals entering the country around 7 million per year. (The Census Bureau, however, estimates half-a-million illegals annually.) The increase in public school enrollments for 2003 came in at 30 times the projected increase,[191] suggesting that the unforeseen increase came from immigration.

Adding the 1.7 million birth rate per year to the 1.5 million *legal* immigrants per year, plus an estimated 3 million illegal immigrants per year, gives 6.2 million additional people *each and every* year. At this rate, the American population doubles in 50 years.

Approximately 90 percent of the U. S. population increase is from immigration plus the descendants of post-1970 immigrants. Almost all of these immigrants come from the Third World.

It has been claimed that America is taking in more *legal* immigrants than all other nations of the world combined. It has also been claimed that more people were admitted to the United States since 1960 than in all the years 1776—1960 combined.

The bottom line is that whether one uses the figures of the pro-immigration people or the anti-immigration people, immigration both as an absolute number and as a proportion of the population is very high.

Immigration is beneficial. Another claim is that immigration is actually beneficial to the United Sates and to the people in the nation. What are these alleged benefits? And *who* is it that benefits?

Democrats want immigrants for their votes. Republicans want immigrants for cheap labor. Many Americans are in favor of immigration because, as with most issues, they have not thought it through. They simply believe what the mass media tells them.

The rest of the people don't want immigrants because Americans want more space for themselves, better and higher paying jobs for themselves, and because they don't want to pay the free healthcare, the free schooling and the food stamps the immigrants consume.

Unskilled Americans, including Black workers, lose jobs to unskilled immigrants because the immigrants are willing to work for lower wages. "An estimated 1,880,000 American workers are displaced from their jobs every year by immigration."[192]

Many skilled Americans are working at jobs below their skill levels because the skilled jobs they would have gotten have been given to skilled immigrants who work for lower wages. This is a benefit to business owners but not to the people at large.

Skills. One Harvard economist, who is himself a Cuban immigrant, has argued that using *family ties* as a basis for admission to the U. S. is not beneficial to the nation. He has proposed instead a *skills* criterion (as well as cutting absolute levels of immigration by one-third).[193] In other words, people who have useful skills to offer to the U. S. economy should be admitted.

Many skilled workers *are* admitted, however, from India and elsewhere, since they work for lower wages than American skilled workers. American skilled workers are then forced to work at jobs that are below their skill levels or lose their careers. Legally, this is not supposed to happen. Corporations must fill out forms declaring that they cannot hire these skills from among the available labor pool. These petitions are almost routinely granted, however.

Legal grounds for immigration. Today, much of the actual immigration is not decided on the basis of benefits to America but on the basis of family ties: having a relative in America, marrying an American. Or on the basis of having been born within the national boundaries of the United States. "An average of 300,000 women annually cross our borders and deliberately birth their children on United States soil—in order to gain citizenship."[194] Once a child has been birthed in the U. S., the law of family reunification brings in the rest of the family. This strategy is known as "anchor babies."

However, it is difficult to see why the fact that a baby has been birthed on this side of the border should be grounds for citizenship. And the costs of such a policy are horrendous as we shall see below.

One program is based on chance: 55,000 random immigrants get green cards without regard to whether they will contribute to this country.[195] This, of course, is a bureaucratic cop-out.

THE PROBLEM IS A PROBLEM

The problem of immigration is a problem, however, because it entails severe costs, because it carries considerable risks to Americans, and because it has already racked up countless American victims.

The costs of immigration. It has been estimated that immigrants cost American taxpayers $93 billion dollars annually above the taxes paid by those immigrants who pay taxes. Health care and the education system are strained by the present level of immigration.[196] As mentioned previously, the increase in public school enrollments for 2003 came in at 30 times above the projected increase,[197] suggesting that the unforeseen increase came from immigration.

There are over 300,000 "anchor babies" born in the U. S. every year. These babies qualify for welfare, subsidized housing, Medicaid, etc., placing "astronomical costs" on taxpayers.[198] These anchor babies then begin a chain of *legal* immigration through the practice of admitting relatives of U. S. citizens.

Education. Another hidden cost is education. With help from the Supreme Court in 1982, school officials cannot ask students whether they are citizens nor refuse them a free public education if they aren't.[199] Since the Constitution gives Congress alone the power to legislate the questions of naturalization, the Court here openly usurped congressional authority.

One study found that 15 percent of California pupils were children of illegals. Texas, Arizona, Illinois and Nevada were close behind.[200] The costs of educating these children were put at $29 billion a year. In one Arizona school district, Mexican residents—yes, Mexican *residents*—were attending Arizona public schools. The school officials objected to turning them in because it would lower their student population and they would get less federal funding! Again, it's the taxpayers who pay, not the employers who employ the illegals.

Medical costs. The federal government has ordered hospitals to provide free health care to illegals.[201] Emergency rooms in the border states are essentially clinics for illegals. Mexican-American citizens have to wait; illegal Mexicans don't, because of the abundance of legal aid organizations eager to sue the hospital on any sign of "discrimination." The federal government, however, does not pay for this ordered free medical care. The result in Los Angeles is that "seven emergency rooms and sixteen clinics closed down in 2004 alone."[202]

Unemployment. President Bush says that illegals take only those jobs Americans don't want. In fact, they merely take *wages* that Americans don't want. American minorities are hardest hit by this illegal labor market, because a larger proportion of minorities work in the same job categories as the illegals.[203]

Increasing immigration also, of course, means increasing population. And increasing population means increasing demand for and consumption of oil, which increases oil dependency and exacerbates all the problems discussed in the previous chapter.

Other than that, the only concrete and specific benefits to America and to Americans that have been pointed out are few and minor, such as ethnic restaurants.

The threats associated with immigration. Two groups of immigrants are especially ominous: the Reconquistadores, those Mexican immigrants who boast that they are going to take over the American Southwest and return it to Mexico, and the Islamic immigrants. Not all Muslims are terrorists but all terrorists so far have been Muslim. Also, as we have seen, there are many other forms of Jihad in addition to terrorism.

La Reconquista. How many Mexican immigrants, legal and illegal, support the Reconquista? A poll of Mexican-American citizens revealed that a *majority* believed the southwestern U. S. properly belongs to Mexico.[204]

That means that many Mexican-Americans do not. Some assimilated Mexican-Americans are unhappy with the way their neighborhoods are being overrun by immigrants.[205] These Mexican-Americans are called racist by the immigrants. One Mexican-American responds, "As a Latino, I am sickened by groups such as [...]. These are racist, anti-American groups."²⁰⁶

Drugs. Immigration is also accompanied by drug smuggling. In addition to the harm that the drugs themselves do, there is the harm of the organization that must exist to obtain and deliver the drugs across the border. Prior to the "War on Terror", there was a "War on Drugs". The latter was no more effective than the former.

Crime. It is estimated that 30,000 illegals with criminal records are in Los Angeles County. The LAPD arrests 2,500 criminally convicted deportees annually.²⁰⁷ It is small wonder that some cities like New York follow a "don't ask, don't tell" policy.

Besides forgery of Social Security numbers and driver's licenses, a common crime is identity theft. For example, a divorced mother of two in Omaha, Nebraska had her Social Security number stolen and sold to an illegal Mexican woman. Soon, the American woman was in trouble with the government, had her credit ruined and had to pay money to straighten the whole thing out. And here's the kicker: the press and the pro-illegal immigration organizations made the *Mexican woman* the *victim* in this story!²⁰⁸

In 2003, there were 46,000 immigrants in federal prison (cost: $1.3 billion), 74,000 in state prisons (cost: $880 million), 147,000 in local jails.²⁰⁹ Looking at 55,332 illegals, this study found that they had been arrested an average of eight times apiece. Twelve percent were for violent crimes such as murder, assault, and rape.²¹⁰ It is also estimated that 95 percent of warrants for homicide in Los Angeles are for illegals.²¹¹

For instance, Russell Kuster, a fifty-year-old off-duty detective, was eating at a Hungarian restaurant in Hollywood when a hostile customer pulled a gun and began threatening the manager and the customers. Kuster tried to calm the situation, but the man shot him four times. Kuster died. He was within a year of retirement. The killer was an illegal who had a long list of arrests in his home country, Hungary, including robbery and rape. A year after he entered the U. S. illegally, he was arrested for homicide. The district attorney dropped the case. He was not deported. A year later, he was convicted on drug charges. When immigration officials finally moved to deport him, the killer applied for political asylum! This application allowed the prisoner to be released back into American society. When he committed sexual assault in Nevada, the INS again tried to deport him, but Hungary refused to take him back. The killer was freed again into American society and continued his life of crime which ended in the killing of detective Kuster.[212]

Tina Kerbrat was a rookie police officer with two children, three and six years old. One night when she stepped out of the cruiser to question two men who were drinking on a public sidewalk, one of the men shot her to death. He was an illegal from El Salvador who had filed a petition for political asylum. The INS denied the request. The man left and immediately crossed the border illegally again. He was arrested at the border but was allowed to remain in this country. After Tina Kerbrat's death, the police chief criticized the immigration authorities for their destructive policies. A Hispanic activists group immediately demanded an apology *from the police chief* and staged a demonstration. "Where's Mommy?" three-year-old Nicole asked as her mother's casket was carried into the church.[213]

During a routine traffic stop, officer James Saunders was shot and killed by an illegal from Mexico. He left behind a pregnant wife and a two-year-old daughter. The illegal who killed him was a convicted drug- and violent-criminal who had been released and deported three times. Washington State authorities arrested him for dealing cocaine and heroin, but the INS failed to pick him up. Two months later, he killed Officer Saunders.[214] The illegal immigrant and drug dealer filed a civil suit claiming his constitutional rights had been violated! There are numerous organizations that encourage illegals to sue whether they have a case or not and that cover the costs of such vindictive civil suits. The purpose is to buy time for the illegal and to inflict heavy costs on the government for daring to enforce immigration laws. And the tactic works.

Police sergeant Ricky Timbrook was shot in Winchester, Virginia while pursuing a suspect with other officers. His wife Kelly was pregnant with his son. The man who killed him was from Jamaica and had been arrested for illegal entry into the U. S. a year earlier. The illegal knew how to work the system and applied for a bail bond reduction. He got it and was released from jail. Over the next year, he won several delays in his deportation proceedings. After being arrested for the murder of Ricky Timbrook, the illegal applied for American citizenship![215]

Of course, American citizens also commit crimes, but the additional crime contributed by illegal immigrants is extra crime we don't need.

Armed incursions. There have also been armed incursions by corrupt elements of the Mexican army and police who have clashed with U. S. Border Patrols. One book also details the trashing of property and victimizing of Americans living near the border.[216] Interestingly, little of this is ever reported in the mainstream media.

"In the Tucson sector, Border Patrol agents are routinely assaulted, shot at, or rammed by smuggler vehicles."[217]

Disease. In the past, immigrants to the U. S. had to pass a health-screening test. No such test is administered today even to legal immigrants.[218] Tuberculosis, Chagas, acute hepatitis B., Chronic hepatitis C, sexually transmitted diseases have been reported.[219] The number of cases of Bubonic Plague are few but rising rapidly.

One author has even argued that immigration is bad for Mexico, because it allows the corrupt Mexican government to export its problems to the U. S. rather than correct those problems in its own society.[220]

Muslim immigration. The numbers will of course be disputed. Are there Americans, other than Muslims, who are in favor of more Muslim immigration? Yes. Generations of young Americans have been taught in schools and colleges to favor any policy that benefits Third-World people. Any proposal to limit immigration (from Third-World countries) is not only viewed as wrong, but the people proposing it are viewed as vile and despicable. Any proposal to increase immigration by Europeans is opposed.

In February, 2005, CIA director Porter Goss testified before Congress that it is only a matter of time before a group of terrorists "attempts to use chemical, biological, radiological and nuclear weapons."[221] In 2004, Border Patrol agents arrested more than 650 suspected terrorists.[222] Assuming the usual 3 to 1 chances of escaping detection, that would mean that 1,950 entered successfully. Recall also that it took only 20 terrorists to give us 9/11.

Canada, which has tried to "smoother terrorism with kindness", has become a major exporter of terrorists.[223] Canadian law does not make it a crime to belong to a terrorist group.[224]

Three Muslim illegals were arrested working as language instructors at the Army Special Operations Command Center at Fort Bragg.[225]

In Arizona, 26 employees of the state Department of Motor Vehicles were arrested for selling phony driver's licenses to smugglers, drug dealers and illegals.[226] A similar case occurred in Virginia. Federal authorities uncovered a crime syndicate selling millions of phony documents of all kinds to illegals (three million in Los Angeles alone).[227]

Many terrorists become legal American citizens simply by marrying an American.

The U. S. has implemented a system of obtaining a fingerprint of persons entering the country before issuing a visa. The fingerprint can be checked against a database. However, since it exempts persons entering from Canada and Mexico, the program applies to only 20% of persons entering.[228] Also, Islamists who become citizens of England, France, Spain or Germany can travel to the U. S. without a visa.

Victims of Immigration. Harder to quantify but more devastating in its emotional effect is the damage to individual people and the suffering to their relatives caused by immigrants. A website called www.ImmigrationsHumanCosts.org has been created and is devoted solely to this problem. Americans can contribute their stories to the site, but the stories must be accompanied by a photograph of the victim and a link to another website where the story is corroborated. We'll confine our cases to illegals.

A forty-year-old actress, Adrienne Shelly, was murdered by an illegal because she asked him not to make so much noise in the next apartment. She lost her life and a promising career. Her three-year-old daughter lost her mother.[229]

Twenty-eight-year-old Ryan Ostendorf was driving to his paramedic job in Topeka, Kansas when he was crashed into by a drunk-driving illegal. He was married to his long-time girlfriend, Meagan. The illegal had no driver's license, had been arrested for drunk driving before and had already been deported once. Drunk driving is a cultural attribute believed to demonstrate machismo, which may explain the large overrepresentation of Hispanics in drunk-driving statistics.[230]

Another indication that illegal immigration is not a victimless crime is the case of Natalie Housand, a 20-year-old nursing assistant who was working on her RN. An SUV traveling at 100 miles per hour plowed into her car head-on and killed her. A witness said the brake lights of the SUV never went on. The illegal immigrant driver said he was too drunk to remember the incident.[231]

Donna and Sean Wilson of Mt. Juliet, Tennessee were killed by another drunk driving illegal who had been arrested fourteen times in five years but never deported. Their daughter Heather, appearing at a press conference, expressed shock that such a "serial criminal" should be allowed to continue to haunt the highways. He was a tragedy looking to happen.[232]

Americans find it difficult to comprehend how anything alleged to be human could chop an axe into an innocent nine-year-old boy, but this happened to Jordin Paulder in Georgia. Jordin was playing with other children in front of the apartment building where they lived when a car with a wobbly tire drove by. Jordin called out to tell them they had a flat tire. The immigrant in the car found this offensive, so naturally he stopped the car, stepped out and slammed an axe into the child's face.[233]

An illegal, who had been ordered deported but never bothered to go, kicked in the apartment door of a Boston woman early one morning and announced, "I'm not here to steal, I'm here to kill." How the woman managed to remain alive has not been revealed, but this illegal turned up later in Minnesota living in a high school and posing as a student. Local Minnesotans rallied to his defense with "Free Francisco" T-shirts,[234] showing again that the problem is not just illegal immigration and is not just the government, but is also (some of) the people. And the press: the local newspaper decided that this was a story about homelessness and never mentioned the young man's criminal record nor his illegal status.

Be careful when you check your mail. Joyce Dargan of Myrtle Beach, South Carolina was at her roadside mail box when she was hit by a car driven by a 14-year-old illegal who was drag-racing another boy at 80 miles an hour. The boy had been stopped twice for traffic violations in the previous six weeks but was still on the road. Joyce's husband, commenting on the uselessness of government where immigration is concerned, vowed to be there six years later when the boy is set free from prison to kill again.[235]

Min Soon Chang, an 18-year-old freshman at UNC Charlotte was hit head-on by an illegal driving on the wrong side of an Interstate highway at 100 miles per hour. Chang was described as outgoing by family and friends. Chang joins young school teacher Scott Gardner of Gastonia, NC and many others killed by drunk illegals. Scott's wife was injured in the crash. When she recovers, she'll have to raise their two small children alone. The illegal had previous DUI arrests.[236]

Debbie Thomas, a mother of three, was killed on Christmas Eve by an illegal driving drunk in a car with no inspection sticker and registered to another person. Slightly injured in the crash, the illegal escaped from his hospital bed and is still at large.[237]

In Spotsylvania, VA, in broad daylight and in front of co-workers, an illegal whistled at a 15-year-old girl. Enraged that she did not respond, he ran after her, hit her in the face, fracturing a bone and producing cuts requiring 30 stitches, and tried to drag her off into nearby woods.[238]

An illegal with a prior cocaine possession conviction was killed in a shootout with police. In the shootout, he used his own small child as a human shield. She was killed too. Naturally, his "community" blamed the police; and his girlfriend, whom he had physically abused, is mounting a multi-million dollar lawsuit against the city of Los Angeles.[239]

A four-year-old girl in Gainesville, GA, was molested, strangled and killed by an illegal who had been deported before and was back again. The sheriff commented that being deported these days was like having an expense-paid trip home to see your relatives.[240]

A well-to-do Saudi couple was arrested for enslaving and sexually abusing an illegal for four years in their Aurora, Colorado home. One source commented that if Saudi Arabia treated a race the way they treat women, they would be as thoroughly condemned as South Africa (although the two nations are hardly parallels: South Africa did not chop off the genitals of Black female children and keep them locked up).[241]

In southern Utah, Travis Smith, 19, was killed as a carload of illegals plowed into his car. The smuggler, who was transporting the illegals to Pennsylvania, fell asleep at the wheel. For ending the life of this innocent teenager, the smuggler received six years in prison.[242]

An eight-year-old girl was raped and buried alive by an illegal who had been arrested three times the previous year for burglary. Had he been deported, this little girl's life would not have been ruined.[243]

Four immigrant gang members in Lynn, Massachusetts broke into a home and shot Amy Dumas, 16 years-old and her wheelchair-bound father.[244]

Mary Nagle was a 42-year-old mother of two young children and had a master's degree. She made the mistake of hiring an illegal immigrant to paint her house. For that, she was raped and killed. The illegal immigrant had been arrested before for assaulting a woman. He skipped his court appearance in that case and obviously he was not deported for being an illegal.[245]

Douglas, Arizona is a border town. Robberies, rape, beatings, etc. are a common occurrence there. Stock is killed, dogs poisons, fences cut, water tanks emptied. One little old lady was robbed fifty-seven times. They've also seen plenty of Arabs among the thousands of illegals who stream through every day. "Years ago they would politely ask you for water outside. Now you come home and someone is in your house, eating your food, trashing your bedroom, stealing your stuff and leaving garbage everywhere." Getting kids to school safely requires guards to follow the school bus, since a mother and daughter were carjacked by an illegal. One young girl was raped in her own home.[246]

Jenny Garcia, an 18-year-old college freshman, was murdered with a butcher knife in her own house by an illegal. The illegal had been arrested earlier for child molestation but was released by Austin, Texas authorities because Austin is a safe haven or sanctuary city for illegal immigrants.[247] A

Congressman introduced a bill to outlaw sanctuary for illegals, but only one fourth of the Congress voted in favor of the bill.

Brittany Binger, a 16-year-old girl in James City, Virginia was raped and murdered by an illegal and was so badly beaten that dental records had to be used to identify her body. The illegal had been arrested previously for drunk driving and possession of a fake Social Security number, but he was not deported. As a result, Brittany died a horrible death.[248]

An illegal immigrant was convicted of raping six people, including two Rutgers students and a 14-year-old girl. He had been arrested a few years before for assaulting a woman but was released on probation and was not deported, as the law requires. His luck ran out when he attempted to rape a young clerk in a music store. He was chased down the street and wrestled to the ground by the store owner's nephew and others.[249]

One Islamist decided to become a one-man Jihadist and tried to purchase guns and explosives. It was a sting operation, however, and the man was arrested.[250]

It is not unusual for Mexican illegals to have a wife and children in both countries.[251]

A number of small towns have been overwhelmed by an influx of immigrants, including gang violence, teen pregnancy, overburdened schools and increased taxes for Americans: Lewiston, Maine by Somalis; Wausau, Wisconsin by Hmong; Owatonna, Minnesota by Somalis. Somalis, although apparently poor, have been investigated by the FBI for contributing millions of dollars to terrorist groups in their homeland.[252]

A MISINFORMED ELECTORATE

One of the most sinister features of this problem and all the other problems facing America today is that most of the people simply do not know what is going on. This is why America is "sleeping."

News media contributions to this problem. Mainstream media, such as The New York Times, NPR, CNN, etc., have contributed to the problem of immigration in three ways: (1) by keeping people uninformed, (2) by keeping people misinformed and (3) by promoting immigration, both legal and illegal.

The Wall Street Journal labels anyone opposing *illegal* immigration as being "anti-immigration."[253] Illegal immigrants are routinely referred to in the mainstream media as "undocumented workers." The Wall Street Journal also condemned a U. S. Senator for proposing an *increase* in immigration of *only* 35 percent, comparing him to a KKK leader.[254]

The New York Times called the Minutemen "clowns."[255] The Los Angeles Times described an illegal immigrant caught in a traffic violation as "an Anaheim woman" instead of as "an illegal immigrant" and spent the majority of the article covering statements condemning the police, the city and the INS.[256] The Los Angeles Times also condemned those Americans who argue that illegal immigrants pose a security threat and take some jobs from Americans.[257]

The New York Times published dire descriptions of an America without illegal workers.[258] The Times also claimed that illegal immigrants were *helping* Social Security.[259]

A Washington Post reporter, after listening to a tape recording of a Congressman's speech about Chinese Communists from China in the U. S., reported that the Congressman had "insulted Chinese Americans, then slurred a fellow congressman, both blatantly false statements, as proved by the tape recording itself."[260]

The Arizona Republic newspaper opposed a bill that would authorize local police to arrest people crossing the border illegally, since that responsibility should be left to the feds (who everyone knows don't have adequate manpower).[261] The Arizona Republic also described two illegals with fake documents as working "aboveboard."[262] The same newspaper also described Minutemen using slanted language: "This is more about Deputy Dawg than effecting change."[263] The paper also calls a proposal that would grant all illegals "guest worker" status as "courageous" and calls enforcing the law "the easy way out."[264]

Another area of relentless misreporting is the issue of bilingual education. A poll that sampled *Latino* opinions in five heavily Hispanic American cities found that the Latinos overwhelmingly desired to have their children taught English as soon as possible and to have all other subjects taught in English. In one school district, Hispanic parents staged a boycott and pulled their children out of school to protest *against* bilingual educational practices. But the news media pay scant attention to such facts. Instead, they editorialize about the imagined virtues of bilingual education, and they rush to publicize those Hispanics who favor bilingual teaching.[265]

A prominent example is the coverage of the Proposition 227 initiative of the voters in California. In spite of polls showing widespread support among voters including Hispanics of the initiative to end bilingual education in California's public schools, the news media focused of those who opposed it, and reported that "bigotry" was the initiative's driving force. They also ignored the fact of teacher incompetence and the fact that many bilingual teachers were severely limited in their own English skills. When the Proposition won by 20 percentage points, including 40% of Hispanics in favor, the media moved to contain this fact from getting out by concentrating on the 60% of Hispanics who voted against the measure.[266]

In fact, even after the Proposition was enacted into law, many school districts simply ignored it and continued doing what they have been doing: handicapping Hispanic children by making it harder for them to succeed in American society. The media, of course, ignored these facts. Any other case where administrators defied the law would have been big news. Not in this case.[267]

WHAT TO DO?

So, is immigration a cost or a benefit, and to whom? Since it benefits some Americans (corporation owners and executives) and hurts others (the people), the question would seem to be one that could only be settled by a direct vote. It would have to be a direct vote by the people of the United States (or I should say, by the citizens of the United States). Not by the representatives, since the politicians are eager for cheap votes or have been bought off by corporations eager for cheap labor.

Force. If immigration is not decided on the basis of benefits or votes, then the issue comes back to one of force. The land was forcibly taken from the Mexicans. They are going to forcibly take it back, either by arms or by votes.

Of these, the more favorable to Americans would be arms, since an armed uprising would break the media code of silence and could be dealt with effectively by the citizens and the government.

The silent accumulation of votes via the birthrate of Hispanic and Muslim immigrants will continue to not be reported in the media and cannot be objected to in any case. And some point, Americans in effect lose their voice because Americans will always be outvoted by Hispanics and Muslims. Americans then become a disenfranchised minority in their own country. This will be a gradual process. It has happened in some cities and at least one state already, and more and more cities and states will be added until the national balance tips, between 2020 and 2030.

Proposed solutions. Four steps would ease the problem: (1) Eliminate the incentives to cross the border. (2) Eliminate the incentives to hire those who cross the border. (3) Punish those who cross the border. (4) Punish those who hire those who cross the border. Illegal immigration would still continue, however. The only way to solve the problem is to seal the borders.

Incentives for illegals. The incentives are jobs, welfare, etc. At present, there are no disincentives. Other nations can refuse the repatriation of their citizens.[268] The Supreme Court has ruled that illegals can only be incarcerated for six months; after that, they must be released back onto the streets.[269] If there are not enough beds for them, they must be released immediately. The number of beds is far fewer than the number of illegals. So, even if an illegal is caught, he still has it made. Even illegals who commit crimes are caught and serve their sentences and then released onto American streets rather than deported![270] These include sex criminals convicted of sexually assaulting young boys and girls.

There are also many American organizations designed to help people in the U. S. illegally![271] This help includes threatening companies with lawsuits if they turn in the illegals. How can they do that? Employment laws that bend over backward to be fair to workers can be twisted to discourage companies from taking action.[272] Another group called Humane Borders even puts water in the desert for illegal border crossers.[273]

Disincentives for corporations and employers. There are none. Phony Social Security Numbers only result in the IRS notifying the employer. The employer is not obligated to do anything about it.[274] The IRS does *not* notify the Department of Homeland Security or the INS about the phony social security numbers.[275]

In 2002, The Social Security Administration sent out a million "no match" letters to employers who filed phony W-2s. Business groups and pro-illegal immigration organizations swung into action condemning the SSA. Result: a 90 percent reduction in such letters.[276]

The incentives are cheap labor and a certain amount of power over the employee. Most of these businesses are eating and drinking establishments, construction companies, agricultural firms, service jobs in businesses, and health service organizations.[277]

One proposal is to tax corporations who hire immigrant labor at below par, and the corresponding law that would impose extra import duties on corporations that run to overseas cheap labor to reduce their costs. Problems with this proposal are that it would be difficult to get Congress to pass such laws[278], given the realities of campaign contributions, etc. Although the House has several times passed by nearly two-thirds a law authorizing troops on the border, the Senate always kills it.[279]

Also, given the continually increasing squeeze that energy costs impose on corporations, businesses have to make up those costs elsewhere. Unfortunately, it is the workers who have to pay the difference. And in this case, it is the costs and threats of immigration that are being increased by this squeeze. Thus, the problem of oil dependency reinforces and increases the problems of immigration.

Use of force. Given the magnitude of the problem, hiring enough Border Patrol agents would result in a mammoth police force in the southern and northern border states. One of the "unthinkable" solutions is to deploy the U. S. Army, or at least to have them ready as backup.

If Mexico says that Mexicans have a right to cross the U. S. border, then Americans have a right to cross the Mexico border. If National Guard units followed the armed gangs and armed drug smugglers across the border and wiped them out, Mexico might change its mind about open borders. A number of towns on the Mexican side of the border are known staging areas for incursions into the U. S.

Disincentives for politicians? Given that most political contests are close, any group of more than 5 percent of the voters wields considerable power, since they could decide whether the contest is won or lost. Thus, Senators and Presidents are loathe to offend Hispanic voters by opposing immigration or favoring limits to it. Do all Hispanics favor immigration? Affluent Hispanics are not thrilled with it, but how do they vote?

And how *could* one set up disincentives for politicians? Politicians would have to vote on it.

Enforcement is another problem. The Border Patrol is understaffed for the enormous task it has to do. And at least one Border Patrol agent in San Diego was himself involved in the illegal smuggling of people. The kicker is that he was himself an illegal who had gotten his job with a fake birth certificate.[280]

Some concerned citizens have become fed up with the federal government's disregard of their safety and have organized.[281] As the problem gets worse, one can expect the behavior of these citizens to become more determined. Will there have to be gunfights between citizens and Mexicans before the U. S. government will act on behalf of citizens or at least stop acting on behalf of illegals?

Another important question concerns the penalty for illegal entry into the United States. If the penalty is merely to be transported back to the border, then there is in effect no disincentive to try again, and in fact most do try again and succeed within the first few tries. Increasing the penalty for attempting to crash the border would probably help more than fences.

Abolishing Self-defense

Ronyale White was in her home at 11:40 P.M. on May 3, 2002 when her ex-husband showed up at the house and threatened to kill her. She called 911 and told them in a panicked voice what was happening and that she had a restraining order that was to be given "Priority 1A". Ronyale was told the police were on their way. She locked her bedroom door, turned on a tape recorder and waited trembling. Five minutes later, she called 911 again and told them her husband had a gun and was threatening to kill her. She pleaded with them to hurry. Five minutes later, she called the police again as her bedroom door was being kicked in. Two shots were heard. The phone went dead. When the police arrived, after 17 minutes, they found Ronyale dead on the floor.[282]

Self-defense is a natural instinct. It is also an inalienable right if there ever was one. But any right, without the means to exercise that right, is no right at all. To tell people they have a right to defend themselves, provided they don't use anything but their bare hands, is to deceive people. In these days when attackers are invariably armed, people who are not allowed to be armed have been deprived of their right of self-defense. Alternatives like pepper spray don't do a lot of good when it is raining; moreover, indoors or when it's windy, a person is as likely to hurt herself as her assailant with such devices.[283] Even karate is useless against a handgun at ten paces.

To persuade people to give up their right of self-defense is a mental coup. Yet, in the United States in the last few decades, this is what has happened.

Self-defense! Who needs it? First, Americans have been persuaded that they do not need to defend themselves because someone else will do it for them, namely, the police or the army. But this is a deception that borders on an outright lie.

Many people do not know that police do not have a legal obligation to protect *individuals*. That's right. Courts have without exception ruled that police only have an obligation to protect the public at large.[284] Just who the public is made up of, if not individuals, is comprehensible only to the legal mind.

In any case, police usually arrive too late to stop a crime or even to apprehend the criminal. The police may be busy, may suffer technological breakdowns or be too far away to respond in time. One book presents cases in which the police were negligent, incompetent or even criminal in their behavior.[285] As a result, criminals "are much more worried about encountering an armed victim than about the police."[286]

At the same time, the U. S. Army has proved twice that it can't cope with terrorist/guerrilla-style warfare. If the Islamists, or the Reconquistadores, or both at the same time opt for taking America by force, the government will need an armed citizenry in order to survive. Some have speculated that Saudi Arabia will cripple the U. S. economy just before the insurgency begins, so that the federal government will be weak and will be preoccupied with economic disasters and can't respond effectively to the insurgency. If citizens do not know how to defend themselves and are ill equipped to do so, guess who will win?

It is an irony of fate that at this critical time, when Reconquistadores and Islamists are pouring across the border with their unregistered, high power guns, the U. S. government is taking steps toward banning gun ownership by Americans.

Fear and loathing. The second prong of the mental coup against Americans has been a massive re-education campaign in the press and in the schools to create and sustain an attitude of fear and loathing of guns per se.[287] For instance, in Jonesboro, Arkansas, an 8-year-old boy was suspended from school for three days for pointing a breaded chicken finger and saying, "Pow, pow, pow."[288] In Irvington, New Jersey, two second-graders playing cops and robbers with paper guns were charged with making terrorist threats. The boys were suspended from school and even charged by police with a crime. "These examples show how a 'zero tolerance' policy can be turned to embarrass, humiliate and punish people for any thought about or contact with anything that even suggests a weapon"[289]

Faking the data. Besides "the media's wholesale demonization of gun-owners",[290] a large number of studies and statistics are done to make it seem that guns are dangerous to gun owners and to children, that guns increase crime, etc.[291] It would be nice to be able to say, as with immigration estimates, that these numbers merely reflect different opinions. Unfortunately, in this case the studies are flawed at best and faked at worst.[292]

One book provides a detailed analysis of the statistics and a discussion of methodological problems in the anti-gun's data-fabrication crusade.[293]

For example, the statistic that says that gun owners are more likely to be killed by guns when their homes are invaded by armed thugs. This study did not distinguish between those who were killed by their own guns and those who were killed by the guns of the armed thugs! If there was a gun in the house and the owner was killed, it counted. The study also included suicides among their data! That's right, suicides. The truth is that gun owners are much *less* likely to be killed by an assailant than people who do not have guns.

Women who own guns are two-and-a-half time *less* likely to be harmed than women who do not own guns.[294]

After England banned guns, according to the British Home Secretary, Jack Straw, "levels of victimisation are higher than in most comparable countries for most categories of crime.... England and Wales were second only to Australia [another gun-control nation] in victimization rates."[295]

The reason is simple: criminals will always get their guns, just as those who wanted a drink during Prohibition got one.

The seventeen states without concealed-carry permits have 81 percent higher rate of violent crime. Restrictive gun laws produce 1,400 more murders, 4,200 more rapes, 12,000 more robberies, and 60,000 more aggravated assaults.[296] One lie is that permitting people to carry a concealed weapon will enable criminals to commit crimes more easily. But less than .001 percent of people with concealed-carry permits commit crimes or have their gun permits revoked.[297]

When a sniper went on a shooting spree in Washington, D. C., the press went on a spree with articles urging the banning of guns without stopping to remember that in Washington, D. C. guns *are* banned. In fact, in D. C., where guns have been banned for thirty years, the homicide rate and violent-crime statistics prove that Washington is more violent and unsafe than Baghdad.[298]

After a criminal/terrorist shot dozens of people on a Long Island train, loading and reloading 15-cartridge magazines into his gun, a New York Times article claimed that lots of lives would have been saved if a law had existed that limited cartridge size to 10 rounds!

Other than anti-gun articles, anti-gun TV programs and movie documentaries, there is almost a media blackout on guns. Few of the stories of people saving their own lives with guns make it into the press and then only in small town newspapers. Americans are learning that if they want accurate information, they have to turn to the Internet, for instance, www.AmericanSelfDefense.com. On the Internet too, of course, one has to be critical and selective. There are many, many anti-gun websites.

What may be the last movie to present citizens owning guns in a favorable light was "Red Dawn" in 1984. In this movie, the infiltrators knew that gun stores were required to keep a government form that listed all the gun owners in town. They simply broke in and grabbed this form, then rounded up all the gun owners, since the gun owners were the ones most likely to resist. A documentary by Larry Elder, entitled "Michael & Me" refutes many of the false claims in Michael Moore's "Bowling for Columbine."

While homicide rates dropped 20% between 1992 and 1996, *reporting* of homicides in the news media increased by 721%.

After September 11, 2001, gun sales surged by 20%. Approximately 60% of the increase is due to sales of guns to women.[299]

For more information, see www.justfacts.org/gun_control.html.

Stealth. But is the U. S. government really moving toward banning guns altogether? America's two most popular newspapers have admitted that the so-called "assault weapons ban" is merely the first step. As one columnist put it, "[The assault weapons ban's] only real justification is not to reduce crime but to desensitize the public to the regulation of weapons in preparation for their ultimate confiscation."[300] A New York Times editorial says the same thing.[301] The former head of Homeland Security, Tom Ridge, in January 2003 proclaimed that any use of a firearm by anyone under any circumstance, is a *terrorist* act.[302]

The Mafia would undoubtedly welcome a ban on guns. They could do a land-office business selling illegal guns to ordinary citizens. It would be a bonanza not seen since the government tried to ban the sale of alcoholic beverages.

If the American colonials had been anti-gun, there would be no United States today. If the early humans had been unwilling to kill those who threatened them, there would be no human race today.

Alienation. The federal government's opposition to gun ownership has also alienated what has traditionally been one of the most patriotic and staunch group of American citizens: gun owners. Quite apart from the merits of having an armed citizenry, it is safe to say that strategically it was a very unwise move on the part of the politicians to alienate this group of Americans, especially at the present time.

The movement to ban guns. After the government passed a law banning "assault" weapons, the sale of semi-automatic weapons immediately doubled. There are indications that gun owners are stashing weapons and ammunition preparatory to an eventual government ban and confiscation of guns. The expectation is a gradual move: rifles with telescopic sights next, weapons with pistol grips next, weapons holding more than 15 rounds, more than 10 rounds, more than 8 rounds, etc.

One gun-ban organization claims a 95% success rate in getting anti-gun candidates elected as Congressmen, Senators, governors and mayors in the 2006 midterm elections. If anti-gun people really believe what they are advocating, they should put a sign in front of their houses saying, "This is a gun-free home." They won't do that, of course, because they know their house would be targeted by criminals. But what if all homes implicitly had such a sign in front of them?[303] That's what a gun ban does.

Mainstream newspapers report shooting sprees but never report that the spree was stopped by the use of a gun. Nor do they try to estimate how many other people, who would have died, are alive because one of the good guys had a gun.

Defending America. To guard against even isolated terrorist attacks on the major targets, like reservoirs, railroads, and trucking, a police force of enormous size would be required. The economic effects of recruiting and training such a police force would be prohibitive. And a police force of that size would turn America into a police state such as the world has never seen.

Citizens must be used to guard against terrorism. There is nothing new in this. Citizen air raid watchers were used in World War II. Even now, neighborhood crime-watch groups exist. Such citizen groups are needed to guard against terrorist attacks. Whether those groups are armed or not should be decided on practical grounds, not on the basis of *a priori* hatred of guns.

Defending ourselves. Many people don't have guns because they believe they don't need them. But the time to buy a gun is *before* you need it. When you need it, it's already too late.

One woman, who was a lobbyist for one of the anti-gun groups until her own personal experience changed her mind, has spent the years since writing books for women on guns and personal safety. In one of her latest, she gives success stories of women saving their own lives and those of their children with handguns. She reports that 37.6 million American women either own or have rapid access to guns. According to Department of Justice figures, 27% of American women keep a gun in the house. She also provides evidence against the media-driven myths (lies) about guns.[304]

Senator Craig of Idaho claims that on average every thirteen seconds someone uses a gun to stop a crime.[305] In one study of six thousand such cases, in 98 percent of the cases, a shot was never fired.[306] For instance, in one case, a homeowner, answering the door at night to find two disreputable looking thugs standing there, simply raised his shirt to show his handgun. The two ran away. The actual number of cases is undoubtedly much higher than is known, since in most cases of successful self-defense, especially where no shot was fired, gun owners do not bother to report the incident.

Another unreported but terribly important fact is that many people are walking around each day never knowing that their own lives were saved because *somebody else* owned and used a gun. For instance, a coed at UNC/Charlotte heard the glass door of her apartment being forced at 3 A.M. one night. A man entered her bedroom, pulled a knife and forced her to submit to rape. While he was enjoying himself, she reached over to her bedside table, opened the drawer, took out her gun and blasted the man. DNA evidence proved that this was the serial rapist who had raped four other coeds in the past year.

Crime statistics show that serial rapists rape an average of 20 women before they are stopped, and some rape as many as 100. By killing this rapist, the unidentified and unsung young woman saved 16 other women from being raped and may have saved as many as 96 other women. These other women, many of whom undoubtedly are opposed to guns and in favor of gun control, will continue to live never knowing that their own bodies were spared because of the use of a gun.[307]

Another example: twenty-seven homes in the Little Rock, Arkansas area had been invaded in six months. But when a couple of middle-age homeowners stopped three men who broke into their home, wounding one of the men in the process, home invasions in Little Rock stopped completely for more than a year.[308]

Since 75 percent of violent crimes are committed by criminals with a history of arrests, it is probable that stopping any one criminal saves the lives and property of countless other people.[309]

Does the Second Amendment guarantee a right to own guns? Another prong in the multi-prong attempt to abolish the right of self-defense is the audacious claim that the Second Amendment of the Constitution does not recognize a right to own a gun.

Anti-gun organizations claim that the Amendment only guarantees a right to have a militia and does not give individuals the right to own a gun. But in the seventeen and eighteen centuries, a militia was different from an army. A militia was raised from the citizens of the local area for a specific, usually emergency, task. If the citizens didn't have guns and know how to use them, you could not raise a militia. To put it another way, the potential militia is the citizenry.

More importantly, the Constitution does not *give* rights. Americans were assumed to *have* those rights, independently of and prior to the Constitution. The War of Independence was not fought to defend the Constitution, because there was no Constitution at the time. The document inspiring the Revolution was the Declaration of Independence. And that document recognized individual human rights as existing prior to itself. "We hold these truths to be self-evident...." They were regarded as self-evidently right as well as already existing.

The Ninth Amendment makes it clear that "The enumeration in the Constitution, of certain rights, shall not be construed to deny or disparage others retained by the people."

The original version of the Constitution did not state a list of individual rights, and many were opposed to doing so, since it could be interpreted to mean that any rights not listed did not exist. Many in fact distrusted the whole idea of the Constitution. Patrick Henry refused to attend the Constitutional Convention, saying he "smelt a rat." Even most of those who did attend distrusted the power of *any* central government. The Constitution reads like what it is: a determined attempt to limit in every possible way the potential power of the central government.

The Bill of Rights does not grant rights. It states *restrictions* on the government and declares explicitly that the government is *not* to *limit* the rights of individuals, thus recognizing that those rights exist prior to and independent of the Constitution. Thomas Jefferson wrote letters to all the State conventions urging them not to ratify the Constitution until a Bill of Rights was attached to it. And many did not.

Thus, whether the Second Amendment is intended to guarantee a militia or not, the Second Amendment prohibits the government from limiting gun ownership, thus implicitly recognizing a right to own guns.

Cases. Stories of successful defensive gun-use rarely make it into the news media, while the media is often willing to actually create news or fabricate stories to promote gun control.[310] Here is some of the news that was not fit to print:

An Israeli housewife saved many lives in 2002 when she shot dead a terrorist about to set off a bomb in a supermarket.[311]

Barbara, a single parent with three children, had her house broken into three times. Reluctantly, she bought a gun. One day when she was home sick with a cold, a man came to her door with a story about having something belonging to her daughter who had just gone off to school. Barbara had no way of knowing that this man had been jailed for raping two women twenty years before but was let out after only four years due to "good behavior." A few months later, he'd raped again, was caught and imprisoned. Fourteen years later, he was on the streets again. Today, Barbara opened the door to him just enough to take the letter he held in his hand. The man burst through the door, slashing Barbara with a rusty blade. Barbara's 11-year-old son jumped on the man's back and Barbara ran for her gun, slipping and sliding in her own blood. She emptied the gun into the man. The judge sentenced the man to life. The police confiscated Barbara's gun, but Barbara was now convinced. She went right out and bought another gun.[312]

It is estimated that one out of every six American women have been or will be the victim of an attempted or completed rape during their lifetimes.[313]

Many other women are victims of American courts' now pro-criminal bias. Sharlotte Pearson had been beaten repeatedly before and after her divorce. She moved from Pensacola to Forest Park to escape her ex-husband, but he found her again and began beating her. She managed to get her gun, shot and killed him. She was arrested and charged with murder! The jury took just 30 minutes to find Sharlotte not guilty.[314]

Denny Halston was dragged kicking and screaming from her mother's car by her ex-husband. Denny's mother pulled out her handgun from her purse and ordered him to stop beating her. She held him at gunpoint until the police arrived.[315] In many more cases, of course, the woman does not have her mother there to save her.

In many cases, a gun in the hand of a woman *able and willing to use it* is enough to save a woman's life. Jeanine in St. Louis had two sons asleep in her third-floor apartment in the middle of the night when she heard a noise. She got her gun and ran into the living room just as the man crashed in through the patio door of her balcony. She was already only six feet away, too close for firing at anything but his head. She chambered a round, flicked the safety off and leveled the sight right between the man's eyes. The man, who was out on bond, ran away. Jeanine called the police and gave them a description and the direction of flight. The man was arrested shortly after.[316]

Brenda Barnett lives near Sun Valley but has to make a business trip once a week on two-lane highways. One October morning, she saw a pickup truck tailing her. The truck pulled along side, and two men began making obscene gestures at her. Brenda picked up her gun, which she always keeps in the car. When the two men saw it, "they were off like greased lightning."[317]

In Dallas in 2002, a retired doctor and his wife turned into their driveway when a man wearing a mask and carrying an AK-47 pulled up in front of the driveway and ordered the old couple down on the ground. The doctor's wife Patricia took out her revolver and began firing. The wannabe terrorist returned fire, jumped in his car and drove away, but the police found the bullet-marked car the next day.[318]

Charmaine Dunbar of Pittsburg, a married mother of three, was walking her dog when a man with a gun came up behind her and ordered her to stop. He had sexually attacked six women in the previous six weeks, completing rape twice and forcing a woman to perform oral sex on him in another case. The women ranged in age from 10 to 33 years of age. But this time was different. His victim was armed. Charmaine fired twice, disabling her wannabe rapist.[319]

There are many, many other cases, almost none of which are broadcast or printed by the news media. A woman, afraid of guns, bought only a .22 caliber pistol. When a man broke into her house and began slashing her face with a knife, she shot him four times without stopping him.

Sometimes, it is armed citizens who save the lives of wounded policemen.

People do not lose their humanity just because they own a gun. One woman allowed herself to be beaten severely before she could bring herself to shoot her assailant. An old man was abducted and forced into the trunk of his own car. Unfortunately for the criminal, the trunk was where he kept his guns. When allowed out of his trunk, miles from nowhere, the old man fired three times, trying to scare off his abductor, before he was forced to shoot him.[320]

Sue Gay, a grandmother in Indiana, was saved from a man who broke into her house and held a box cutter to her throat. Her 11-year-old grandson ran upstairs, got a gun, and shot the man.[321]

Erin Moul, the owner of a small bookstore, was approached by a customer in her store who demanded that she open her cash register and give him all her money. "I don't think so," she said and pulled out the gun she kept in her purse. The would-be robber saw the gun, freaked out and ran out of the store.[322]

Minnie Dorsey was in her Florida home one night when a man kicked in her door and threatened her, demanding her money. The 83-year-old grandmother pulled her handgun, and the intruder ran out of the house.[323]

In Kentucky, a serial robber picked a Deli Mart as his next victim. It was a bad choice, even though the robber was armed. The clerk was armed too and defended himself. The robber was wounded, fatally as it turned out.[324]

Out of 12 stories that ran in small town newspapers over a five-day period, four of the intended victims were women, one was Black, one was Oriental, and another was Indian. The researcher quipped, "Self-defense is an equal opportunity emancipator."[325]

Michelle Ayres was raped in 1994 when could not defend herself. When another attempt was made in 2000 by another man, Michelle was armed. Her husband was at work. Her two children were asleep in their home, both sick. Michelle had nursed them for two days and was exhausted. In the middle of the night, a man broke the window of a rear door, unlocked the dead bolt and got in. He punched Michelle repeatedly and tried to rape her. Fortunately, her husband kept his gun under the pillow. She was able to get the gun and fire it at the rapist. The man ran out of the house.[326]

Ann Barry, a 60-year-old single woman, taught night courses and knew she needed protection. She bought a gun and took lessons. When a man broke into her house, her first thought was to call 911, but there was no time. She saw a man creeping down the hallway with a gun in his hand. She raised her gun, fired and ducked back behind the door frame of her bedroom. The man swung towards her and started shooting. When the shooting stopped, Ann prepared to take another shot, but the man had turned and started back toward the kitchen, staggered, but made his way out of the house. Ann then called 911, but her hands were shaking so badly that it took her three tries to get the number right. There were two other bad guys with this one, but they all tried to run away when the shooting started. They were so flustered by this resistance that they backed their car into a ditch. They fled on foot but were eventually rounded up by the police.[327]

A young man stopped his car at a red light. Suddenly, two men appeared at his window with guns and ordered him to get out of his car. Instead, the young man picked up his licensed handgun and shot one of the men. The other man fled. The two men had just robbed some other men on the street.[328]

Convenience stores are the target of choice for criminals, yet many store chains do not allow their employees to be armed. Many of the employees are teenagers and laws do not permit them to have guns. In Houston, after five convenience stores were robbed in five days, store clerks began arming themselves. When two armed men entered a Texaco gas station convenience store and began to pistol-whip one of the employees, the other, Khoa Nguyen, pulled his handgun from beneath the counter, and a shoot-out took place. Khoa won.[329]

Some people have to learn the hard way. Lisa Liev, a clerk, had been robbed and beaten a month earlier. She got a gun. When another robber entered the store where she worked, Lisa still wore a bandage on her head. The robber raised his gun to shoot Lisa. She dropped to the floor and got her gun. The man jumped the counter to get at Lisa, but she fired. The man died at the scene.[330]

Even gated, security-conscious developments are not immune. Near Orlando, Florida, Elizabeth Magruder lived with her husband Ron. A registered sexual predator, who was awaiting trial for raping his own 13-year-old daughter but was allowed out on the street by a judge, was stalking Elizabeth. As Elizabeth and Ron were sitting out by the pool, the predator entered the yard, grabbed Elizabeth by the throat and dragged her into the house, pointing a gun at Ron to keep him off. Ron ran to a neighbor's to dial 911, and the distraction enabled Elizabeth to twist herself free and run down the hall and into her bedroom. She reached her gun just as the predator grabbed her from behind in a choke-hold. Elizabeth twisted toward him and fired. The career of this career sexual predator was over. No judge will ever be able to release him again.[331]

A few months after Maria Pittaras finally was able to buy her dream house in an *upscale development* in Florida, she woke up to find a man on top of her. The man was a *neighbor*, a married man. He held a knife to her throat and ordered her to cooperate as he pulled the covers off her and began to grope her. Maria felt around on her nightstand for the revolver her father had given her the year before. With one hand, she cocked it, pointed and fired. The man slumped off of her. By the time the police arrived, he was dead.[332]

Another serial rapist was operating in the Colorado Springs area. In the space of a few months, he had attacked a fifty-six-year-old woman coming out of her bathroom at about 11 P.M. He tied her up and repeatedly raped her. In another town, he grabbed a 51-year-old woman as she came out of her bathroom. She struggled and he choked and stabbed her in the neck and abdomen. Then he raped her for hours. Finally, he picked Jean Zamarripa. But this 72-year-old woman was armed. When she heard a noise on her back porch, she called 911. But as usual, before anyone could get there, the man crashed in, breaking two locks including a dead bolt. Jean was ready with her revolver. She fired several times, and the man ran. He was so flustered that he drove recklessly, attracting police attention, and the police caught him. DNA linked him to the series of rapes. He was sentenced to four life sentences.[333]

Lessons from the past. Significantly, when Islam conquers a nation or a people, they disarm them, even though the Muslims remain armed. Dhimmis are forbidden from owning guns or bearing arms.[334]

Historically, one of the first things governments do when they interfere with the rights of some of their citizens is to disarm them. It is usually done gradually, as in Nazi Germany. First, the Nazis passed a seemingly innocuous law requiring registration or licensing of guns. This provides the government with a list of the names and addresses of the people who own guns. Second, they imposed tighter restrictions on easily concealed guns, such as handguns. Third, they passed a gun ban. The Jews dutifully turned in their guns to show that they were law-abiding and harmless citizens. After they did so, the Nazis rounded them up and put them into concentration camps.[335]

The same pattern was followed in Ottoman Turkey in 1915-1917. The Turks, who were Muslims, ordered the Armenians, most of whom were Christian, to obtain permits to carry guns. The Armenians complied. This provided the government with a list of gun owners. Then, the government passed a gun ban and confiscated all the guns. Once the government had the guns, they slaughtered the Armenians.[336] (A current exercise of *taqiyya* denies that any genocide of Armenians ever took place. The Armenians, however, have a different opinion about that.)

The Soviet Union followed the same pattern: licensing in 1918, a ban in 1920, severe penalties in 1926. From then until 1945, 20 million people (class enemies) were exterminated.[337]

Uganda, from 1971-1979, established registration of all guns and owners, then licenses for transactions involving guns. This was followed by confiscation and searches without a warrant. After that, 300,000 Christians were slaughtered.[338]

In 1994, Rwanda required registration of guns, owners, and ammunition. Then, it outlawed the carrying of concealed guns. Then, it gave itself the power to confiscate guns. Then, 800,000 Tutsis were exterminated.[339]

Nationalist China required gun permits in 1914. In 1935, they established a ban on gun ownership. Ten million people were rounded up and killed. Communist China picked up where the Nationalists left off, establishing tougher laws in 1951 and 1957. Twenty to thirty-five million enemies of the state were wiped out.[340]

Guatemala passed laws requiring the registration of guns and owners with high licensing fees in 1932. In 1947, the government passed laws prohibiting the carrying of guns. In 1964, Guatemala passed a law banning guns and sharp tools. After that, between one and two hundred thousand Mayas and other Indians were slaughtered.[341]

The list goes on and on, but the path followed is the same. In the United States, the government has begun to follow the same path, starting with registration and licensing.

Subordinating Ourselves

In Illinois, a little girl named Jessica had been longing to transfer to a certain elementary school, so her parents applied for the transfer. One day a letter arrived informing her parents that Jessica could transfer to the school. The phone rang soon after, and a school official interviewed Jessica over the phone. After the interview, he told Jessica that she was approved. Jessica was very excited. The next morning, with optimism in her heart, she dressed and went off to school. But after the orientation session, a teacher took Jessica aside and told her that she could not be admitted to the school. Why? Jessica wanted to know. Because you are white.[342]

A strange thing happened in America in the 1970s. A new principle was introduced into the national consciousness. It was different from the principles on which the nation was founded and had always lived by. But the principle was staunchly defended, because it formed the basis of a new plan for the benefit of Black people.

How we got here. In 1954, the Supreme Court had decided in *Brown vs. Board of Education* that separate was inherently unequal. This was a milestone in the struggle to promote the equality of Black people. The decision was based on a diagnosis of a problem and on a prediction of results that would bring solution. The problem was believed to be prejudice. Prejudice is forming judgments on the basis of inadequate evidence or no evidence. White people were believed to have condescending or demeaning opinions about Black people because they didn't know any Black people or had not spent enough time with them. The cause of this was that the two groups were segregated from each other: they lived in different parts of town, attended different schools, etc.

The solution was to be integration. If people were required to attend the same schools, live in the same neighborhoods, etc., they would get to know each other, and white people would see that Black people were the same in all important ways. It was also believed that Black people would then be attending better quality schools and getting a better education—although this was not explicitly stated. In the Brown case, the two schools were chosen because they *were* essentially of the same quality. The NAACP, in selecting this case to pursue, wanted to make sure that the court did not simply order the district to improve the quality of the Black school to make it equal to the white school. They got what they sought: the Court declared that separation itself was fundamentally the problem and ordered integration.

The consequences are now well known: white flight from cities to county schools and neighborhoods, which was countered by Court-ordered bussing of city kids to county schools, which was countered by the explosion of private schools. The nation we live in today—crumbling cities surrounded by relatively pleasant suburbs—is the consequence of this program to improve the lot of Black people.

In short, it didn't work.

What to do? In the 1960s, various other programs were tried. Educational programs like "head start" were funded to provide crash courses in remedial studies to bring the preparation of Black students entering college up to the level of the white (i.e. non-Black) students. These programs included psychological counseling to remove any problems of self-esteem or other blocks to successful performance.

TV and the movies got involved and portrayed Black people in more and more programs and movies and only in favorable ways. This probably did more than anything to remove stereotyped perceptions of Black people, because in these shows Black actors were not allowed to behave in stereotyped ways.

All of this helped, but it still wasn't enough to achieve equality. The failure was blamed on a "culture of poverty" which involved inculcating attitudes of low self-esteem, expectations of failure, a dislike of reading, etc. These attitudes were reproduced from one generation to the next and thus the cycle of poverty recurred. A massive "War on Poverty" was mounted. This resulted in welfare dependency, father desertion thanks to "aid to dependent children", and welfare exploitation by poor people (who were smarter than the politicians thought they were).

With the murder of Martin Luther King, Jr., the Civil Rights Movement took a different turn. It gave way to Black Power. But what to do? Everything had been tried.

The coalition of organizations driving the movement at this time came up with a drastic plan. (Whenever group planning or networking are mentioned, someone always yells, "Conspiracy!" There was no "conspiracy." Just because a large number of people are working to solve a problem and they occasionally communicate their results to each other and argue with each other, doesn't mean they are conspiring.)

A temporary plan. The plan was to be temporary: Put Black people into the best schools, including professional schools like law, medicine and business administration, even if their admissions qualifications were lower than other applicants. Require the hiring of Black people into managerial positions and their promotion to higher and higher positions, qualifications notwithstanding. In order to do this, race had to be, not only one of, but the overriding criterion of college admissions and of corporate hiring and promotion.

It seemed like a good scheme. These Black people would get better jobs, make more money, establish an achieving and supportive home environment for their children, featuring attitudes of eagerness to learn and love of reading. Those children would do well on their own, have other children who would do well, etc. After that, the plan could be dropped, because it would no longer be needed.

One small problem. There was just one little problem, but it was merely a philosophical one: this program meant adopting the very *opposite* of the fundamental principle that had guided the Civil Rights Movement. That principle had been: *no discrimination based on race*. It was a principle that appealed to the notion of fair play of all Americans, including white people. The principle was now to be: discriminate on the basis of race. And the people to be discriminated against were white people!

The intellectual merits of this idea began to be debated by academics, and the controversy over it shattered the unity that had existed among liberals for the past twenty years. Academics are still trying to come up with clever arguments in favor of this idea. But this debate need not detain us here, because we can now concern ourselves with the *actual* consequences of this program.

A tough sell. In the 1970s, this new scheme presented tactical problems: how to sell this idea to people in general, and how to hold together the coalition of white and Black people who had supported and worked for equality and civil rights for twenty years?

The people running the organizations were politically experienced by the 1970s and knew from their experience the power of slogans and labels. How to sell the idea of unequal treatment to people who had fought for equal treatment for so long? How to persuade people to accept preferment based explicitly on race when they had fought for twenty years against handing out privileges based on race? And more ticklish still: how to get Americans to accept a scheme of *subordinating themselves* to a small minority when Americans are deeply opposed to subordinating themselves to anybody?

It was going to be a tough sell. They couldn't call it "racial preference" even though that's what it was. They couldn't call it "racial quotas", even though quotas were to be the criteria they would use in arguments to force schools, politicians and corporations to implement this plan. In fact, the word "race" must not appear in the label at all, even though race was to be the overriding criterion. How to swing it?

What's in a name? Everything! Some ingenious person, whose name has been lost to history, came up with the label "affirmative action." It was brilliant. It didn't really *say* anything, so it couldn't be refuted. And it sounded great. Action was what was needed, and lots of people were in favor of doing something. And affirmative—who could be against anything that was affirmative?

And so the campaign was launched. "Affirmative action" was the new program for helping those less fortunate than we, helping those in need. The people who had worked for years and voted for years for just such an idea—helping those in need—accepted this new slogan with open arms, open hearts and open pocketbooks. And the media jumped on the bandwagon.

Even today, the term still works its magic. In 1997, the city council of Houston proposed a measure that would end "racial preferences". Polls showed the public in favor of the motion by a substantial margin. Activists got busy and persuaded the city council to change the wording of the proposal to "ending affirmative action." The wording was changed, and the measure was defeated by a substantial margin.[343]

But until a few intrepid souls began to get the word out that America had been sold a program of discrimination, discrimination against the "white" race was carried on behind the scenes. For instance, a Pentagon hiring directive actually read: "Special permission will be required for promotion of all white males without disabilities."[344]

In the 1970s, no one stopped to ask, but isn't "affirmative action" really preferential treatment based on race? And isn't the race being discriminated against the white race? In fact, *all* races and cultures except one were being discriminated against. Most people didn't notice. They were turned down for admission. Okay, well, their grades weren't *that* good and they didn't do *that* well on the SATs. They didn't get the job they applied for. Well, the company must have found a better person.

But as the program began to go into effect around the nation, the reality of what this wonderful term actually meant began to be driven home to a few individuals who just couldn't rationalize it away.

Victims of race preferences. In 1987, Yat-pang Au was a Chinese-American high school graduate who was the top of his class, with SAT scores higher than 50% of the UC Berkeley student body. Yet he was turned down for admission to Berkeley. He and his father decided to fight back.[345]

Cases like this began to get the word out to white people, Jews, Asians and others that they were being discriminated against on the basis of their race or ethnic group. People with higher scores were being penalized because they belonged to the wrong race! As recently as 2003, the Supreme Court ruled that universities can continue to discriminate against student applicants based on their race.

Boston Latin School, one of the highly desirable schools in the Boston area, denied admission on the basis of race to white students with high exam scores in favor of minority students with lower exam scores. Julia McLaughlin's father sued the school, citing the fact that over a hundred minority students with scores lower than hers were admitted. Luckily for Julia, a district court judge ruled the admission policy racist and unconstitutional.[346]

Discrimination against people who were not the right race was not confined to students. Sandy Atkins taught school for five years, then raised her children, then returned to teaching while still raising her children. When she had obtained a Master's in educational leadership, she began applying for the job of principal at various schools. She was repeatedly passed over for less experienced and less qualified Black candidates because she was white.[347]

A hundred and ninety-two teachers at Northern Arizona University sued the college for denying them pay raises because of their race. All had been earning salaries below the midpoint of their salary range, but none had been given raises. At the same time, almost all minorities in that same categories were given raises. The white teachers lost in court but won on appeal.[348]

Some airlines are so intimidated by the power of minorities that they have lowered their qualifications for pilots to the extent that the lives of passengers and crew are endangered. The stories are told here in the words of some insiders:

"I myself was an airline pilot and knew many good people with plenty of heavy jet experience, who interviewed at ... and were turned down as a result of quotas. [This airline] has been the worst airline in the past many years to hire young inexperienced minorities over very experienced pilots. As an example, [this airline's] requirements for pilots were 350 hours of total flight time with no captain or turbine time required, compared to Delta and TWA who required 1500 hours captain time in a multi-engine turbine aircraft. 350 hours of total flight time is the equivalent of having the candy striper in the hospital conducting triple bypass surgery."

"In 1999, a ... 747 departed SFO, lost an engine on takeoff and came within 300 feet of hitting a hill in the Bay area. This was a minority co-pilot flying the aircraft and the individual assumed they had blown tires on takeoff, rather than realizing that an engine failed ..., and the result was improper technique in recovering from an engine failure which almost killed an estimated 3000 people in the Bay area."

"Here's the funny thing ... this co-pilot from the above incident was suing [the airline] due to the harassment that he received from the other pilots regarding this situation."

"I sat in the cockpit of a ... 727 and a minority pilot ... had to have the captain help him in what to say and how to pick the clearance up. I was amazed.... Another time ... another minority co-pilot was doing the best he could do on the radio with his broken English."

"There are so many stories of minority pilots being given so many chances on checkrides in order to pass them, the story that a minority pilot who thought he was transferring fuel from one tank to the other when in actuality he was dumping the fuel overboard on a 747 going across the Atlantic."[349]

And you thought your only problem on an airplane was terrorists.

Michael Ryan was in favor of "affirmative action" and "diversity" until he was repeatedly denied promotions by his employer, the FAA, due to its policy of racial discrimination. One of the promotions was given to a Black woman with 13 years less seniority than he had. Ryan finally sued the FAA. As the testimony in court against the FAA mounted to staggering proportions, the FAA decided to settle the case out of court in Ryan's favor to avoid further bad publicity.[350]

In the rest of the business world, your chances are no better. Edward Blum was a successful stockbroker at a major nationwide brokerage firm when the city of Houston was fighting a voter referendum to end preferential treatment based on race. The mayor threatened the brokerage firm with loss of city contracts unless their employee Blum stopped supporting the referendum. The company was also intimidated by Jesse Jackson's "Wall Street project" and did not want to antagonize the EEOC or attract attention from the Office of Civil Rights of the U. S. Department of Justice. The company ordered Blum to stop exercising his right to free speech and political activity and began to harass him in various ways. Blum fought back for a long time but ultimately resigned.[351]

Patricia Steffes joined an international corporation as an 18-year-old billing clerk in 1972, following her father and other relatives, and worked her way up to operations support manager for manufacturing. During that time, Steffes graduated from college in finance and accounting and had been promised the next promotion which opened in Lansing, Michigan. She didn't get the promotion even though she was more qualified for the position than the person promoted. She wrote letters appealing to the managers above her. The company retaliated by "reviewing" her performance with a view to "helping" her develop the right attitudes, etc. Finally, she sued. In retaliation, the company gave her demeaning work to do. Ms. Steffes eventually took a doctor-recommended leave of absence to deal with post-traumatic stress caused by the company's treatment of her. She returned to work but was forced to quit after only one day.[352]

The proportion of minorities at companies like Xerox, Bausch & Lomb and Eastman Kodak is far above their percentage of the American population, yet the proportion keeps rising even while the total employment at these companies decreased by one-third.[353]

The situation in government is no better for those who are of the wrong race. Lawyer Joseph Ray Terry had spent many years fighting discrimination against minorities. His employer, the EEOC, had consistently given Mr. Terry "superior" and "excellent" performance reviews. But Mr. Terry was white, and after applying for a promotion for 10 years, he finally sued the EEOC. One of those promoted over him did not even have a high school diploma.[354]

In another case involving four white employees passed over in favor of less qualified candidates, a District Court ruled that the IRS's "affirmative action" policies had encouraged "institutional discrimination against white male employees."[355]

In another case, Jennifer Long testified before the Senate about cases in which citizens who were under investigation by the Houston office of the IRS killed themselves after prolonged, unnecessary and often illegal "tax harassment" by the IRS. Long says that her Black supervisor "screamed at her and called her a lazy, stupid liar." He also discriminated against her because of her race until she was forced to sue.[356]

In another case, a Black IRS collection division chief was charged by revenue officer Kathy Howe and ex-employees Mona Meier, Gary Hoeffken and Norma Woodward of retaliating against employees who refused to promote less qualified minorities over whites. Also, although using number of property seizures as a factor in employee evaluations is against the law, Bonnie Carson, one of his revenue officers, testified that "He just came right out and said we would be evaluated on how many property seizures we did, and if we didn't have one in the previous year, we wouldn't get a satisfactory rating."[357]

Things are no better at HUD. Larry Price mortgaged his home to hire a lawyer to sue HUD for discriminating against him because he is white. After six hours of depositions, HUD's attorney agreed to a settlement. Price was awarded a promotion with back pay and interest, plus $141,000 in attorney fees, plus $10,000 in compensatory damages. After his settlement, HUD managers retaliated by giving Mr. Price distasteful work assignments such as 30 day travel assignments with no provision for flying home on the weekends to maintain his property. Mr. Price was ultimately forced to retire.[358]

Dennis Worth got help from the Center for Individual Rights to bring a class-action lawsuit seeking to enjoin both HUD and the EEOC from giving job preferences on the basis of race.[359]

Jerry Henry was a painting contractor in Ohio, a large percentage of whose business came from Ohio State University. In the 1980s he began to lose painting contracts because of his race. By 1989, he was told that the University had set aside 100 percent of the painting jobs for minority bidders. Not only was Henry to be handicapped because of his race, but "Because of his race, he was not even allowed to compete."[360]

Cheryl Hopwood worked hard to make something of herself and had accumulated a long list of achievements. She applied to Law School at the University of Texas, School of Law. Her LSATs and grades were good, as was her background. She was rejected, while 84 other individuals with credentials below hers (in some cases far below) were admitted.[361]

The list goes on and on with no end in sight. See www.adversity.net for more. These are not isolated incidents.

Reactions to self-subordination. Several of the consequences of this policy of discriminating against white people are relevant to the weakening of America. In the late 1980s, a sociologist did a simulation experiment, control-group design, using 30 white males. The reactions to being discriminated against reflected those of white society at large: some were angry, most accepted that they were inferior, a few were depressed.[362]

Racial antagonism. This program of race subordination began to produce antagonism between the races. White people who had been neutral or even supportive of Civil Rights now began to resent Black people. Black people sensed this resentment and resented being resented. For instance, on college campuses, racial hostility began to appear for the first time in decades.[363]

One hundred and seventy-five colleges reported a rise in incidents of racist graffiti, jokes, anonymous hate notes and brawls.[364]

A dean at Middlebury College in Vermont reported that, for the first time in nineteen years, she was being asked by white students not to assign them a black roommate.[365]

A professor at UC Berkeley said that he'd been seeing racist graffiti for the first time in eighteen years.[366]

Another Berkeley professor reminiscing about the glory days of the civil rights movement said, "Twenty years later, what have we got? Hate mail and racist talk."[367]

At UMass, a group of white students chased a group of Blacks.[368]

A Tufts University student said, "Many of my friends wouldn't care if they never saw a black person again in their lives."[369]

One Black college professor writes, "What is new are the frequency, the places, and the class of people involved in an unprecedented escalation of overt racial hostility."[370]

Self-doubt. Black people who had been shoe-horned into colleges with students far more qualified than they were could not, of course, perform up to the level of their fellow students. They felt inferior, where before they had felt competent or even superior.[371] They looked around for something to blame. More about this in the next chapter.

Clyde Summers of Yale Law School, a proponent of minority rights, identified the problem as a pervasive mismatching between students and institutions, due to preferential admissions, thereby fostering failure among students with the qualifications to succeed.[372]

Offers of remedial help are further blows to the students' self-esteem.

Black students react with absenteeism and an attitude of disparagement toward the curriculum as irrelevant. To combat the resulting high drop-out rates of these otherwise qualified Black students, schools employ what David Riesman called "affirmative grading:" giving the students grades they didn't merit.[373]

Perceptions of inferiority. The perceptions of white students are also affected, as they begin to get the impression that Black students really *are* inferior. Thus, double standards in admissions "perpetuate the very ideas and prejudices it is designed to combat."[374] Black students react with demands for reduced standards and easier courses.[375]

Devaluing of academic credentials. The use of race discrimination and the lowering of academic standards led employers to question the competence of Black applicants for jobs.[376]

Blaming the objective measures of quality. "When disproportionately large numbers of black law school graduates failed their bar examinations, that simply set off more cries of 'cultural bias' in the tests. In short, the prevailing dogmatism remained unmovable and impervious to any evidence."[377] Data on college performance is so bad that it is now being kept secret by colleges.[378]

When it is recalled that the same affirmative admissions and affirmative grading to pass Black students who have failed examinations are also used in *medical schools*, the problem becomes somewhat more than academic. The lower academic standards in medical schools affect the white and Asian students as well, since the tests are easier, the material is simplified, and the quantity of knowledge required is smaller. Those who ultimately suffer are the patients, in other words, you and me. One professor called it "cruel" to "allow the trusting patients to pay for our irresponsibility."[379]

The Association of American Medical Colleges is firmly *in favor of* race preferences. Lower grades in colleges and lower scores on the Medical College Admission Test by a factor of 30 percent are no bar to being admitted to medical school for Blacks and Hispanics. And "entrance into medical school virtually assures an M.D. degree and a license to practice."[380]

The flaw in the strategy of race discrimination. Some famous crusaders for civil rights, like Bayard Rustin, were among the first of those who criticized race preference.[381] He too held that the problem was mismatching: the highest level schools could not find enough Blacks to meet their quota so they admitted Blacks qualified for level 2 schools. This left level 2 schools empty-handed, so they admitted Blacks qualified for level 3. The level 3 schools admitted Blacks qualified for level 4. In other words, Blacks all up and down the spectrum were in schools that were inappropriate for them, with the usual results of feelings of inadequacy, resentment against whites, anger at the curriculum, and high dropout rates.[382]

One Black professor predicted the failure of preferential racism in 1970.[383] Roy Wilkins condemned the creation of "sealed-off black studies centers" for "racial breast-beating."[384] The issue is not whether there should be more Black people in colleges, but *which* colleges they should be in and whether preferential treatment should be the mechanism of that increase.

No power to the people. When the people of California soundly voted down race preferences in admissions to the state's colleges, the True Believers[385] at Berkeley were busy trying to find "how to reinstate racial preferences in other guises."[386]

Contributions of the press to the problem. None of these negative results were allowed to be printed in the press. "The mass media has created a reality in which the issue and its attendant problems do not exist."[387] In the sixties, the media was *against* preferential treatment, especially after John F. Kennedy and Hubert Humphrey made their celebrated denunciations of quotas and other race-based programs.[388] One New York

Times columnist warned against giving the federal government power to supervise corporate hiring practices.[389]

Now, the mainstream press is "one of the nation's most ardent institutional champions of" racial preferences.[390] And that has meant that few, if any, stories about victims of race preferences ever get printed or broadcast; and few articles report the divide between how the policies were supposed to work and "their actual everyday impact on real people in the real world."[391]

When the president of Rutgers University let it slip that Black SAT scores were on average 350 points lower than average non-Black scores, the press had a feeding frenzy condemning the "racism" of the president, of white society and of America in general. *Never* once did the press mention *the data*, the 350 point difference in scores.[392] When reporting of facts is replaced by mouthing of slogans (as though they were facts), the nation is weakened.

When high-profile lawsuits are mounted against universities, the press breaks its silence on race preferences with articles condemning the white *victims* of race preferences and castigating them for seeking justice in the courts.[393]

When a law student at Georgetown published data in the school newspaper proving racial discrimination against non-Blacks, Black law students rallied and demanded that the entire editorial board of the school newspaper be expelled. Georgetown University administrators themselves confiscated every issue of the newspaper, and law school professors who had offered to help the white law student were targeted for protests and backed off. It was not long before the mainstream media got involved—not to expose the injustice, the violation of freedom of the press, or the mob rule that had surfaced at Georgetown—but to condemn the law student for exposing the truth.[394]

For instance, one of the unexamined "explanations" of the disparity in performance that is routinely recited by the media is the supposed poverty background of the Black or Hispanic students. The truth is, however, that "a large percentage of those admitted ... share the socio-economic profile of their white schoolmates.... Most of the Blacks and Latinos admitted come from middle- and professional-class families."[395]

Another response of the press to the exposing of the use of race preferences in American universities is to loose a barrage of news stories on preferences given to the children of the rich, on the theory that this justifies visiting injustice upon middle-class white students. In other words, two wrongs make a right.[396]

Another example of misleading reporting is the news that average test scores at Berkeley had *gone up* over the years of preferential treatment. The press did not see fit to report that this same data, if broken down by minority versus majority, showed that the average test scores of minority students at Berkeley had actually gone *down* during this period.[397]

When California banned race discrimination against whites and Asians, the press went wild. The New York Times called it "Segregation Anew". Time Magazine predicted enrollment of minorities plummeting to 1963 levels. The networks and NPR followed suit. But while reporting the decreased numbers at Berkeley's Law School, for instance, they ignored the fact that minority enrollment at California's second-tier law schools had actually gone up.[398] And in fact the *total* admissions of "students of color" had actually gone up across the board, due to the huge increases in admissions of Asians who could get in now that they were no longer being discriminated against.[399] Still, the media continued to refer to "campus white-outs" and to cover up the facts with headlines like "Some Minority Admissions Drop in California."[400]

When a study of bar examinations was published that purported to show no difference between students admitted under preference and those admitted on the basis of merit, the news media trumpeted the news. None of them looked at the actual data, which showed huge disparities between the two groups in rates of *passing* the exams.[401]

In some cases, the press was busy fanning the flames of race antagonism. For instance, the "epidemic" of Black-church burnings in 1996 was "largely press-created."[402] And the press was too embarrassed, when the truth finally came out, to print corrections.[403]

Race preferences and immigration. Another embarrassing development arose. The status of privileged race was extended to Hispanics (probably to increase the voting and political power of those who favored race preferences). But as the floodgates of immigration opened in 1967 and reached crisis proportions in the 1990s, more and more of the admissions, hiring, contracts, etc. that had previously gone to Black candidates were being given to Hispanics and other immigrants. In 1970, Blacks made up 66 percent of the people to be preferred because of race. By 1990, their proportion was down to 49 percent. Today, it is even smaller and will continue to shrink, assuming nothing is done about legal and illegal immigration (which seems a certainty).[404]

Hispanics have begun mounting lawsuits against local, state and the federal government for giving too large a proportion of jobs and contracts to Blacks rather than to them.[405] As we shall see in the next chapter, these unfair policies have been extended to more and more groups, and these groups have learned to use the tactics of punitive lawsuits and mass protests with the result that the functioning of many governmental and private organizations has been virtually crippled.

The leadership and the proletariat. By 1995, according to an opinion survey commissioned by the Washington Post and undertaken by Harvard University, huge majorities of Blacks, Hispanics and Asians oppose using race even as "a factor in college admissions or employment."[406] Still, the leaders continue to push preferment based on race and to castigate anyone, Black or white, who says otherwise.

The leadership also continues to use the persuasive technique of portraying poor Ghetto Blacks and their miserable lives as a reason for continuing to discriminate against whites and in favor of Blacks. But in fact, such poverty-stricken Black people are rarely the beneficiaries of race preference programs, simply because they lack even the threshold level of skills needed to qualify under the preference programs. Middle-class Black people are the beneficiaries of these programs. The impoverished are left untouched by them.[407] A Black professor of economics at Boston University agrees, claiming that the bottom one-fifth of the African-American community has not been helped at all by affirmative action.[408]

Lasting consequences. This abandonment of the principles of fair play and of individualism represents a diametric shift in the political views of a large number of Americans. And as we shall see in the next two chapters, these are not the only changes in American belief systems.

Also, the longer preferential treatment failed to produce equality and the more it produced poorer education and decreased competence for Blacks and whites, the more firmly its supporters advocated it and the more adamantly they condemned any opposition to it. This hardening of the mind was one of the most damaging consequences of this misguided policy and one of the least visible. More will be said about this mental set in a later chapter.

Subordinating Our Culture

Elisa, a six-year-old girl, was beaten to death in 1996 in New York City. This case would have been shocking enough, but Elisa was beaten to death by her mother. Her mother had been beating her for years. Even more shocking is the reason for the beatings: to purge demons out of Elisa. That such a thing could happen in America is dismaying. What is more dismaying is that the New York City Child Welfare Administration knew about the beatings all the time! The city agency, supposedly responsible for the welfare of children, had done nothing about it out of respect for the non-Western culture of the mother![409]

This is only one example of another fundamental change in the mindset of Americans. For Americans, the rights of the individual had always been uppermost. Now, a culture was allowed to be more important that the individual, even to the point of the death of that individual. .

How did this total about-face develop? During the 1970s and 1980s, the list of groups that were to benefit from preferential treatment was enlarged to include Hispanics, then women, then Middle-Easterners. But to include these other groups, other justifications had to be created. Past discrimination wouldn't apply.

At about this time, another term began to be heard more and more often. It was another seemingly innocuous word that turned out to mean something other than what it sounded like. The term was "multiculturalism."

"Multiculturalism" sounded like it meant becoming familiar with all cultures. And this is how the program was sold to the public. Courses on non-Western cultures began to be introduced in college departments. The content of existing courses in grade schools and colleges began to be modified to include time spent on ideas, historical events, or customs of non-Western cultures. Whole departments were created: Islamic Studies, Middle Eastern Studies, Black Studies, etc. Schoolbooks for grade schools began to be required to talk about non-Western cultures.

In practice, however, from the content of these courses and these textbooks and schoolbooks, it can be seen that "multiculturalism" has a different meaning from what it sounds like. It means praising all non-Western cultures. Even more interesting, it means more than being neutral to Western culture, it means condemning Western culture![410] And this is the aspect of the plan that raises suspicions: why the attack on Western culture? Surely, one can praise other cultures without condemning our own.

For one instance among many, Barbara Johnson defines multiculturalism as "the deconstruction of the foundational ideals of Western civilization."[411]

The Hispanic student group MEChA with affiliates at 400 colleges in the U. S. has a motto: "For our race, everything. For those outside our race, nothing."[412]

The required re-education course at Penn spelled out the agenda for "multiculturalism" as: "prejudice; racism; racist behavior; American racial and ethnic groups; racial supremacy groups; racism at Penn; stereotypes; race as social construct; ethnicity; minority vs. majority."[413] That's it. That is the sum total of what "multiculturalism" was to mean at Penn.

But the situation gets more extreme. This practice was so fervently held to that it included praising even inhumane cultures by ignoring any of their practices that violated Western notions of fair play, gender equality, minority rights, humane treatment of offenders, or tolerance of diverse opinions. For instance, genital mutilation of young girls by Islamic cultures was ignored, along with the lack of other rights of women. One book describes these practices in detail.[414]

In other words, Western culture was being subordinated to other cultures, and Americans are being taught to esteem other cultures and denigrate their own. Interestingly enough, the people pushing this curious program were themselves of Western culture: they too are subordinating their own culture.

Promoting ignorance of other cultures. Another curious feature of "multiculturalism" is that the *classics* of non-Western cultures cannot be taught, since many of these non-Western classics glorify war or dominance over other groups or accept slavery or promote values of hard work, self-reliance, responsibility and other personal virtues which this coalition (for whatever reason) wants to downplay. Hence, only *current* writings from these non-Western cultures are included, and only certain of the current writings, namely those that promote the kinds of values, attitudes and characteristics which the members of the coalition favor.

The result is ironic. Because of the sanitized version of these cultures being taught and because of the selectivity with which they are presented, students are getting not only an inaccurate view of other cultures but a patently false view. In short, they are led to believe that the people in other cultures hold the same views as their professors.

This means that the people pouring out of schools and colleges year after year do *not* understand other cultures. In particular, it means that they have a self-defeating view of Islam. They know nothing of the slavery, the brutal treatment of women, genital mutilation, forced abortions, imprisonment of *victims* of rape, the stoning of homosexuals, the vicious treatment of criminals, the public enthusiasm for terrorism, the lack of democracy, or the absence of political freedom in these societies. They believe that Islam seeks world peace, the rights of all people, men and women, etc. In other words, the Islamists—or at least the "moderate" Islamists—are just like us multiculturalists.

Causes of multiculturalism. The overwhelming question, of course, is why. Why did anyone come up with a scheme of praising all other cultures and condemning our own? There were different motives of several different groups in the coalition that was driving the movement for change in America at the time.

Supporters of the Black-race preference program saw that they were in trouble and needed to broaden their base of support. They decided to incorporate Hispanics as a group that was also entitled to preferment. Since Hispanics had not been legally segregated and had not been enslaved, it was less easy to show that they had been discriminated against and were entitled to preferential treatment. And since they were not of a different race from the "white" race, the preferential treatment could not be based on race. "Multiculturalism" allowed Hispanics to be included. And new labels and slogans began to be created to promote these policies: "diversity"[415], "inclusiveness", etc. College student bodies, corporate work settings, etc. were supposed to reflect the "diversity" of the American population. At the same time, these groups became active in pro-immigration initiatives to insure that America became more and more "diverse" all the time. The pro-immigration bill of 1967 had laid the groundwork, and the slogan became "Give us your *third-world* tired and poor...."

Another large group of supporters were the typically American good-hearted people who simply wanted to help others in need. The idea of world peace had been drilled into them in grade school in the 1950s, they had shouted it till they were hoarse in the anti-war demonstrations of the late 1960s and early 1970s, and multiculturalism, globalization, international interdependency, and a world governed by one set of laws seemed to be the way to go.

There were also those from the anti-war movement who simply had never forgiven their government for having put their lives at risk by threatening to draft them to fight what they perceived as a pernicious war. Their hatred of the government had turned into hatred of the United States and of its culture—Western culture.

Finally, there were the dedicated Marxists (who had been called "communists" until the 1960s). They were frustrated that the Soviet model was not selling. They tried the Chinese model briefly during the 1960s, but it sold even less well to most people. Someone rediscovered an obscure Italian communist named Gramsci, who had written in the 1930s that the reason socialism had not caught on properly in the Soviet Union and was converting only a minority in Europe was that the culture of these countries was incompatible with socialism. Eradicate the underlying culture (i.e. Western culture), Gramsci claimed, and people will wholeheartedly embrace socialism. The Marxists saw in "multiculturalism" a legitimate excuse to condemn America and to begin to cleanse Americans of the taint of Western culture.

Of course, they could not present this as a reason to the other groups in the coalition, but since those groups had their own motives for promoting "multiculturalism," all that the Marxists had to do was to continually harp on the negative aspects of Western culture.

What were these alleged negative aspects? Well, to the Marxists, there was obviously the allegation of imperialism. So, they railed against Western dominance of third-world countries, talked colonialism, exploitation, etc.

There was the practice of slavery. Even though the practice was abandoned over a century ago, they could get a lot of mileage out of it. Interestingly, one would think it never occurred to them that the Arabic cultures were prominent in the slave trade at that time and at the present time. Since the coalition had made the curious decision not to admit faults in any third-world cultures, Arabic slave trading could not be mentioned or acknowledged. And all negative statements, for instance, that the prophet Mohammed had himself owned slaves, are labeled as allegations and cited as proof of Western bias.

There was the alleged American discrimination against third-world people. Since Blacks and Hispanics in America were being given *preferential* treatment based on the fact that they or their ancestors had been third-world people, one would think that this would be a hard sell. It wasn't. They simply focused on other groups, particularly immigrants. Any proposal to limit, much less stop, immigration was cited as proof of anti-third-world bias. The charge of bias alone, quite apart from any data that might support it, was enough to strike cold terror into the hearts of most people.

To consolidate the new large base of support for the program, all non-white people were lumped together using a new coined term. It the U. S., it was "people of color." In Canada, it was "visible minorities." In other words, "us" and "them". Ironically, the "us" were the ones being subordinated.

Multiculturalism and immigration policy. Another policy assumption of the multiculturalists, which we learn from what they advocate, is that people of all cultures should immigrate to the United States. This is a curious position. If other cultures are so fine and American culture so foul, it is unclear why other people would want to immigrate to it. But obviously, they are eager to do so.

Two other assumptions this immigration policy rests on are that: (1) all cultures are *compatible* with Western culture and (2) all cultures are compatible with each other. Is this true? Is every culture in the world compatible with every other culture? Is the Islamic practice of genital mutilation of women compatible with American policies of women's liberation, for instance? As we read daily news reports of Sunnis and Shiites killing each other, may we not be forgiven for wondering whether even these two subcultures are compatible with each other? To say nothing of Hindus and Muslims.

Should we not demand some positive evidence that a culture is compatible *before* admitting members of that culture into America? All the examples that are usually cited of past successful immigration into America and how it made America great are examples of members of a nation with Western culture immigrating to this nation, another nation with Western culture.

Another fact that should give Americans pause is that multicultural societies have usually (invariably?) erupted in genocidal violence. Shouldn't these cases make Americans stop and think before throwing the doors open to all comers?

Another troublesome feature of the policy is that it includes a determination that immigrant groups *not* assimilate to American culture. This policy is promoted by such programs as multilingualism. California public schools were required to teach in 42 different languages. Three million children are taught in a foreign language, and the number has been rising by 10 percent every year.[416] This is done in the face of immigrant parents' opposition to the program.[417] A New York State Education commission report asserted: "Multicultural perspectives should *infuse the entire curriculum, pre-kindergarten through grade 12.*" The Supreme Court turned the program into a requirement.[418] A number of lawsuits have been filed to allow workers to speak a foreign language on the job, whether or not anyone else can understand them.[419] This movement is ironic considering that students throughout the world are struggling to learn English, because English is becoming the universal language of international commerce.[420]

At Stanford, some courses even bordered on reverse racism, with one course entitled "Black Hair as Culture and History."[421]

By making the "seams" within the United States more pronounced and institutionalizing these seams, and by making it less likely that different fragments can be knitted together, "multiculturalism" also contributes to our nation coming apart at the seams.

News media contributions to the problem. Media gush in favor of "diversity" and "multiculturalism" but do not look too closely at the consequences of programs putting such ideas into practice.[422] Nor do they focus on any facts that do not favor those ethnic groups singled out as special (for example, Blacks, Hispanics, Muslims).

For instance, the high illiteracy rate among Hispanics is taboo.[423]

Similarly, the high rate of teen pregnancy among Hispanic teenagers is ignored or explained away with the usual clichés about poverty and racism.[424]

There seems to be no limit to how far media will go to come up with excuses in support of multiculturalism. One of the most dangerous is the promotion of "folk medicine." These practices endanger the very people the journalists are so eager to help. "The journalists I've spoken to usually have their minds made up already. They don't allow objective data to override their prejudices," one doctor said.[425]

One of the most clear-cut cases of cover-up was the case of a mental patient who was exorcised by a Haitian "prophet" using $12,000 in New York State funds. The patient had hacked his girl friend to pieces in front of her children and then set her on fire. The press mentioned the exorcism as justified religious counseling to the patient.[426]

Another multicultural issue is genital mutilation of females in some Muslim immigrants to the United States. Congress cannot bring itself to outlaw the practice, and the press refuses to do any investigation to determine the extent of the practice in the U. S. or to observe its consequences.[427]

The case of six-year-old Elisa, reported earlier, who was beaten to death by her mother to purge demons out of her, resulted in a doctored version in the press. But the fact that the Child Welfare agency in New York City knew about this and *did nothing to stop it*, was *not* reported. The case worker spoke little English and was from the same culture that favored such treatment of children.[428]

Multiculturalism and freedom of speech. Another unfortunate side-effect of this program is that, because of the obvious bias in these beliefs (against Western culture) and because of the patent selectivity in the presentation of other cultures, the proponents of multiculturalism cannot allow open discussion of these views or permit open dissent. These views, thus, have to be taught, accepted and practiced, but not discussed or debated.

Suppression of discussion, however, breeds resentment and opposition. As more and more questioning of these views is met with denunciations and punitive re-education sessions, resentment and opposition to multiculturalism has grown.[429] And the stronger the resistance becomes, the more fervently the proponents cling to these beliefs, and the most rigidified these beliefs become.[430]

Selling the idea. *How* the proponents are getting a growing number of Americans to accept the subordination of our culture is the subject of a later chapter.

Subordinating Our Country

On September 11, 2001, student Zewdalem Kebede was arrested by San Diego State University police for disagreeing with people *who applauded* the attack on America. He was threatened with expulsion.[431] The Ethiopian student was not alone. "Professors were removed from the classroom, students were hauled before kangaroo courts, and campus organizations were threatened with disbandment."[432] All this punishment and harassment was *for expressing loyalty* and support for America! Madison, Wisconsin barred its public school teachers from leading students in the Pledge of Allegiance.[433]

To say that these official moves against America represent a change in beliefs and attitudes about the United States would be an understatement. The question is how did our country get into such a state? And why do most Americans still not know about it?

As the race preference policies produced more failures, and resentment among Blacks intensified, the members of the coalition were mortified. How could they admit such a fiasco? How could they take the blame for having damaged so many of the Black people they were trying to help? They couldn't and they wouldn't!

Someone came up with a way out, an explanation for the results of these policies. Discrimination against white people didn't work because America was *inherently* racist. Racism was somehow so ingrained into the American people, into the institutions and into the practices of America that nothing short of a complete transformation of the nation and of the people could change it.

A hard sell. In order to sell Americans the idea that their nation, which had freed the slaves over a century ago and had recently turned itself inside out to advance Black people, was inherently racist, some ingenuity was called for. To convince those people that they were *really* anti-Black was going to be a challenge. History had to be re-written. Literature had to be re-selected and reinterpreted. New "studies" had to be done.

The new history. Even though only a small fraction of Americans ever owned slaves, a few of the Founders had, so the neo-historians made the most of that. All historical evidence that counted against the foreordained conclusion could easily be *left out* of the new history books. After all, how many people read original sources? For instance, Jefferson in his original draft of the Declaration of Independence devoted several paragraphs to *freeing the slaves* and the evils of slavery. To gain unanimity and appease the Southern delegates, however, the Continental Congress deleted those paragraphs.

The Abolitionists, those working to free the slaves, setting up the "underground railway," hiding runaway slaves in their houses at great risk to themselves, etc. were a clear refutation of *inherent* American racism. What to do? It was decided that audacity was the best approach. Condemn the Abolitionists as racists! If they were racist, then surely everybody else was.

The efforts of the United States on behalf of minorities around the world had to be re-perceived as imperialistic—we were really after the oil or the ivory or whatever—even though we didn't take the oil and even in countries which had no oil. America was power-mad and out to dominate the world—even though we left the countries and didn't dominate them.

Those annoying facts. The idea that the dominant white majority makes it impossible for others to succeed "is hard to square with the fact that some despised, downtrodden groups have won the game at the expense of the supposedly dominant culture."[434] The prime example, of course, is Jews. But every other group that has come to this country (Asians, etc.) has done quite well for themselves. In fact, Africans, South Americans, Cubans and Jamaicans have done well for themselves, learned English without any trouble, attained advancement on their merits, and so on.

The only groups that appear not to have done well are African-Americans, Mexicans and Puerto Ricans. But even this is too broad a statement. Those African-Americans and Hispanics *who have rejected the ideas of this chapter and the two previous chapters* have done well for themselves. Perhaps, therefore, it is not America or race or ethnicity that is the problem, but the ideas advanced in these three chapters that have held back these Blacks and Hispanics. It may be that these ideas are as self-defeating for Blacks and Hispanics as they are for the rest of Americans. It is a possibility Blacks and Hispanics might want to consider.

The success of the program. But are Americans really buying the idea that America is evil? Are we actually being brought to subordinate America to the rest of the world?

A UMass Amherst Professor informed his students that "This class will be consistently anti-American."[435]

A distinguished professor of political science at SUNY/Binghamton called America "a breeding ground of racism, exploitation and genocide."[436]

One Smith College graduate firmly believed that America dropped the bomb on Hiroshima *after* Japan had surrendered! Another Smith College graduate was shocked to learn about Woodrow Wilson's attempts to create a permanent peace and a League of Nations. She was also surprised that Teddy Roosevelt worked in partnership with his wife rather than keeping her in the background.

The New Jersey state legislature voted down a bill requiring schoolchildren to recite brief passages from the Declaration of Independence. A state senator in New Jersey said the document was "offensive to my community."[437]

Visible displays of this anti-American sentiment occurred after 9/11. Some even blamed the attack on America itself.[438]

One person wrote that America is "an imperialist nation which exploits, starves and kills civilians around the world—daily."[439]

At Marquette University, students were blocked by the University from holding a moment of silence around an American flag.[440]

Lehigh University's vice provost banned school employees from displaying the American flag.[441]

Florida Gulf Coast University's head librarian forbade her employees from wearing "I'm proud to be an American" stickers.[442]

American flags and other patriotic symbols were banned at Central Michigan University, Arizona State, Holy Cross College, and Amherst College.[443]

A University of Hawaii professor said, "Why should we support the United States, whose hands in history are soaked with blood?"[444]

University of New Mexico professor Richard Berthold told his students, "Anyone who can blow up the Pentagon would get my vote."[445]

These anti-American statements and actions brought no punishment from university administrators. However, a Johns Hopkins University professor was fired for remarks supporting the war *against* terror.[446]

Duke University removed a professor's website merely for linking to articles proposing a military response to the attack.[447]

"America is not a 'nice' country," one student at Wake Forest University said.[448]

A Duke student said that "the sight of the flag burning would be preferable to its display."[449]

A University of Colorado student said, "We had it coming."[450]

To prove how bad America is, an Islamic student at Arizona State University actually inflicted injuries on himself, claiming they were attacks done by Americans.[451]

UC Berkeley's student newspaper ran a cartoon depicting the 9/11 hijackers burning in hell and wondering where their virgins were. A mob stormed the newspaper's offices.[452]

A school teacher in Sacramento burned an American flag in front of his sixth-grade class.[453]

Bobby Fischer said, "This is all wonderful news. It is time to finish off the U. S. once and for all."[454]

An introductory course in politics at Johns Hopkins University had a reading list filled with books on American oppression, the evils of the CIA, etc.[455]

At Stanford, one course entitled Gender and Nationalism preached that nationalism is a male creation designed to oppress women.[456]

Putting America at risk. Some of the members of the coalition genuinely hate America, and merely creating anti-American sentiments among the American people is not enough for them. They want America brought down.

This seems an extreme statement. Unfortunately, there is all too much evidence of its truth.

One of their targets, understandably, is to cripple the military. For economic reasons, many military bases were closed in the 1990s, but since the 1960s, anti-American militants have co-opted the environmental movement as a mechanism to restrict the training of soldiers and sailors.

For instance, to protect the birds, soldiers at Fort Bragg, America's largest base, "are limited to a maximum of two hours while operating in any one area of the reservation. They aren't allowed to dig into the earth and are allowed to fire only small-caliber blank ammunition."[457]

At Fort Hood, Texas, only 17 percent of the reservation is "unaffected by one environmental constraint or another."[458]

At Camp Lejeune, "Marines are restricted from using the beaches during the turtle nesting season, making amphibious landing exercises (traditionally the core mission of the USMC) impossible."[459] Because of concern for the "desert tortoise", the military at Yuma, Arizona, Fort Irwin, California, and Nellis Air Force Base, Nevada are forbidden to train at night.

At Camp Pendleton, California, the Marines' most important amphibious training base, "only one mile of the seventeen miles of beach is available for use," due to concern for the gnatcatcher, the fairy shrimp, the tidewater goby and others.[460]

A suit was filed against the Navy for using a new sonar system which allegedly disturbed dolphins, in spite of a six-year, $10 million study that proved the system had negligible impact on marine mammals. Without this new system, "U. S. Navy ships are vulnerable to the new, ultra-quiet diesel submarines operated by China, North Korea, and Iran."[461]

A section of the island of Vieques, Puerto Rico, was "the only area where ships, submarines, fighters, bombers, and amphibious ground forces could train together in realistic terrain using live ammunition." It was lost to environmentalists, who called the Navy "rapists."[462]

At Fort Lewis, Washington, 72 percent of the military reservation is given over to the spotted owl. Makua Military Reservation in Hawaii has been closed to protect a tree snail. At Pacific Missile Range in Kauai, Hawaii, ballistic missile defense testing has been severely compromised to protect a species of grass.[463]

The Navy's Pinecastle Bombing Range in Florida and a bombing range in Arizona are threatened with closure or severe limitations. On Coronado Island, California, where most SEAL training is done, "training is severely limited for most of the year."[464]

Americans against America. *How* the proponents are getting a growing number of Americans to accept the subordination of their own nation is the subject of a later chapter.

An Ideology of Submission

These views on the duty of subordinating ourselves, subordinating our culture and subordinating our nation have been reiterated for so long, defended so adamantly and taught so passionately to the young that they now amount to an ideology. This ideology is new. Nothing like it has ever appeared in any nation or culture before. Every nation, every culture has placed itself first or at least viewed itself as the equal of every other culture and every other people. This ideology of subordination does the opposite.

Since this is a new ideology, it needs a new name, one that is unique. The name chosen should not be pejorative. An epithet merely says that the speaker does not like the ideology; it does not say what the ideology is. The name chosen should be as value-neutral as possible. A label is a poor way to argue against a position.

Since this ideology is in fact an ideology of self-subordination or submission, I propose to call it **Dhimmism**. But any name will do, so long as that name has not already been used to designate other political ideologies and is not merely an epithet.

Bat Ye'or defines dhimmitude thus: "(1) the inequality of rights in all domains between Muslims and dhimmis [in this case, between nonwhites and whites], (2) the social and economic discrimination against the dhimmis [discrimination against whites]; and (3) the degradation and vulnerability of the dhimmis [the repeated accusations of inherent racism, etc.]."[465] Since this is an ideology that advocates the condition of dhimmitude for Americans or at least for "white" Americans, the neologism "Dhimmism" is not inappropriate.

No one is saying that this subordination was done deliberately or that there was any conspiracy to do it. Maybe it was just a side-effect of what the zealots were trying to do. Maybe the activists' hatred of America influenced their choice of policies. How it came about does not matter. It has now become so ingrained and has been taught to so many Americans that what we must do is to understand it.

"LIBERAL"

The most important thing to note about this new ideology is that it is *not* liberalism. Not only it is *not* liberalism, but it is *incompatible* with liberalism.

This is an important point for two reasons. First, the people who came up with these views in the 1960s *were* originally liberals or Marxists. (The Marxists rarely identified themselves as such in those days. They too called themselves "liberals.") As these people struggled to solve problems and came up with proposed policies, they thought of their policies as liberal. Most of these people were not political philosophers and did not know the actual definition of liberalism. They had always thought of themselves as liberals. They continued to do so. And whatever they came up with—that too was liberalism.

Second, a large number of other people identified themselves as liberals. The easiest way to get these people to agree with the new policies was to call these policies "liberal." Most of the people developing these ideas probably did not think of this, since they already regarded their ideas as "liberalism." For most people, the word "liberalism" probably meant "helping people less fortunate, particularly Black people."

Most conservatives are as ignorant of the meaning of "liberalism" as these Dhimmists are and fell into line with the practice of calling these ideas "liberal." They thus played right into the hands of these people. And as the unfortunate consequences of the new policies began to be felt, the conservatives became more and more outraged, and the word "liberal" for them became one of the highest condemnations they could think of, though they came up with additional epithets such as "political correctness" which insinuates that these ideas are Marxist, which as we shall see, they are not.

It is important, therefore, to spell out the differences between Dhimmism and liberalism.

Liberalism: no discrimination on the basis of race, creed, color or country of national origin.

Dhimmism: discriminate in favor of the Black race on the basis of race and discriminate in favor of people of third-world origin on the basis of ethnicity or country of national origin.

Liberalism: the freedom of speech of the individual shall not be curtailed.

Dhimmism: no one may say anything that might offend or hurt the feelings of Black people, women or persons of third-world origin.

Liberalism: the clash of opinions, the marketplace of ideas, is essential to the vitality and progress of a people.

Dhimmism: disagreement about the details of Dhimmist policies and programs is permitted; but alleging unfortunate consequences of these programs or questioning of the fundamental ideology on which the policies are based is forbidden.

Liberalism: the rights of the individual are paramount. No group may impinge upon the rights of the individual.

Dhimmism: the group is paramount. The word "individual" is a red-flag word.

Liberalism: individual preferences are the bedrock of democracy.

Dhimmism: "If individual desires and interests are socially constituted … the ultimate authority of individual judgment comes into question."[466] Popular preferences are often not "authentic."[467]

Liberalism: no one may be condemned without a trial before a jury of his peers. The accused has a right to be assumed innocent until proven guilty, and has the right to face and cross-examine his accuser and the right to counsel. In other words, everyone has a right to "due process."

Dhimmism: If anyone is accused of racism or sexual harassment, he is probably guilty. The accuser is not required to confront the accused because it might hurt the accuser's feelings. A jury is unnecessary, and the verdict and punishment may be decided by a Dhimmist administrator or other person in authority.

Liberalism: the freedom of the press shall not be infringed.
Dhimmism: presses that print articles in conflict with Dhimmism may be smashed, their editors assaulted and their newspapers destroyed. Books criticizing or exposing Dhimmism should be burned. Every effort should be made to fire radio commentators who criticize Dhimmism. Doing these things is merely an expression of the freedom of Dhimmists.

It should also be pointed out that Dhimmism does not fit on the simplistic one-dimensional analysis of political ideologies. It is neither "left," nor "right," nor "centrist." It is a new ideology. There have been many political philosophies which do not fit the one-dimensional classification scheme. Dhimmism is one of them.

"CONSERVATIVE"

The traditional term "conservative" too has acquired a new meaning, depending on the source that uses the term. For the Dhimmists, anyone who disagrees with or questions Dhimmism is labeled a "conservative".

Thus, "conservatives" are those who are opposed to *affirmative* action, opposed to *diversity*, opposed to *inclusiveness*, opposed to giving the tired and poor of other countries that same opportunities of U. S. citizenship which they or their ancestors enjoyed. Anyone who is a "conservative" is thus a despicable person.

Thus, the word "conservative" has become an effective label for vilifying anyone who dares question Dhimmism or its policies.

Conservatives have fallen for this trick too and proudly *agree* when they are labeled "conservatives." They fail to realize that the term they are being labeled with has a very different meaning for their attackers and the adherents of the Dhimmists than it does for them, the conservatives.

Traditionally, the term "conservative" referred to people who accepted conservatism, the tenets of which loosely included such things as laissez-faire economies, private enterprise, minimal government, pro-religion, pro traditional nuclear families, anti-birth control, anti-abortion, anti-sex, etc.

Even today, conservative polemicists cannot help mixing in these favorite policies of theirs with their criticisms of the Dhimmists' mistakes, thus setting themselves up for easy dismissal by their opponents. Their books thus appeal only to those who already accept conservatism. They are books that "preach to the choir" and do not change anything. Nor do they reach the people in the middle, the undecideds, the moderates, the independents, the few remaining actual liberals. Conservatives even make matters worse by labeling anyone who does not buy the whole conservative agenda as a "liberal," thus ensuring that they will not reach anyone who does not already agree with conservatism.

The Dhimmists exploit this *naiveté* by labeling everyone who disagrees with or questions or attempts to expose Dhimmism as a "conservative." This, of course, includes all the traditional liberals, since liberalism is incompatible with Dhimmism. As Harry Stein put it, "many of us were soon startled to find ourselves tagged conservatives (and often worse) for holding firm to the values of old-fashioned liberalism: a bedrock commitment to fairness and individual liberty."[468]

"LEFTISM"

The leftist or Marxist is concerned with opposing capitalism in whatever nation it is found. Leftism aims to be worldwide, yet it condemns as "imperialism" every other attempt to go global. Marxism condemns a class or stratified society and aims to achieve a classless society in which everyone belongs to the working class. Leftists oppose "the" ruling class and strive for a society in which the working class or proletariat dominates (rules?) society.

As you can see, Dhimmism is quite different from leftism, even though today in America most leftists work seamlessly with the Dhimmists to oppose liberals and conservatives. And both leftists and Dhimmists call themselves "liberals." Conservatives fall for this and call both liberals and leftists and indeed anyone who disagrees with conservatism "leftists." The confusion in naming makes it easy for leftists and Dhimmists to operate under cover and accomplish their work of undermining America.

ENTITLEMENT AND OUTRAGE

While Dhimmism is being taught to "white" Americans, a doctrine of entitlement and outrage is being taught to Blacks and Hispanics. Hispanics are entitled to the whole of the western hemisphere on the grounds that their ancestors, the Native Americans, were here first. They should be outraged that their land was forcibly taken from them by the gringos. Blacks are taught to be outraged because their ancestors were enslaved. As reparation for this outrage, they are entitled to whatever they want. This E-O Ideology is being taught in colleges and schools throughout the United States.

THE POINT OF VIEW OF THIS BOOK

The reader may want to know where the present author stands on all this. The only adequate way to know is to read my book *What Freedom Is*. The author's position also does not fit neatly into the one-dimensional scheme of political views. It is not conservatism, nor Marxism, nor quite equivalent to liberalism, and it is certainly not Dhimmism.

Enforcing the Ideology

In 1990, the University of Cincinnati held a meeting of the whole faculty to increase the faculty's "sensitivity" to the new Ideology. The "facilitator" told a young woman professor to stand. Because of her high academic qualifications, the "facilitator" singled her out as a member of the privileged white elite. He lashed out at her white skin, her blonde hair and blue eyes and sneered that she could win a beauty contest. Later, the "facilitator" demanded that the young woman stand up again for some more abuse, but she only sat sobbing while the "facilitator" went on castigating her for such things as wearing a string of pearls. The rest of the faculty were already so cowed by 1990 that no one would stand up to defend her against these Dhimmist tactics, not even the vaunted feminists, not even the tenured professors.[469]

Unfortunately, such a case is not the exception, but the rule. How did we allow America to degenerate to such a point? The various groups that have worked together since the 1960s form a network. They have founded many organizations around various causes and interests, and these organizations work together as a loose coalition. There was and is no conspiracy. These people have networked together for years; and although they disagree on many things, they do agree on the basic policies, programs and assumptions of the Ideology.

Over time, they have developed various methods for handling problems such as disagreement, questioning and rebellion. Some of these methods were effective and got passed around until they are now widespread. They were never officially adopted by any of the groups because they did not need to be.

VILIFYING THOSE WHO DISAGREE

As the policies of the Dhimmists continued to produce unfortunate effects, more people criticized, questioned, doubted. Like all True Believers[470] on shaky ground, the Dhimmists responded vehemently to these critics. The goal, of course, is to silence dissenters so that other people will not begin to have doubts about the Ideology.

The basic approach is to conclude that anyone who disagrees, instead of being merely mistaken or wrong, is a *bad person*. To make these charges work, epithets had to be found that no one could defend himself against because: (a) no evidence could possibly be offered that would count, (b) offering any evidence or arguments to the contrary would sound self-serving, and (c) since the label would be wielded only when someone disagrees with a policy (for instance, a policy that appears to favor one of the privileged groups), the *disagreement itself* would appear to condemn the person.

Of course, the First Amendment acknowledges that even a bad person has a right to speak; but in practice, if the person is labeled as bad, then what he says has no effect anyway.

A more direct approach is simply not to provide dissenters with the opportunity to be heard. For example, a caller to the NPR program "Talk of the Nation" said quite sincerely that Dinesh D'Souza should not be allowed to speak on the air. What was D'Souza's crime, the moderator asked. He is a conservative, the caller said earnestly. It is extremely rare that a conservative is invited to speak on NPR, and even this one time was objected to.

Even silently disapproving of something a student or teacher says is unacceptable to the True Believers. They need everyone to accept the Ideology. Silence is liable to punishment. This deprives everyone not only of the right to free speech but of the right to freedom of thought, the right to an opinion! One Black educator recognizes this: "To say that **A** has a right to **B**'s approval is to say that **B** has no right to his own opinion."[471]

Racism. Anyone who questions the doctrine of subordinating white people on the basis of their race is labeled a "racist." This includes the Black people who recognize the disastrous consequences inherent in discriminating against *anyone* based on their race. Ironically, since a racist is by definition someone who discriminates on the basis of race, the actual racists are the Dhimmists themselves. The meaning of the word "racism," thus, had to change. It now had to mean: anyone who opposes any program that favors Black people or that appears to favor Black people.

It was and is an effective tactic. Denial is futile: a racist *would* deny it. Even prior civil-rights activity is no defense: the person has *changed*, has become "conservative." And in fact, many people who devoted years of service and sacrifice working for civil rights have been castigated as "racists" for pointing out the Dhimmist programs' harmful effects on Black people. And Black people themselves who criticize Dhimmism are vilified as "Uncle Toms" or "Jim Crows" or "Oreos". Oreo is the worst because it insinuates that, although the person's skin is Black, he is really a *white* person. What could be worse than that?

Sexism. In the early 1980s, the feminists also became converted to Dhimmism and began vilifying those women who still advocated equal rights between the sexes. Women, they claimed, deserved "affirmative action" too. Anyone who disagreed was labeled a "sexist" or even a "rapist".[472]

_____**phobia**. (Fill in the blank.) An all-purpose epithet for anyone disagreeing with the growing list of privileged groups can be generated from this suffix. For instance, anyone who questions specially favorable treatment for homosexuals is guilty of Homophobia. Anyone who opposes special favors for Muslims is said to be crippled with Islamophobia. Anyone who values America and wants to defend it is guilty of Xenophobia.

Elitism. This is another double-jointed word. It sounds like snobbism, condescension, feelings of superiority. In fact, it is used to condemn anyone who favors introducing standards into education, admissions, hiring or promotion. This term is interesting because its use implicitly presupposes that Black people and Hispanics are incapable of meeting the standards. (In other words, the accusers are again betraying their own racism.) People advocating *standardized* testing are also routinely accused of "racism."

To say that there is "great" literature or "great" art is to be guilty of "hierarchical" thinking, which is elitist.[473]

Fascism. Anyone who attempts to oppose the anti-American activities of the Dhimmists is labeled a "fascist." This is another example of the Big Lie technique, since many of the activities of the Dhimmists, as we shall see in this chapter, are explicit examples of fascist activity.

To head off any attempt to save America from their anti-democratic activities, the Dhimmists regularly accuse the U. S. of being "fascist." Naturally, they do not cite any evidence to support their claim.

RE-EDUCATING THOSE WHO QUESTION

Vilifying those who disagree is all very well, but it doesn't really do anything except isolate the person who would introduce doubt among the faithful. This is important, but it is even more important to convert the people who have doubts, strengthen the faith of the people who are wavering, and punish those who try to escape notice by paying lip service to the Ideology while in fact thinking their own thoughts.

At first, as the policies of the Dhimmists continued to produce unfortunate results for the very people they were designed to help, the Dhimmists required every student to take courses in "Studies" departments. The unfortunate results continued, of course, because the results came about as a consequence of the policies. Still, the Dhimmists would not admit that they'd made a mistake. Something more drastic was needed to purge the racism out of the people. Ideally, what was needed was thought control, but of course they couldn't do that. They needed some procedures that would: (a) convince the people that they harbor racist attitudes and (b) cleanse these attitudes out of them.

Naturally, the Dhimmists needed an effective word for these procedures, otherwise, someone would recognize that what they were doing was identical to what the Chinese communists do. For this process, the communists used "brainwashing," which is not regarded by them as a bad thing. On the contrary, it is believed to be good for the person and good for the society. Still, the term "brainwashing" had gotten a bad press in America at the time of the Korean War. The Dhimmists decided on the term "sensitivity training." These training sessions are now required of everyone under the control of the Dhimmists.

Convincing students and employees that racism exists. One speaker at a Harvard re-education workshop told the students and faculty that 15 percent of whites were overt racists and 85 percent were subtle racists. In other words, every white person is a racist whether they engage in racist behavior or not. Another speaker informed Blacks that "Overreacting and being paranoid is the only way we can deal with this system.... Never think that you imagined it, because chances are that you didn't."[474]

"The ultimate in brainwashing … is getting you to believe something about yourself [e.g. that you are a racist] that you know to be untrue."[475]

Regular training. "a growing number of schools even mandate credits in … courses about 'diversity' as graduation requirements." Colleges also enforce the ideology by using "the *in loco parentis* apparatus of the university to reform their private consciences and minds."[476]

Colleges transformed their freshman orientation programs, lengthening them to up to a year and focusing on "racism, homophobia, statusism [elitism], sexism and ageism."[477]

Punitive training. A president of Smith College mandated that "Where insensitive speech (not harassing) is at issue … educational strategies will be preferred." If students did not accept re-education, "suspension or permanent separation from the College" was the alternative.[478] Other colleges have similar intensive training programs. At Sarah Lawrence, a student was forced to watch a video on "homophobia" and write a paper on it as part of his re-education for having laughed at the wrong time.[479]

Training the faculty. The University of Cincinnati required its staff and faculty to endure "sensitivity training". At the session, the Vice Provost condemned the silence of the white males among them. In other words, even the freedom not to speak was revoked. Also, staff and faculty were required to write an essay on the topic "What I can do to help our department demonstrate our appreciation for diversity." She also advised anyone who disagreed with what was going on to find employment elsewhere.[480]

The University of Cincinnati was the same one which, at another "racial sensitivity" session, forced a white woman professor to stand while the speaker harassed her for her blonde hair and blue eyes. This example is indicative of the fervor with which the college administration has embraced the new Ideology. And the fact that no one on the faculty rose to defend her is either an indication of the extent of faculty approval or of lack of academic freedom or both.[481]

Specialists in such re-education training sessions have become a new growth occupation in higher education with hundreds of colleges seeking job applicants.

Cases. A student at Sarah Lawrence College who laughed at a joke deemed to violate the Ideology of Submission was sentenced to read material to correct his thinking and to write a paper expressing the right views.[482]

At Carnegie Mellon, a student refused to wear a pink triangle during the required "sensitivity training". He was fired from his university job.[483]

Carnegie Mellon also barred Internet access by its students to eighty-one websites that had the word "sex" in their title.[484]

West Virginia University has its own version of a loyalty oath: "I will practice … cultural diversity."[485]

FORCIBLY PREVENTING DISSENT

"When I bring up the idea of people speaking their minds, many of my … friends panic and talk as if encouraging people to say what they think will destroy civilization."[486]

Limiting freedom of speech. One way of preventing dissent is to limit what students and faculty members are allowed to say. It may be hard to credit that such blatant violations of academic freedom, not to mention First Amendment rights of freedom of speech, would be allowed; but on America's campuses not only are they allowed, they have been codified into university rules and are known as "speech codes."

Anyone opposing such anti-American codes is reviled as a racist, sexist, etc. Recently, the few academics who are trying to change campuses back to liberalism have found themselves having to fight battles of definition with the Dhimmists. Dhimmists try to defend the speech codes by blurring the distinction between speech and action. Saying certain things or posting fliers or writing in student or independent newspapers is *not* free speech but instead is sexual harassment or racial harassment.[487] Destroying the newspapers, however, or disrupting speeches by non-Dhimmists is not action but an exercise of "free speech."[488] Those who have read George Orwell may be forgiven for remembering his neologism "doublethink" at this point.

In 1993, a professor at Hampshire College introduced a motion affirming "the right of all members of the College community to the free expression of views in speech". The faculty voted down the motion. One professor (now a dean) said "the First Amendment was written by a rich, white, male slave owner." Another professor said he would favor the free expression motion only if it did not specify "without regard to the content or views expressed" because freedom of speech should be reserved for views that are "unobjectionable."[489] This is explicit proof that the Dhimmists do not even know what liberalism is.

The University of Connecticut's "speech" code outlaws "inappropriately directed laughter" and the "conspicuous exclusion" of individuals from conversations.[490] The University of Nebraska ordered a graduate student to remove from his desk a five-by-seven picture of his wife in a bikini because it created a "hostile environment".[491]

An editorial in a student newspaper at Vassar College was met with charges of "political harassment."[492] "*Political*" harassment? Yes, political harassment.

One professor at the University of New Hampshire, commenting on the university's violation of another professor's rights of free speech, which continued through four levels of appeal and was struck down in the law courts, said, "a perfectly decent group of people, because of the climate or the way they were trained … can't see clearly anymore."[493] This is terribly important and insightful. They can't "see" clearly anymore, meaning they can't think clearly anymore. This claim cannot be accepted at face value, but it is possibility that bears thinking about.

The U. S. government's Office of Civil Rights is now also run by Dhimmists and threatens colleges with loss of government contracts and grants if they do not enact codes that forbid harassment or a hostile environment by students or faculty saying things, laughing, printing articles in newspapers or otherwise communicating anti-Dhimmists sentiments.

What about privacy? One confidential and membership only online computer discussion group at Santa Rosa Junior College got into trouble because the group contained an internal spy who broke confidentiality and reported some of the members of the male-only discussion group who said derogatory things about women. A number of women sued. The school paid the women $15,000 each to avoid the legal expenses of the threatened suit.[494]

Judith Kleinfeld was a professor of psychology at the University of Alaska at Fairbanks who specialized in the education of Native American Alaskans. When she publicly complained that the university's "equity pressures" were graduating these students prematurely without adequately preparing them for the job market, there were demonstrations against her for "racism." She was suspended from teaching, and the university launched an "investigation" against her. The university finally concluded that they had no case, but by then the damage was done. *The process is the punishment.* Then, the U. S. government's Office of Civil Rights opened a four-month investigation of Prof. Kleinfeld and concluded that it had no case. But the process worked. Prof. Kleinfeld now has "declined to address even in the broadest of terms the educational issues that affect Native students." "I constantly worry about what I can say in the classroom."[495] In other words, even though the Dhimmists lost the case, they achieved their objective: to suppress the voicing of views that challenge the Ideology.

"One of the professors [at Harvard Divinity School] was sharply interrupted, mid-sentence, by an angry T. A. [teaching assistant] who 'corrected' him because he had referred to God as 'he'. 'I was ... even more aghast as I saw how much power she could wield with such petty rudeness when the professor meekly corrected himself and apologized.' "[496]

Limiting freedom of the press. Student newspapers that print any articles that hint that the policies of the Dhimmists are having unfortunate effects are ripped from news boxes or stolen directly from the newspaper offices. The Dhimmists engaging in these acts of suppression of the freedom of the press are said by administrators to be exercising their right to "free speech." Note that such attacks are not deemed "harassment", nor are they deemed to create "a hostile environment."

One group found 205 such incidents between 1993 and 2001. "At UC/Berkeley, copies of the student paper were stolen six times in the 1996-97 academic year."[497] This is further proof that the students themselves are not being taught what liberalism is, nor the basic principles of democracy.

An alternative student newspaper at Penn State, for instance, ran a cartoon poking fun at a militant feminist who in the official student newspaper had warned anyone who dared to criticize her, "I'll kick your ass." "Campus activists reacted [to the cartoon] by seizing and destroying all six thousand copies of" the alternative newspaper "and burning them in a bonfire."[498] What is more telling is that the editor of the *official* student newspaper labeled this imitation of Nazism as an expression of free speech. What is worse, a member of the faculty agreed.

Shadow classes. When it fails to silence a dissenting professor by means of harassing charges and investigations, universities create "shadow classes" and "invite" students to register for those sections instead of the professor's, because the professor's views might "offend" them. In one such case, Michael Levin, a philosophy professor at City University of New York, filed suit in court, won and was upheld on appeal. The appeals court ruled that "the shadow classes were established with the intent and consequence of stigmatizing professor Levin solely because of his expression of ideas."[499]

A dean at the University of Delaware told a reporter from the Delaware State News that the university had every right to ban external funding if the monies came from a politically objectionable source.[500] In this case, the funding organization was objectionable because it was conservative.

A Dartmouth College spokesman defended the stealing of copies of the conservative *Dartmouth Review* from delivery sites, saying it did not violate the code of student conduct because *The Dartmouth Review* was "litter."[501] The same happened at SUNY Binghamton.[502]

A Tufts University student was placed on probation for two years for selling a T-shirt with the words: "Why Beer is Better Than Women at Tufts."[503] Tufts students fought back and marked off "free speech zones" with tape and chalk on the campus sidewalks and invited the media in. The university backed down in this instance. Now that the news media has been transformed and has accepted the Ideology of Dhimmism, it is not clear that such a tactic would work.

The student newspaper at the University of Massachusetts at Amherst had its offices invaded by students who smashed windows, destroyed property and attacked staff. The chancellor put the position of the university more bluntly than colleges usually do. He said that there was a conflict between two values ... protection of free expression and the creation of a multicultural community." It's clear from the actions that were permitted and the students who were not defended which side the university was in fact on. The New York Times in 1995, a year before the new owner took over, wrote that the UMass policy created "a totalitarian atmosphere in which every one would have to guard his tongue all the time lest he say something that someone finds offensive."[504]

Affirmative speech. The University of Buffalo, Law School ruled that student free speech must be limited by "the responsibility to promote equality and justice."[505] In other words, as long as what you say is Dhimmism, you have a right to say it; otherwise not.

The University of Maryland lists among "unacceptable verbal behaviors ... idle chatter of a sexual nature." Unacceptable behavior, however, does not include stealing and trashing conservative newspapers at the University of Maryland.[506]

At Carnegie Mellon, a student who criticized the policies of one of the student leaders, a woman, was charged with sexual harassment. The student leader accusing him cited the large body of publications in the Ideology of Submission in her defense.[507] The Ideology has become its own justification.

At Vanderbilt, a conservative student organization was ousted from the university for refusing to report the racial composition of its staff to the administration,[508] saying it was none of their business.

At a Midwestern college, an assistant professor, who requested anonymity, told a researcher that it is "suicidal" to criticize campus militant feminists in any way. "They want people to be scared. Then you keep quiet and they don't have to deal with you." He described the atmosphere as "McCarthyist."[509]

At the University of Minnesota, a professor of social science, also speaking on condition of anonymity, told a researcher, "At faculty meetings, we have learned to speak in code: you say things that alert other faculty members that you do not agree … but you say nothing that could bring a charge of … insensitivity. People are out for control and power."[510]

At the same university, Norman Fruman, a distinguished scholar in the English department, said: "With the rise of poststructuralism, Derrida, Foucault, Althusser, you have the basis for a Stalinist position.… All of the literary masterpieces, including the very notion of aesthetic quality, are said to be a means of patriarchal control."[511]

At California Polytechnic Institute in 2003, a student was found guilty of "disruption" for posting a flier advertising an upcoming speech by Mason Weaver, a Black independent thinker.[512] FIRE entered the case and the university agreed to purge the conviction from the student's records and pay the student $40,000 in legal fees.

Fighting fire with FIRE. FIRE, the Foundation for Individual Rights in Education, was founded by Alan Kors, a history professor at the University of Pennsylvania. They have a website, www.theFIRE.org, where students and faculty can notify them of cases of violations of the First Amendment or the Fourth Amendment and where anyone can look up any college in the nation to find FIRE's rating of that college on its respect for individual rights. FIRE continues to receive hundreds of complaints every week[513] and can respond to only a few of them. They first write a letter to college administrators reporting the allegations. In most cases, the colleges back off when they find out that FIRE is onto them, and cease and desist from their unconstitutional practices. When they don't, FIRE sues them. They maintain a staff of pro bono lawyers for this purpose. They virtually always win. They also try to give the colleges the publicity they deserve and in some cases succeed in doing so.

Attacking books. Whenever a book is published exposing or arguing against or even questioning the dogmas of the new ideology, the Dhimmist hordes descend on the book, labeling it "conservative" or "racist," and reeling off a list of standard "criticisms": that the book is boring, that it contains little information, that its information has been published before, and that it is poorly written or difficult to read. It is not necessary to read the book ahead of time to make these accusations, since these "criticisms" are sufficiently elastic that they *might* be true of any given book.

These tactics discourage readers from risking the price of the book. Hence, the information in the book is, for all practical purposes, effectively eliminated.

Attacking professors. Professors who do not follow the prescriptions of Dhimmists may be subjected to smear campaigns, as happened to Stephan Thernstrom at Harvard and to Reynolds Farley at Michigan.[514]

Or they may have their classrooms invaded by students not enrolled in the course who then disrupt the proceedings of the class.[515]

Colleges are selective in their punishing of these outrages. Disrupting or smearing the non-Dhimmist classes or professors results in little or no punishment to those doing the disrupting. Doing the same to Dhimmists would be a disaster for the students. But such disruptions never happen, partly out of fear and partly because the non-Dhimmists are law-abiding and respectful students who believe in free speech and open discussion.

Attacking speakers. Another way of preventing dissent is to prevent speakers whose views differ from the Ideology of Dhimmism from speaking on campus. When it was impossible to prevent such speeches from being set up, the speakers themselves are shouted down and the meetings broken up. Some speakers are physically assaulted. These incidents are cited with pride by administrators as showing that the students breaking up these meetings are not afraid to exercise their right of free speech. These reactions prove that not only the students but college administrators these days have no idea what democracy is.

Ambassador Jeanne Kirkpatrick has been driven off the stage at Berkeley, the University of Wisconsin and the University of Washington.[516]

Eldridge Cleaver was welcome on campus in the days when he supported the Dhimmist ideology. After living in nations where the Dhimmists ruled, however, he changed his mind and began to speak out against Dhimmism. Now, Eldridge Cleaver is unwelcome and has been prevented by disruptions from speaking at Berkeley, Wisconsin and Minnesota.[517]

Ward Connerly was prevented from speaking at Columbia.[518] Columbia banned the audience rather than the speakers from the rented lecture hall, thus claiming that they were not engaging in censorship, since the speakers were free to speak (to an empty hall) if they chose. Such doublethink is common in American universities these days.

Third-world author Dinesh D'Souza was surrounded and shouted down at Columbia.[519]

Daniel Flynn was ejected from a meeting at the University of the District of Columbia when it was discovered he was a conservative. A mob at Georgia State University grabbed copies of Flynn's booklet Enemies Within. They claimed that it was racist because it had a picture of an Arab on the cover, being ignorant of the fact that the Arab pictured was Osama bin Laden and not feeling it appropriate to find out before condemning the book. As a further irony, Flynn was also physically assaulted at a press conference outside the Supreme Court building. [520]

Other speakers routinely attacked include Ann Coulter, Reginald Jones and David Horowitz.[521]

PURGING DISSENTERS

Those who do not respond to re-education are purged. Employees are simply fired. Tenured professors who cannot be fired are set up in situations where they can be accused of sexual harassment and forced to resign.[522]

Sexual harassment of faculty members. For instance, at the University of Minnesota, four female graduate students filed sexual harassment charges against six tenured faculty members, five men and a woman. The basis for two of the charges was not having given the women higher grades. The basis for another charge was having given a "patriarchal" interpretation of Isak Dinesen's work. Six months later, the charges were dropped for lack of a case, but the experience still cost the professors thousands of dollars in attorney fees.[523] Again, the process is the punishment.

In many cases, universities have suspended virtually all of the provisions of Constitutional due process rights of the accused. In one study, 36.2% did not allow cross-examination by the accused, 37.9% did not allow the accused to have legal counsel, 55.2% did not provide an impartial judge,

60.3% did not guarantee a right of the accused to confront accusers, and 91.4% did not provide accused students with legal counsel or assistance of any kind.[524] Since many of the accusations brought against faculty and students are for transgressing the Ideology of Submission in one way or another, these violations of due process are especially telling.

Cornell University established a Judicial System which included an array of due process protections. "Discrimination", however, including allegations of sexual harassment, were handled by a different office which offered no due process protections to accused faculty and students. This is now the case at hundreds of universities.[525] Many professors, faced with these persecutions or allegations of harassment, sue the universities in civil court. Rather than open their internal documents to the scrutiny of an impartial court, colleges usually choose to settle and pay costs to the professor in amounts that "have ranged from hundreds of thousands to two million dollars."[526]

The case of James B. Maas is one of the most curious. Maas, a distinguished professor of psychology, was voted by his students the best professor at Cornell. But he was accused of sexual harassment, including grabbing a student's breast, kissing, etc. The Faculty Ethics Committee found that none of these charges held up but convicted him anyway on the grounds that the fact that the accusations were made showed that he had made the women feel very uncomfortable. It even barred Maas' "advisor", a professor of law at Cornell, on the ground that he was "too much of an expert."[527]

Another male professor at the University of Hawaii made the mistake of having an honest discussion of the issue of sexual harassment in one of his classes. Three women were offended and tried to disrupt the discussion, but other students objected to these women rather than to the discussion, so the attempt failed. The women then brought charges that the professor had created a "hostile environment." The women then beefed up their charge by accusing the professor of sexual extortion: scholarships for sexual favors. Two months later, one of the three women added the charge of rape. The professor was not permitted to call witnesses nor to cross-examine. A set of university offices was already in place to help the *accusers*. Students at the university held several demonstrations against the professor. This torment continued for thirteen months until a vice-president of the university exonerated the professor, finding that the student charges were internally inconsistent and unsupported by evidence. The student who issued the rape charge now sued the professor *and* the university in civil court! The university quickly settled with her, paying her $175,000. The professor countersued the student. The jury of four men and four women decided in fifteen minutes that the student's story was a tissue of inconsistencies and absurdities (including classes on days when in fact there were no classes held, etc.) and awarded the professor $133,000.[528] So, the student made $42,000 on the deal.[529]

Dhimmism pays.

Harassment of students. One woman student of Hispanic decent at San Diego State University made the mistake of being a Republican, campaigning *against* racial preferences in admission to San Diego State and debating the issue with La Raza. She got a phone call from her dorm advisor at 2 A. M., saying he wanted to discuss her "drug use." She informed him that she had never used drugs. To gather evidence, she went to the university clinic and tested negative for all drugs, but that changed nothing. She was informed that she would be evicted from her dorm.[530]

Naturally, people who disagree with the Ideology of Submission almost always keep quiet about it.

Disabling Americans

On one international test, America's most advanced students scored *lower* than those in *any other country* involved in the test, lower than students in Latvia and in Cyprus.[531] How did this situation come about? And how will the United States defend itself if its citizens have been rendered incompetent?

As we shall see in this chapter, this mental disability on the part of America's young people was no accident, and it was no reflection on the native ability of Americans. Getting people to subordinate themselves, their culture and their country is a hard sell. The usual methods of mass-market propaganda cannot bring enough people to agree. There are bound to be people who simply won't go along. Vilifying them and preventing them from speaking are essential, but these methods only isolate and contain the dissenters. They don't convert others. Also, these methods risk attracting attention (which they have) and generating opposition.

The American people needed to be "transformed" into Dhimmists. Adults are too practical and too mature to accept the unsupported claims of the Ideology. The Dhimmists determined to transform America by transforming the curricula of the colleges and the K12 schools[532] to instill the Ideology into those too ignorant to have formed any opinions yet and too young to have acquired the cognitive skills to defend themselves. (A narrative account of how this happened can be found in my novel *The Rape of Alma Mater*.)

Of course, the Dhimmists do not intend to produce any debilitating side-effects. As many have observed, they are so desperate to promote their ideology that they are blind to all side-effects their programs have. They simply want to further the Ideology, which they are convinced is good and helpful.

As of today, the transformation of the schools and colleges of America is an accomplished fact. Hundreds of public school curricula all over the United States had been transformed. Some state governments have officially required the new transformed curricula to be adopted by all the public schools in their states. Already in 1993, a conference of over eight hundred teachers, college professors, administrators and state officials met in a "celebration of twenty years of curriculum transformation."[533]

"When future historians go back to find out what happened to American universities at the end of the twentieth century that so weakened them, politicized them and rendered them illiberal, anti-intellectual and humorless places,"[534] they will find the fanatical proponents of the Ideology of Submission, by whatever name they are then called.

What exactly have these transformations been?

Transforming the Students

"The most successful tyranny is not the one that uses force to assure uniformity, but the one that removes the awareness of other possibilities."[535]

In order to instill the Ideology of Submission into students, the Dhimmists needed those students *not* to ask the Dhimmists what evidence they had to support the claims of the Ideology or even to know that evidence is needed to establish the truth or falsity of a statement. They needed the students to accept the ideology. This was easy enough to accomplish once they had become dominant (or as they like to put it, attained a "hegemony") in academia and in the K12 schools.

Don't confuse me with facts. Ask a Dhimmist for evidence and you will get a lecture on the evils of science.[536] Ask "How do you *know* that?" and you will be informed that "knowledge is a patriarchal construction."[537] Charge them with bias, and they will condescend to remind you that "bias is a condition of consciousness."[538]

"Why do we have to have a fact-finding commission before we respond to student demands?" a speaker at a faculty "sensitivity" program at Harvard asked rhetorically.[539]

How can you solve or even discuss serious problems like terrorism, the energy crisis, or immigration with someone whose basic thought processes have no place for evidence, support or statistical analysis?[540] How can you educate people who have been taught that to learn such subjects as logic, scientific method, and language analysis is to participate in "the rape of our minds?"[541] The American Council of Learned Societies proudly proclaims that "precisely those things now identified as failings in the humanities actually indicate enlivening transformations."[542]

Militant feminists, among other Dhimmists, have been at work for the past two decades "transforming the knowledge base."[543] They have rejected the "hegemony of Greco-Euro-American standards."[544] They have rejected science because they allege its subject matter to be male dominated. Women have other ways of knowing, ways that are not narrowed down by facts.[545] Sandra Harding holds that Newton's Principles of Mechanics should be called "Newton's Rape Manual."[546] For Harding, science is part of a "discredited bourgeois Christian legacy practically indistinguishable from imperialism, its cognitive core tainted by sexism and racism."[547]

Some Dhimmists attempt to persuade their colleagues and students by the logical fallacy known as "appeal to authority." In this case, they appeal to the "authority" of physicist Thomas Kuhn and claim that Kuhn holds that scientific theories and facts are merely the beliefs of the scientific community. This is a misreading of Kuhn, but even if it were accurate, Kuhn's saying something does not make it true. Kuhn himself was appalled at the misunderstanding of his book by nonscientists. In a new postscript to the second edition, he took pains to correct the impression: "I am a convinced believer in scientific progress."[548] But the damage had been (and continues to be) done.

One recent example of anti-scientific thinking urges a "global mind change" that would eliminate science and objectivity (which the author claims are "Western constructs") from the minds of third-world people. He asserts that they are obstacles to "progress" and globalization.[549] Thus, third-world countries, which already have enough problems, are being saddled with thinking that bars them from all possibility of making the progress that Western countries have made. Japan and now China, however, are having none of this. They are grabbing all the Western science and technology they can lay their hands on.

All of this seems rather abstract. Does it have any practical consequences? Answer: of course. In 1987 a Black teenager falsely accused several white police officers of raping her. Even after it was discovered that she fabricated the whole story, the Dhimmists *still* supported her accusation, claiming "that the actual facts did not ultimately matter."[550]

Other militant feminists reject the "doubting game" of science and advocate a "believing game" because "many women find it easier to believe than to doubt."[551] Males aim at "exact thinking"—which is bad. Women's thinking is more "inclusive."[552]

Another response is simply faking the facts. For instance, a sociologist at the University of North Carolina published a study in the New York University Law Review claiming that there was "little to no difference" on bar exam passage rates between people admitted to law schools under preference programs and those admitted on merit. Problem was that those who examined her data discovered that even her own data showed a three-to-one difference.[553]

One militant feminist wonders whether Western philosophy has anything at all to offer women. "We might begin to question the import of Descartes' stress on logic and mathematics as the ideal types of rationality, in a society in which only a tiny percentage of people could realistically spend time developing skills in those fields."[554] As we shall see below, America today is indeed a society in which only a tiny percentage of people have basic skills in math. And even fewer have basic skills in logic.

Militant feminists claim that women have an "epistemic" advantage over men. In other words, they are better "knowers"[555] and "might give us a quite different understanding of even physical reality"[556] once they have developed different epistemologies.[557] What exactly a female epistemology would look like, its proponents do not say. But this does not seem to be a practical problem, since this as yet nonexistent field already has many enthusiastic adherents.

In place of previous subject matters, "One begins to study quilts, bread-loaf shapes, clothing, pots, or songs and dances that people who had no musical literacy or training took for granted."[558] This change also presupposes changes in the standards and criteria of what is considered an achievement. This transvaluation of all values is at the heart of the transformationist movement. One course insinuated that the aboriginal concept of "dream time" as an explanation of cause and effect was superior to the "'logocentric' approach of Western philosophers like Aristotle and Descartes."[559]

"Having denied the very possibility of objective learning ... serves them very well indeed, by leaving them free to do what they please in their classrooms."[560]

How extensive is this transformation of academia? In the 1970s, there were fewer than twenty courses in women's studies. Twenty years later, there were tens of thousands of such courses. But their revolution is not confined to women's studies. They are at work on hundreds of transformation projects for changing university curricula and public school curricula. "The whole knowledge base must be transformed."[561] One book chronicles the triumphs of the transformation movement.[562] At this point, the English departments, foreign language departments, history, education, law, journalism, religion, and art departments have been transformed. The social sciences are riddled with transformations. The Dhimmists are even trying to infiltrate and undermine the physical and biological sciences.[563]

Some academics became enamored of the notions of a school of German Marxist thought known as Critical Theory. Using this school's name, they began to transform a number of traditional fields into what are essentially new fields or dogmas: Critical Legal Theory, Critical Race Theory, etc. To give an idea of the sorts of doctrines contained in these new transformed fields: "Critical Legal Study's critique of liberal law ... strives to show how such concepts as individualism and the rule of law (which assumes law's autonomy, coherence, consistency, and neutrality) are fundamentally untenable. Law is power."[564] "Postmodernism questions the integrity and viability of the ultimate foundation of liberal freedom: the autonomous, self-determining individual."[565]

Transformationists have also entered the administrations of colleges and reward and protect those who promote transformationist work at the college. They have set up transformationist retreats where "outside facilitators are brought in to help selected faculty and administrators "rethink how they teach."[566] "We now find deans and college presidents admonishing students not to be taken in by claims of objectivity.... Learning and teaching have less to do with truth, reality and objectivity than we had assumed."[567]

Students who have accepted these basic premises of Dhimmist thinking are "virtually unteachable". As one English professor put it, "For them *reason* itself is patriarchal, linear and oppressive. You cannot argue with them."[568]

Education and indoctrination. To put it another way, students in colleges and high schools at the present time are being indoctrinated, not educated. What is the difference?

Indoctrination consists in bringing students to believe what the teacher believes: in this case the various precepts of the Ideology of Submission.[569] One of the earmarks of indoctrination is the blurring of distinctions. Another mark of indoctrination is that the statements being advanced are immune to criticism. Any statements offered as criticism are attributed to personal failings in the person offering the criticism. Any counterexamples offered are interpreted as attacks on the teacher and further demonstrate that the student is hostile. If such efforts at rational discussion are persisted in, the student is silenced by threats. "[T]his comment [is] an example of sexual harassment..... Any future comments, in a paper, in a class or in any dealings will be interpreted as sexual harassment and formal steps will be taken. You are forewarned!"[570]

Education, by contrast, consists of enabling students to form their own conclusions by teaching them to clarify the words used in making a claim, weigh evidence for and against the claim, and evaluate arguments for and against the claim.

Most Dhimmist teachers deny that they are indoctrinating. This is certainly the safest course of action. But some admit that they are indoctrinating but claim that all teaching is indoctrination and their efforts are "counter-indoctrination" of the teachings of non-Dhimmists.[571]

Result. Having students who are unaware that they need evidence in order to assess whether a statement is worthy of belief or not is useful to Dhimmists, since the students have no basis for rejecting the statements of the Ideology that they are being taught.

That doesn't sound reasonable to me. A lot of people have wondered: why do reasonable arguments seem to have no effect on the people who advocate these strange contra-American policies? It should be simple to point out to these people how their beliefs are wrong. Any reasonable person would abandon these beliefs and come up with something different, even if it is something else that is also wrong. But argument and reasons do not work with the Dhimmists. Why?

The Dhimmists needed their students to be unable to discern when an argument is invalid, since many of the arguments they use to persuade the students are well-known logical fallacies such as the ad hominem argument, the appeal to authority, etc.

"They also regard logic and rationality as phallocentric."[572] As a result of this failure to teach logic and forbidding students to study it, a number of kinds of fallacious thinking have become commonplace.

Guilt by association. For instance, book **B** is praised by person **P**. Person **P** is a conservative. Therefore, book **B** is conservative.

What is wrong with thinking this way? First, the praise of person **P** does not imply that all the statements in the book are false or wrong. It does not even make it probable. Second, person P may be game-playing. He may have praised it publicly to make sure nobody reads it. A book's truth or falsity, rightness or wrongness depends on the statements in the book.

Again, book **B** quotes person **P**. Person **P** is a conservative. Therefore, book **B** is conservative.

What is wrong with this way of thinking? This thinking presupposes that if one quote in the book is from a conservative, they all are. If five percent of the quotes in the book are from conservatives, it hardly follows that the book is conservative, since ninety-five percent are from non-conservatives. Furthermore, this argument presupposes that all statements by all conservatives are false or wrong. Such a belief needs to be supported, not presupposed. Presuppositions have a dramatic effect on beliefs and on thinking. Being unaware of one's presuppositions is therefore risky. Thinking that is guided by a large number of presuppositions of which the person is unaware is one of the characteristics of the authoritarian personality (of which more below).

Contradictions. Two statements contradict each other when one of the statements cannot be true unless the other is false and vice versa. They may *both* be false, but not both can be true. In other words, one statement makes a claim the truth of which the other denies.

In the recent past, for an academic to make a mistake in elementary logic was such a gross blunder that it virtually ruined that academic's reputation. To contradict oneself was even worse. Yet, today, even the most imminent of academics publish contradictions and no one objects.

For instance, Stanley Fish holds that the task is "not to decide ... by ... disinterested evidence but to establish by political and persuasive means."[573] "Does might make right? In a sense the answer I must give is yes."[574] "Political justifications are the only kind there are."[575] In short, Fish is claiming that statements cannot be said to be true or false but are established only by means of political persuasion. So, where is the contradiction? The problem is that Fish's statements are statements. If *all* statements are merely forced on other people by political power, then that holds for Fish's statements. To put it more starkly: statement S_F claims that all statements S_1, S_2, S_3, ..., S_n (where n is the number of all the statements in the world) cannot be known to be true. But S_F is one of the statements in the world. Therefore, S_F cannot be known to be true. In other words, statement S_F denies its own truth.

Again, "there is no such thing as literal meaning."[576] If that statement is true, then that statement too is without literal meaning.

Another case is that of Barbara Herrnstein Smith. "If there is no truth-value to what anyone says, then ... are you not making truth-claims in the very act of presenting your views, and isn't your account self-refuting?"[577] The answer, of course, is yes. But Smith still doesn't see it. She claims that she is merely providing a description. What she doesn't see is that her "description" is a description of a contradictory position. In other words, the question whether statements can be known to be true is still up in the air, and that includes her own claim, *viz.* that statements *cannot* be known to be true.

Duke University calls a new series "Post-Contemporary Interventions" with no awareness that "contemporary" means the present moment. "Post" means after. An intervention cannot both happen at the present moment and also happen tomorrow.

The genetic fallacy. Book **B** was published by a publisher that often publishes conservative books. Therefore, every statement in book **B** is false and every recommendation in the book is wrongheaded.

This way of thinking presupposes that points of view other than Dhimmism are not worth considering.

This assumption insolates the Dhimmists from any ideas that might cause them to re-think their position. Such tactics of *containing the believers* are often used by movements that are offering their followers beliefs that will not stand up to scrutiny. In the case of Dhimmism, such a tactic of mentally isolating the faithful is absolutely necessary for the continued survival of the Ideology of Submission.

Ad hominem attacks. Person **P** is a racist. Therefore, what he says is false. This side-tracks the discussion onto whether person **P** is a racist, and the point he made is forgotten.

If even a racist says that 2 plus 2 is equal to 4, it still does not follow that his statement is false. To know whether the statement is true, you have to do some arithmetic, not delve into the background of the person making the statement. But in most uses of this tactic, the attacker does not know whether person **P** is a racist or not and does not care. The objective is merely to win the argument and humiliate person **P**.

This is only a small sample of handicapped thinking. For more types and examples, see *Crimes Against Logic*.[578]

Result. Having students who accept statements on the basis of authority and who can be easily brought to reject statements by *ad hominem* attacks and other tricks is useful to Dhimmists in getting students to accept the Ideology. The Dhimmist teacher himself is regarded as the authority, whereas anyone who disagrees or questions is a vile racist, sexist, Xenophobe or whatever.

Don't you dare ask me what I mean! Many movements over time have learned the usefulness of obfuscation in furthering their aims and in protecting themselves from criticism. And as all ideologists have, the Dhimmists also found vagueness to be a powerful means of putting across their new ways of thinking. They coined terms and never attempted to define them except in terms of other undefined expressions. That meant that they had to make sure their students did not ask for definitions or even know the requirements of an adequate definition.

Of course, not just any word will do for a useful and successful bit of jargon. The word chosen must have emotional appeal, for instance, "transformative", "empowering", subjectivity, inclusiveness, lateral thinking, relatedness. "There is also lots of metaphorical talk about windows and mirrors and voices."[579]

Immunity. An ideology, all of whose terms are obscure, is *immune to criticism*, since any claim made against it can always be deflected with the excuse that the critic misunderstands the position. The believers in the ideology, the Dhimmists in this case, think that this makes their position strong. In fact, this makes their position hopelessly weak, because their ideology is nonfalsifiable.

In the late 1960s and early 1970s, a number of eccentric intellectual trends that had come to prominence in Germany and France were attracting attention in the U. S. These trends were not adopted in America as rapidly as a new fashion in clothes, but the process was essentially the same. Soon, these trends were regarded as the cutting edge, and everyone in the publish-or-perish world of academia wanted to be at the forefront. These trends of Critical Theory, Deconstructionism,[580] Postmodernism, and the like, turned out to have great usefulness for the Dhimmists, and by the early 1980s, more and more of them were eagerly exploiting their potential. For instance, to justify their use of vague terms, the Dhimmists claim that "there is no such thing as meaning."[581]

One of the most difficult tasks facing those who are fighting rules restricting freedom of speech on campuses (i.e. speech codes) "was winning the battle over definitions, which meant … getting people to admit that the code was indeed a *speech* code."[582]

One set of transformations of the fields of knowledge began to be dubbed "postmodernism." This term is so amorphous that even those who use the term cannot agree on what sort of thing it refers to. For many, it is a movement in art. For others, it is a whole worldview. Working hand in hand with similar movements in literature, the upshot of this movement is the evisceration of human knowledge.

"Postmodernism challenges such intellectual ... tenets as universal reason, objective truth, empiricism, science, individual autonomy and rights."[583]

Postmodernism is guided by a sense of the dehumanization of the Planet and the End of Man. Its preoccupations include anti-elitism, diffusion of the ego, participation. Postmodernists produce open, discontinuous, improvisational, indeterminate, or aleatory structures. Not surprisingly, they are "against interpretation." Among their themes are the absent center, ontological uncertainty, the death of the "subject". Neither the world nor the self possess unity, coherence, meaning.[584]

The reader may think that such phrases and statements would make sense if one had background in this subject and knew what the coined terms meant. But that is exactly the point. These terms are never defined. When the terms are first introduced, they are characterized using other coined terms which are equally inscrutable but which are evocative and have an air of profundity.

The Dhimmists created whole new "fields" to replace the standard bodies of knowledge that had so painstakingly been developed over the centuries: for instance, "Coordinated Management of Meaning Theory," "Experience, Identity and Interaction," "Postmodernism and Media," "American Rhetorical Theory," "Introduction to Multiculturalism," "Racism," "Sexism," "Social Justice," "Bilingualism and Biculturalism," "Social Inequality and Diversity," "Responsibility and Critical Theory," "The Postmodern Moments in the Marxist Tradition," "Feminism, Queer Theory and Postmodernism," "Postmodernism and Management," "Anti/post-colonialism," "Hip-hop and the politics of Postmodernism," etc.

Those fields that it was impractical or inadvisable to replace were revised until they were unrecognizable: for example, "Radical Ecology and

Critical Theory," "Knowledge Underground: Gossipy Epistemology," "Political philosophy: politics, gender and race," and the like.

To say that there are people who oppose reason itself and reject that whole idea that objective evidence is necessary to support a belief and who refuse to define or even to clarify the terms they use—all of this strains credibility. But sadly, it is all true. It is called rejecting "Western thinking", rejecting "male-dominated thinking", or sometimes simply "postmodernism."

It is very useful to the Dhimmists, since the students have no criteria for assessing the claims of the Ideology and are easily brought to accept the Ideology by what appear to be arguments (which the students have no cognitive tools for assessing). Also, they have the comfort of believing that they are being taught something profound, since the vague words are very evocative. And they can believe themselves to be good persons, because they are being so kindly disposed toward the downtrodden of the earth.

Unfortunately, functioning competently in almost any occupation requires the ability to sort out reliable statements from unreliable ones and recognizing when a statement simply does not make sense. And solving problems requires reasoning—valid reasoning—from one set of statements to others.

Result. Each generation of students (except perhaps those in the physical and biological sciences) have been and continue to be transformed. Thus, more and more Americans cannot function competently, thanks to the work of the Dhimmists. This mental handicapping is probably the single most effective means of rendering America weak and vulnerable.

DUMBING DOWN

As conditions began to improve for Black and Hispanic people, the Dhimmists expected that differences in school performance between these groups and other groups would diminish. They didn't. The Dhimmists decided that the explanation was that Black children and Hispanic children had low self-esteem. Improve their self-esteem and they would learn better.

Textbooks and classroom methods were completely transformed and geared to producing acceptance of and valuing of oneself. Grades still didn't improve. The teachers tried harder. Feeling good about oneself began to take over as an end in itself. Expectations were lowered. Pupils were urged to set "realistic" goals, that is, ones that anyone could achieve. Aiming high was discouraged. No one noticed that setting lower goals would almost guarantee lower performance. Also, the Dhimmists didn't notice that the implicit message of these practices insinuated that the pupils were not very bright, but pupils got the message and performed accordingly. They felt good about themselves. They didn't learn very much.

Affirmative teaching. Classroom teaching began to be geared to the slowest and least interested pupils. This not only wasted the time of the average students and was excruciating for the few bright students, but it failed to benefit the slowest pupils. Learning requires action on the part of the pupil. There is no way to get information through to children who simply do not want to know.

Classes began to focus on feelings and opinions rather than facts, grammatical rules and arithmetic operations. There is no way a feeling can be wrong. And everyone has a right to his or her opinion. By focusing on feelings and opinions, everybody wins. The pupils can't fail. The teacher can't fail. The school can't fail. The "feel-good" curriculum was sold as good for the kids, but it also had the beneficial side-effect that it covered up or obscured the failures of the pupils and avoided making the teacher and the school look bad.

To teach math, calculators are introduced as early as kindergarten. "Teachers let children debate the solution to simple math problems among themselves." "[M]any teachers do not require exact answers on math tests."[585] Many schools teach "creative spelling" and tell children there is no one correct way to spell a word.[586] Reading is taught, not by learning the alphabet, but by learning to recognize a few simple words by having those words used repeatedly in their reading books.

Public schools are now teaching New Age religions to children. This involves giving them exercises to alter their consciousness through guided imagery, visualizations, and contact with spirit guides.[587] Many teachers across the country require pupils to log their daily horoscope, learn palmistry, tarot cards and other means to tap into secret sources of wisdom. Children learn to "see" their personal animal spirits. Others are taught the value of sacrificing themselves for the common good.[588]

Brainwashing. In addition, the brainwashing techniques developed in China are used to break down children's defenses and get them to accept what the teacher wants them to believe and feel how the teacher wants them to feel. These include emotional shock, desensitization, psychological isolation from sources of support, and manipulative cross-examination.[589] For an example of emotional shock and desensitization, one California teacher gave children the assignment of describing how they would kill their best friend and how they felt doing it.[590] Other exercises involve imagining committing suicide, euthanasia, homosexual acts, and occult practices. An interesting question is whether this could have anything to do with the fact that suicide rates of teenagers have gone up.

The journalist who introduced the term "brainwashing" into the English language commented that "no person has ever been brainwashed whose mind had not first been put into a fog."[591] The pupil first has to be shaken loose from whatever beliefs and convictions he might have by being assured that truth and facts are "social constructs," in other words, that facts are whatever a society says they are. Half-truths and even lies sound convincing to people who have no knowledge at all about a subject. The pupil is then taught "tolerance" which is defined as getting along with others, avoiding the stigma of being "antisocial," and comprising. Compromising requires bending or abandoning fixed principles.[592]

What's in a name? As with other practices of the Dhimmists, educationists have coined affirmative-sounding words and phrases to cover what they are doing. For example, "values clarification" does not mean to clarify a child's values but to convince the child that there are no values, only preferences. And this is preparatory to getting the child to adopt the attitudes and preferences prescribed by Dhimmism. "Tolerance" and being "non-judgmental" mean not condemning other cultures no matter how inhumane their practices are. An example of the success of these programs is a group of Yale students watching the destruction of the World Trade Center towers in New York City. They were unable to bring themselves to condemn the perpetrators.[593] Other examples are "higher order thinking skills," "cooperative learning," "the Delphi Technique," "Dialoguing to Consensus," etc.

Schools teach a false notion of third-world cultures as innocent while they teach an image of America as guilty. In particular, they do not teach the truth about Islamic cultures in their treatment of women, among other things. At the same time, they have National Standards for United States History developed by an organization called the National Center for History in the Schools, which standards require presenting America and Western civilization as the bad guys of history, and all others as innocent victims of American greed.[594]

Affirmative promoting. Even so, a few things have to be learned to avoid attracting the attention of parents. This raised a problem: what to do with the kids who failed the grade. The solution was easy for everybody: promote them anyway. Use affirmative grading to give them good marks and promote them. This program was sold under the heartrending slogan: "no child left behind." Since many of these children were Black or Hispanic, this program also had the advantage of avoiding charges of "racism."

The result was that the kids who hadn't been able to do the work of the previous year found the next year's work even more difficult to comprehend. Consequently, they fell further behind, in spite of the fact that the next year's teaching had to be slower to try to help the failing pupils and they failed again at the end of the year. The solution? Promote them anyway, again. Year after year the kids were promoted, and classes became slower and duller for the other kids. Eventually, the beneficiaries of affirmative promoting simply dropped out of school.

Affirmative testing. Of course, this failure showed up in various ways, the drop-out rates being one. But more seriously, it showed up when the kids finally took objective tests for college admissions. The SAT (Scholastic Aptitude Test) had been administered by testing specialists for years. Each question on the test itself had been subjected to extensive testing, and the test as a whole had been scrutinized for its predictive validity in terms of college performance. The composite verbal-and-quantitative score was 980 in 1963 and declined steadily to 890 in 1980.[595] This decline also showed up in another test, the ACT exam, as well as in the Iowa Test of Educational Development.[596]

The sagging test scores on the SAT began to attract attention in the late 1970s and alarmed a number of parents and politicians. Objective tests began to be administered to all high school students, and the results were shocking. High school students could not read, could not do math, and could not write a grammatical sentence.

The "educators" had no problem with this: they simply attacked the tests. Tests were "racist" and biased toward "Western" values of analytical competence, ignoring the more important values of self-esteem.

An international study of thirteen-year-olds showed that Americans fell further and further behind, the more they were required to think (in this case, apply simple principles, analyze experiments).[597] In other studies, not only were American pupils unable to give reasons for their beliefs, but many were unaware of even the need for such. Similarly, they could not tell the difference between knowledge and opinion.[598]

After much hand-wringing, a solution was found: make the SAT easier! The SAT was revised in the late 1970s, and not surprisingly, SAT scores went up slightly. But then, the scores continued to decline on the new easier SAT. In the late 1980s, the test was "revised" again, to make it more "multicultural" by requiring students to be familiar with Black street slang. Again, scores went up. Again, scores continued to decline on the new revised test.[599]

In 1995, they extended the time allowed for taking the test, dropped some of the more challenging questions and allowed the use of calculators. The students were also given a bonus of 95 points.[600] The new "recentered" test has been renamed the Scholastic Assessment Test. Obviously, scores on this new test cannot be meaningfully compared to scores on the previous SAT.

The final solution has been to avoid giving the SAT or to allow substitute "tests" which put more emphasis of feelings.

Results. In one survey of Ivy League students, three out of four did not know that Thomas Jefferson was the author of the Declaration of Independence.[601]

One-third of American 17-year-olds did not know that Abraham Lincoln wrote the Emancipation Proclamation. Thirty percent could not locate Britain on a map of Europe.[602]

As previously pointed out, on one international test, America's most advanced students scored *lower* than those in *any other country* involved in the test, lower than students in Latvia and in Cyprus.[603]

School officials, when unable to get out of giving objective tests, have come up with a creative way out: *cheat*! Fifty percent of the pupils at one elementary school routinely failed the TAAS test until 1997. Then, 100% of the pupils passed the test. After an investigation, one teacher was fired and two principals were reprimanded.[604]

In 1999, the entire school district in Austin, Texas was indicted on criminal charges of manipulating test data used to rate Texas schools.[605] Meanwhile, Houston officials are investigating similar charges in their own 15 schools.

No matter how much evidence one piles up, the Dhimmists have ways of dismissing it: "isolated incident," "the exception not the rule," "special case." Mayor Guiliani of New York City said, "There comes a point, after 15 years of tragically plummeting graduation rates and a total evisceration of standards, that somebody has to say, 'This isn't working.' "The school board did vote to exclude from four-year colleges any student who couldn't read, write or do math, but the meeting was interrupted by demonstrators who protested the decision.[606]

At the same time, the behavior of school children has changed. In 1940, pupil behavior problems in California were listed as: talking, chewing gum, making noise, running in the halls, and getting out of turn in line. In 1990, the problems were: drug abuse, alcohol abuse, pregnancy, suicide, rape.[607] Indeed, the times they are a-changin'.

"Teachers" not only are incapable of producing competent students, they are opposed to doing so. Peggy McIntosh, an educationist at Wellesley College, claims that "excellence" represents a white-male culture of "vertical thinking." She heads a program called "Seeking Educational Equity and Diversity" which holds seminars for thousands of teachers from 30 states on making schools free of "the ideal of excellence."[608]

AUTHORITARIAN THINKING OR CLOSED-MINDEDNESS

What is closed-minded mental functioning? It is a particular type of mental handicap that not only affects a person's ability to do certain things but predisposes a person to accept certain types of conclusions and to accept claims when presented in a certain way.

Inability to solve certain problems. One of the most striking discoveries in research on the closed mind was the discovery that people who scored high on the various scales that had been developed to measure authoritarianism could not solve certain types of problems. This result was demonstrated by Rokeach and his associates with the Denny Doodlebug problem.[609] Without going into details, this was a board-game type of puzzle which closed-minded people could not solve because (a) they made certain assumptions which were not stated in the specification of the puzzle and (b) they were unaware of these assumptions and hence could not question them and try other possible courses of actions that appeared when one removed the assumptions.

Compartmentalized thinking. The ten-year research program by Rokeach also turned up the startling fact that closed-minded people were able to hold two incompatible beliefs at the same time even when the two beliefs contradicted each other. This research finding and others led Rokeach to posit the theory that the mental functioning of authoritarians is such that certain sets of information were never brought into contact with other sets of information in the person's mind. In other words, their minds were "compartmentalized."

If this seems abstract, consider some actual cases. Conservative author Daniel Flynn was invited to speak on the UC/Berkeley campus on September 27, 2000. The Dhimmists shouted him down and burned copies of his book. Simultaneously, they held up signs saying "Fight Racial Censorship." The act of censoring speech was to them compatible with opposing censorship.[610]

Another example: Dhimmists are able to believe that printing a newspaper that criticizes Dhimmism is "action," while destroying that newspaper is "speech."

Another example: Discriminating on the basis of race is racism. Discriminating against white people on the basis of race is not racism.

Inability to question one's assumptions. Another prominent feature of closed-mindedness is the inability to question one's own beliefs, even in the face of serious disconfirming evidence. Rokeach went on to study this in the real-life setting of a mental hospital in Ypsilanti, Michigan. In the Michigan state system, there were three men each of whom believed he was the one and only Jesus Christ. Rokeach had all three moved to the Ypsilanti facility and under his observation had them brought into the same room. How would they react when they encountered other men each of whom was also thoroughly convinced that *he* was Christ? The result was that the experience did not cause the slightest doubt in any of the three men. Each continued to believe that he was Christ and that the other two were "crazy."[611]

Inability to take the role of the other. Another severe handicap of the closed-minded person is the inability to take the role of another person. In order to see another's point of view, one has to mentally adopt the position of that person, mentally play the role of that person. Authoritarians have difficulty doing this.

Susceptibility to authority. One of the first features of the authoritarian personality to be noticed and studied was the propensity to accept statements if the person asserting the statement was perceived as an authority figure. More seriously, certain people tended to follow directives if the person issuing that directive was perceived to be an authority figure.[612] At that point, in the late 1940s, it was thought that only Nazis were authoritarians. It was quickly discovered that the problem is much more extensive.

At that time, to *head off* any tendency to develop authoritarianism, games were devised and played even with toddlers. One of these was called "horses fly." The teacher would ask the three-year-olds to stand, then she would say, "Birds fly," and flap her arms like wings. The children were supposed to repeat the words and flap their arms too. Then, the teacher would say, "Geese fly," and flap her arms. The children did too. "Ducks fly." And so on. Then, she would say, "Horses fly," and flap her arms. At this, the children were supposed *not* to flap their arms. Why? Because horses do not in fact fly. In other words, the children were being taught to think for themselves rather than to follow the leader. Those children who were blindly following the teacher and flapping their arms were laughed at by the other children. This exercise was repeated over and over until all the children were flapping their arms only when the animal in question actually flies and not otherwise, that is until all the children had learned to think for themselves. I wonder if such games are played with children now.

Stereotyping. Authoritarians think in terms of labels. They tend to lump together individual items or people under a label and hold beliefs about all of the people in the set based on the label. When encountering an individual, they do not see an individual but an instance of the set. To the authoritarian, all Black people are alike, all Jews are alike, all conservatives are alike.

Prejudice. This type of thinking is also associated with prejudging. Authoritarians typically judge a book without reading it, judge a person without knowing the person, judge a position without knowing anything about it. How do they do this? Labels is one way. If they can label or categorize a book, a person or a position, then they do not need to know any more. They "know" what the book says, what the person is, and that the position is wrong. It does not occur to them that they arrived at the label in the first place, because some other person placed the label on the book, person or position. They do not question the other person's judgment.

Result. Authoritarians, thus, are easily led. Once they have been brought to hate the labels, they can be controlled to a large degree. The usefulness to the Dhimmists of having authoritarian followers is, thus, obvious.

RESULTS

The consequence of all this is that America is becoming a nation of dumbed-down, cognitively disabled people who are wedded to an Ideology that prescribes the subordination of America and Western culture to others. But how extensive is this change? Are we talking about a phenomenon that affects only a lunatic fringe?

Spreading the Ideology

A teacher at a school in California was shocked when she saw what her seventh grade son was being taught at that same school. All pupils in California are required to be taught a version of Islam that the school wants the children to accept as official Islam. To do this, the children have to pick a Muslim name for themselves, wear a robe, memorize passages from the Quran, and go on an imaginary pilgrimage to Mecca. They are taught how to pray to Allah and are required to pray to Allah and are graded on how well they pray. They are required to fast. They have a textbook on Islam, adopted statewide. The alleged "miracles" of Islam are taught as facts. They are *not* taught anything about the Muslim treatment of women or of nonbelievers, of the lack of freedom, etc. Nor is there any discussion of why Muslims hate America. Obviously, as this teacher observed, if Christianity were taught this way, the ACLU would sue the school system. In fact, Christianity is taught in a wholly negative way emphasizing the Inquisition, witch hunts, etc. in bold type. When parents complain, the school administrators and teachers ridicule them.[613]

Is the Ideology of Submission a fringe phenomenon in the United States that affects only a few oddballs? Or is it pervasive, extending into almost every aspect of American life? Judge for yourself.

Besides their goal of transforming Americans, the Dhimmists, like all True Believers,[614] need to convert as many people as possible to agree with them to reassure themselves that they are right.[615] So, it is not surprising that the Ideology of Submission spread into the content of many fields, such as education, journalism, law, criminal justice, religion, history, literature, and library science, while more and more people in those fields became converts to the Ideology. And it spread into more areas of American society: colleges, public schools, news rooms, motion pictures and TV, courts, law enforcement, government agencies, foundations, book publishers, bookstore chains, public libraries, and even pulpits.

TRANSFORMING THE SCHOOLS

Education departments in the universities across the country were transformed. Public and private schools and school procedures were transformed. Schoolbooks were transformed. Also, the Modern Languages Association, a respected organization whose recommendations are often implemented in secondary schools, was transformed.

Transformed education departments. Schools of education have become so objectionable that some universities, including Yale, Johns Hopkins, and the University of Chicago have closed their schools of education.

A recent participant-observer study of education departments found a "large-scale attack on wisdom and knowledge."[616] Education courses consist instead of slogans and theories. For instance, one instructor objected to Hans Christian Andersen's "The Ugly Duckling" because after the duckling was transformed into a swan, "he never questioned the system."[617] Students are taught that the negative words in education are "conservative," "merit," and "standards."[618]

A faculty member in the school of education at Brooklyn College opposes grammatical English, which she claims is the language of white oppressors, and favors the language of rap and hip-hop instead. She refers to "manipulative open-mindedness" and ignores all who disagree with her.[619]

Public schools themselves have, as a result, become so bad that pupils in California were not learning reading, writing and arithmetic. Its fourth-graders tied for last place in the nation with schools in Louisiana. California created a basic skills test *for their teachers*! Naturally, this test was challenged in the courts as being discriminatory. As a result, some questions on algebra and geometry were removed and more time to complete the test was allowed, but that still did not mollify the teachers.[620]

A "distinguished" professor of early childhood education at the University of Illinois/Chicago is a former member of the Weather Underground and boasts of bombing many sites in America. He argues against expelling disruptive children from classrooms, especially if they are Black or Latino, and lectures students on what they should be for and what they should be against.[621]

Another professor of education at the University of Cincinnati advocates eradicating "Eurocentricity" from the curriculum. Also, with other Marxists he heads a center for "Peace Education" which blames whites for non-white violence. Yes, you read that right. The non-whites are driven to be violent by whites.[622]

Transformed schoolbooks. Textbooks in the kindergarten through 12th grades are required to present other cultures throughout the world and to point out ways in which these cultures are superior to Western culture without saying as much explicitly. These textbooks also emphasize the achievements of non-white people. And they lose no opportunity to exploit every event and action which will make America look bad.

Transformed teachers and administrators. One indicator of what has happened to public education in American is the quality and character of the teachers, principals and superintendents who run the system.

Schools cheat. Faced with objective standardized tests, the failure of schools is apparent. In Virginia, only 7 percent of schools met the standards. In Arizona, 90 percent of students failed the math test. To meet these problems, schools cheat in various ways. Poor pupils are excluded from taking the tests. Teachers assign the tests as homework ahead of time. Test security is minimal. Pupils are allowed more time than the standard prescribes. Teachers tell pupils answers during tests, etc. And the standard for a passing grade is lowered. One study estimated as many as 42 percent of teachers were guilty of cheating.[623]

There are none so blind. Some parents sided with the schools by demanding that their children not be given the tests. School administrators in New York, Wisconsin and Massachusetts bowed to these pressures by watering down the tests or scrapping them altogether.[624]

Shining examples. To give some idea of the character of present-day school administrators: In Dallas, superintendent Yvonne Gonzalez was convicted of stealing money from the Dallas school district and sentenced to prison.[625]

Houston had to buy out the contract of its superintendent, Joan Raymond, at a cost of nearly half a million dollars.[626]

Sacramento had to pay over a quarter of a million to get rid of one of their superintendents and he had only been on the job nine months.[627]

New Orleans paid $210,000 to get rid of a superintendent. The "turnover among big-district superintendents is frequent all over the U. S."[628]

The California Department of Education faked its drop-out rates by reporting the rates over a *one*-year period! The rate was 3.3 percent. Under pressure, they reported the drop-out rate for four years. It was 29.2 percent. The drop-out rates for Los Angeles were 53 percent.[629]

Some states have passed laws forbidding automatic promotion to the next grade. Schools get around this by affirmative grading: grading the "overall" performance, including a lot of other criteria than mere knowledge.[630]

Transformed school procedures. Another indicator of the type of people running public schools today is the case of an Intermediate School in Pennsylvania which required the genital examination of 11-year-old girls, without full consent of the girls or their parents. Semi-hysterical girls who begged to be allowed to call their mothers were not allowed to do so.[631]

Outcome Based Education (OBE) allows pupils to repeat an assignment until they get it right. The class does not move on until every pupil gets it right. OBE "facilitators" are also careful to protect the children's feelings. One of Minnesota's outcomes called for "integration of physical, emotional and spiritual wellness," including a "positive self-concept" and a "multicultural" worldview.[632] OBE usually brushes aside reading, writing and arithmetic as unimportant. "Students will project anti-racist, anti-biased attitudes through their participation in a multi-lingual multi-ethnic, culturally diverse curriculum," say Milwaukee schools.[633] These mandated attitudes are the real goal of OBE and are, of course, the doctrines of the Dhimmist Ideology.

North Carolina educators were given a list of the values teachers should try to instill in pupils: "There is no right or wrong ... The collective good is more important than the individual. Consensus is more important than principle. Flexibility is more important than accomplishment. Nothing is permanent except change. All ethics are situational; there are no moral absolutes. There are no perpetrators, only victims."[634] These "values" are useful for promoting Dhimmism: Consensus forces compromises. Compromises weaken convictions and force individuals to abandon principles.[635]

Just say NO. From 4 to 6 million children in the U. S. are being given mind-altering drugs in school or by parents at the school's direction. The excuse is an alleged "disease" called Attention Deficit Hyperactivity Disorder (ADHD).[636] Some experience with young children shows you that when kids are bored, their attention wanders. Given what we have seen of schools, children of average mental ability (to say nothing of bright kids) will be bored in school. When anyone is bored, they begin to fidget. In the old days of Hollywood, movie studios used to pre-screen their movies in special theaters with seats that were wired to record movement. These measurements of fidgeting were synchronized with the movie, so the filmmakers could tell when in the movie the audience grew restless. They would then re-shoot those portions or cut them out. Schools do not cut out the boring parts. And they have no sympathy for kids of average ability. And they positively detest bright kids.[637] (Remember that students who major in education in college are generally the least bright college students.)

Some medical professionals question whether ADHD is a valid medical condition at all.[638] Psychiatric drugs are potentially toxic to a child's brain. In one study attempting to prove the existence of ADHD, children alleged to have the "disease" had different brain scans from children who hadn't been so diagnosed. It turned out that all of those children had been on psychiatric drugs prior to the brain scans.[639]

The side-effects of these mind-altering drugs are then countered with other drugs, the side-effects of those drugs with other drugs, etc. "The cocktail of medications was guaranteed to ruin the child's mental life ... Yet this 'polypharmacy' approach has become too commonplace."[640] The FDA MedWatch program notes 186 deaths from long-term (e.g. 7 year) use of these drugs. It estimates this is only 10 to 20 percent of the actual deaths.[641]

These drugs may also produce violence as a side-effect. One of the teenage killers at Columbine High School, the boy at Heritage High School in Georgia, a boy in Notus, Idaho and a boy in Oregon were all on, or had been on, mind-altering drugs prescribed by the schools prior to their violent shooting spree.[642]

Yet, schools pressure parents into giving these drugs to their children. How? By threatening to expel the child, put the child into a special-education class, or threatening the parents with prosecution for child abuse or even to have child welfare workers take their child away from them.[643] For human stories of children and parents subjected to these pressures, go to www.AbleChild.org.

Why do schools do this? By inventing a "disease" called ADHD, schools can claim that their own failure is the child's fault. Also, since ADHD is now officially classified as a disability, schools "can get from $10,000 to $90,000 per year in additional ... funds" from the federal government. Of course, the pharmaceutical companies profit. The manufacturer of one of these drugs contributed $748,000 to an organization of "parents" pushing the use of this drug.[644] In the 1980s, the American Psychiatric Association, which had been suffering heavy losses from the growth of clinical psychology, social workers, etc., formed a partnership with drug companies to push the idea that mental disorders are physiological in origin. They also revised their official diagnostic manual to that effect. Further, they held "workshops" for teachers and guidance counselors to sell them on the idea that children needed drugs.[645]

Turning children against parents. In Oregon, pupils are asked if they ever wanted to beat up their parents. Some were shown a movie in which children were fighting with their parents. In Tucson, teachers asked pupils how many of them hated their parents. These actions insert a wedge between children and their parents. In California, some pupils were given worksheets to report whether their parents had a history of alcoholism or mental illness. Even though Federal law prohibits schools from asking children for very personal information, many schools disregard that law or quibble on the weasel term "very personal." In some schools, teachers explicitly instruct pupils not to tell their parents what is discussed in class.[646]

Child spies. "School authorities instruct teachers to ask children questions about their parents' behavior and actions toward them at home.... and report incidents that make them feel 'uncomfortable'."[647] "Often, children are disturbed and emotionally traumatized by the insinuations school authorities put into their heads."[648] "[C]hild advocates have succeeded in convincing school teachers, doctors, your neighbors ... that three out of four parents are child abusers."[649] They coach children on reporting such incidents to school officials.[650] See the website www.ParentsRightsCoalition.org/Horror_Stories.html for additional information.

If even a hint of child abuse can be detected, the Dhimmists go berserk. In one notorious case that concerned a daycare center in Massachusetts, prosecutors questioned children who repeatedly said "no" to the questions. But prosecutors kept asking the questions over and over in other words until they got the answers they wanted. Even though judges repeatedly ruled against the case, the accused daycare centers workers spent twenty years in prison before they were exonerated. The Wall Street Journal's Dorothy Rabinowitz won a Pulitzer Prize for her investigative reports on such manufactured child-abuse cases.[651]

Anti-self-defense. Many schools also indoctrinate their pupils to reject the Second Amendment. The instilling of attitudes of fear and loathing of guns extends to punishing kids who point fingers at each other and say, "Bang,"[652] as happened in New Jersey. In Wisconsin, a third grader was suspended because he had a key chain with a replica of a gun. In Michigan, an academically advanced 12-year-old boy was listed as dangerous because, while other pupils signed it, he refused to sign a vow renouncing the Second Amendment. He also made things worse by defending himself in a fistfight against three schoolyard attackers.[653]

Violence. One schoolteacher in Michigan wrote: "The public would not believe what goes on in the average classroom."[654] Fifty years ago, schools had more leeway to expel students. Today, fear of legal retaliation, fear of charges of racism result in few expulsions. And the pupils know it.

Results. More than 90 percent of American school districts claim to be performing above average (which of course is a contradiction)! More than 70 percent of American pupils are being told that they are "above average" (another statistical impossibility).[655] Few school administrators recognize the mathematical impossibility of such "facts." The truth is that *illiteracy* rates at many schools are 50%. Not only knowledge is suffering, but decency as well. In one study, 25 to 40 percent of pupils saw nothing wrong with cheating on exams or stealing from employers.[656]

TRANSFORMING THE COLLEGES AND THE INFORMATION BASE

In order to convert people to Dhimmism, "The whole knowledge base must be transformed."[657]

How did this happen? How did what once was called a "fringe phenomenon" become a dominant force in America? To avoid the draft, many people went into education in the late 1960s and early 1970s. Many went to graduate schools. By the time the war ended, they had their PhDs. The fashion at the time was to hate the business world and blame it for everything. The education graduates got jobs teaching school. The young PhDs got jobs in academia.

The jobs were well-paid. The hours were minimal. They kept up their contacts with others in the anti-war movement and began to formalize these relations by creating new academic societies and professional associations. Colleges generously paid their travel expenses.

But how did the Dhimmists manage to take over the colleges when in the 1970s they were still only a minority? Academics hate committee assignments and any other departmental duties that take them away from their work. So, by volunteering to serve on search committees, the people who developed the ideology of Dhimmism were able to stack the list of candidates to be invited for interviews entirely with other people who generally agreed with them.

Since academics seldom agree with each other, the emerging Dhimmists were able, by surreptitiously operating as a block, to influence the other faculty members by praising the same candidate and voting for the candidate they had previously agreed-upon. Since the other faculty members had only the information contained in the applicant's folder, there was little basis for judging them. And since academics were seldom enthusiastic about any of the candidates, the enthusiasm of the Dhimmists for the same candidate had a good chance of swaying the outcomes of departmental votes even though they were still a minority.

In decisions on tenure, they appeared to operate separately, as all their colleagues did, but in fact agreed ahead of time on their choice and voted as a block. In this way, over time more and more of the members of departments were in agreement with them. Eventually, they attained a majority in their departments and were able to elect the chair.

An example is the Philosophy Department at Temple University. The department chair and another activist professor have been able to transform the traditional philosophy curriculum into one dominated by "subjects" such as Critical Race Theory, "postcolonial thought," "philosophy of liberation", "theories of race and racism." To aid in transforming the students, one of these professors founded an Institute for the Study of Race and Social Thought. (To give some idea of the thought of this professor: when he was a professor at Brown University, he defended students who stole an entire issue of the student newspaper and destroyed it, saying, "If something is free, you can take as many copies as you like.... This is not a free speech issue."[658]

Once they had sufficient numbers in the college departments, the Dhimmists began to implement their political agenda of "transforming the academy" and "transforming the curricula."[659] Other faculty members resisted at first, but "they quickly wearied of being placed in the unenviable position of explaining that they were not fascists, racists, tormentors of homosexuals and God knows what else."[660] "Rather than being content with their victory, the victors shifted their tactics of harassment, badgering traditionalists when they encountered them in the hallways, classrooms and other domains."[661]

A few students manage to maintain their mental independence, and various websites have been set up to allow a minimum of backtalk. One of these is www.RateMyProfessors.com. Also, www.theFIRE.org runs a companion website where students can rate their professors and report abuses.

Academic freedom vs. freedom of speech. The Dhimmists hid behind academic freedom to render themselves immune to criticism by those independent academics that had not yet retired or been refused tenure and thus forced out. But *academic freedom* is different from *freedom of speech*.[662] Freedom of speech gives people, including teachers, the right to say whatever they want whether it is true or false, because the assumption is that the speaker is only expressing an opinion. Teachers, on the other hand, are assumed to be teaching knowledge that has been proven, supported or for which there is overwhelming evidence, and they have a duty to make clear to students when the theories are not yet highly supported. Academic freedom is to protect the teacher from nonacademic influences. It is not intended to protect the teaching of lies as facts. Any geography professor teaching that the earth is flat or that the sun goes around the earth would be violating academic freedom, not protected by it.

Packing the college administrations. During the 1980s, the Dhimmists took over the administrations of colleges as well, both by getting their faithful into administrative positions and by intimidating the administrators who were already in place. After that, a vast bureaucracy developed. "A host of 'race experts,' diversity consultants, and sensitivity … advisors" began to operate.[663] "Racial identity theory, oppression pedagogy, interracial etiquette, ethno-therapy—these are only a few examples of the ministrations of the self-appointed liberation experts."[664] As Donald Downs dryly remarks of these new administrators, "The academic credentials of such individuals often do not compare favorably with the faculties they govern."[665]

History. One strategy of the Dhimmists was to re-engineer history courses to subordinate men, white people, Western society and America to other people, cultures and nations. The most bizarre of these attempts was a movement to claim that all of Western civilization derived from Africa. "Afrocentrism," as the doctrine is called, claims that the ancient Egyptians were black and that Alexandria was the intellectual center of the Mediterranean world from early times. Aristotle is said to have learned all he knew by studying in Alexandria.

There is one small difficulty with this claim. Alexandria did not exist until years later when it was founded by Alexander, a pupil of Aristotle. Even then, Alexandria did not become an intellectual hub until several centuries later. The doctrines of Afrocentrism have been given an exhaustive and scholarly treatment by historian Mary Lefkowitz, who refutes them point by point, citing original sources.[666] The concept of evidence has become so unknown in colleges these days that Lefkowitz has to explain to students and to the public why evidence is necessary to historical scholarship! Ironically, "the Afrocentrists make Africa the source of the [European] culture that they blame for their own trouble."[667] "The Egyptian universities described by James and Diop never existed."[668]

In spite of all this evidence, "Afrocentrism" is still widely taught in schools and colleges in America. Anyone disagreeing with it is, of course, called a racist, a Xenophobe, a McCarthyist, intolerant, or any other epithet that will silence the critic. The really frightening question is what will happen when the fringe of professors who still rely on evidence have retired and there is no one to tell students that such a thing as evidence is even required?

In many cases, the change to history textbooks has been one of emphasis or of inclusion and exclusion. For instance, in one high school textbook a minor nineteenth century woman astronomer who discovered a comet gets more attention than Albert Einstein.[669] Often, the exclusions and inclusions are politically motivated, as in a prominent college American history text that omits anything positive about America such as Alexander Graham Bell, Jonas Salk, the Wright Brothers or the walk on the moon and instead devotes a great deal of space to Speckled Snake, Joan Baez, and Daniel Berrigan. It also portrays the exploitation of immigrants without mentioning that immigrants created Hollywood and the Federal Bank. Normandy and Gettysburg are omitted but My Lai gets several pages. More serious is the omission of footnotes which surreptitiously teaches students that it is unimportant to back up one's historical claims with evidence.[670]

Literature. The Dhimmists not only purged most of classical literature but soon felt strong enough to attack even Shakespeare. A favorite whipping boy was "The Tempest", which was said to be a play about Western imperialism and was further said to exhibit racism in its treatment of Caliban. Caliban is portrayed in the play as a psychopath; but since he was a native of the island, portraying him thus was therefore racist.

George Eliot, who by her own account placed realism as the highest goal of literary art, is portrayed as an anti-realist. "She also wishes to challenge the realist assumption that there is a world 'out there'."[671] "there is no 'demonstrable truth'. "It is this world of 'mental needs', inaccessible to the rigid male mind, which the novel explores, needs which the patriarchal regime of 'facts' and economic progress has no language to describe."[672] "Maggie ... makes the mistake of thinking that it is the knowledge itself, rather than the gendered, social position of the possessor, that is significant."[673] George Eliot is faulted too: "The text is peppered with references to 'true manliness', treated as an unproblematic and indeed positive quality."[674] For shame! She is also faulted for holding that womanhood included "tenderness and a loving, maternal role."[675]

A professor of English literature at Penn State holds that current fiction isn't "postmodern enough." Although acknowledging that English departments have been losing students over the years and are regarded as "laughingstocks" by other academics because of their absurd "theories," this professor's solution is more theory.[676]

A professor of world literature at N. C. State uses a syllabus for "Contemporary World Literature" that consists entirely of Communists and left-wing poets.[677] He started his own literary journal in 2003 to push his Marxist views to the academic community.

Frederic Jameson, a Maoist Marxist at Duke University, holds that the task of a literary critic is to impose a political framework on a given text. "[T]he political perspective is the absolute horizon of all reading and interpretation."[678]

"Cultural studies". A plethora of new college departments have been created: Cultural Studies, Islamic Studies, Middle-eastern Studies, Black Studies, Gender Studies, Peace Studies, etc. One of the professors of cultural studies teaches that science is just an instrument of the ruling class.[679]

A professor of "peace" studies at the University of Washington advocates revolutionary violence against the United States.[680] A director of the "Peace Studies" program at Purdue teaches what are in effect training courses for activists, where students learn the "essential functions" of "transforming perceptions of reality; altering self-perceptions" and "legitimizing the social movement." "We have a real chance to change all levels of education," he said.[681]

A Middle Eastern history professor at Stanford, even after 9/11, congratulated his fellow professors of Middle-East studies for refusing to recognize terrorism as a threat.[682]

A professor of Middle East history at the University of Michigan and a much sought-after source for the major media (including the New York Times, Washington Post and NPR), holds that "half the American public is terminally stupid" and also claims that "chemical weapons are not weapons of mass destruction."[683]

A professor of Islamic Studies at Columbia condemns all Israelis as cold-blooded and physically repulsive, and claims that the U. S. went into Iraq simply to get the oil. He also teaches other anti-American allegations as fact.[684]

A professor of Islamic Studies at Georgetown teaches that 9/11 is a result of America's "not addressing ... tolerance and pluralism."[685] He has served as a Muslim affairs consultant to the Department of State as well as to corporations and universities worldwide.

A professor at Western Washington University and a speaker on other campuses such as Yale is a founder of MEChA, an organization which according to its website has the goal of "liberating" the "occupied" state of Atzlan (in other words, California, Arizona, New Mexico, etc.) from the U. S. Among his listed academic interests is "the U.S./Mexican Border."[686]

Indoctrination. Some of the professors are frank about their mission to indoctrinate. One professor boasts in capital letters in his class handout: "I'M OPEN ABOUT BRINGING MY IDEOLOGY INTO THIS CLASSROOM BECAUSE I SEE THAT ALL EDUCATIONAL SYSTEMS ARE IDEOLOGICAL TO THE CORE."[687]

The University of California/Santa Cruz created a "history of consciousness" program "to demonstrate the PhD is a fraud" and awarded the doctorate to rapist, crack-addict and murderer Huey P. Newton. A professor of this fraudulent field is Angela Davis, who was influenced by Marxist Herbert Marcuse's theory of "repressive tolerance", the view that anti-communist ideas should be repressed because they express the view of the dominant class. She claims that all minorities in jail are actually "political prisoners." She was held up by Aleksandr Solzhenitzen as a prime example of what is wrong with communism.[688]

A professor of "feminist geography" at Temple University practices what she calls "service learning", which requires students to participate in "community and grassroots efforts at social transformation."[689]

A Black activist, who started an organization because the Black Panthers were not radical enough and held a shoot-out with them, was convicted of torturing two women in 1971. After getting out of prison, he was hired as chairman of the Black Studies Department at Cal State Long Beach, where he developed his own "cultural philosophy" stated using terms in Swahili, and established the Black holiday Kwanzaa.[690]

Jihad. A number of professors in American universities "teach" that jihadists are patriots of the Islamic cause fighting to defend Islam. These professors are at University of California/Berkeley, Northeastern University, Columbia University, University of South Florida, Brandeis, University of Kentucky, Georgetown University, Arcadia University, Cal State, among others.[691]

Reconquista. The chair of the Department of History and of the Ethnic Studies Departments at the University of Colorado/Boulder opposes assimilation to American white society and the speaking of English. She also regards criticisms of Ward Churchill's anti-American statements as a neo-conservative campaign to establish ideological control over the University of Colorado. Since conservatives are a splinter group at UC, it is unclear how they could control it.[692]

Professor Armando Navarro at the University of California/Riverside claims that America belongs to Mexico. He is an ardent supporter of La

Raza Unida and advocates "supporting policies that weaken America's ability to secure its borders against illegal immigration."[693]

A tenured professor of political science at the University of Texas/Arlington and a licensed attorney teaches that "We have got to eliminate the *gringo*, and what I mean by that is ... we have got to kill him."[694] He also teaches that the southwestern United States rightfully belongs to Mexico. He claims that Mexicans cannot be made illegal in "our own homeland". "We are migrants, free to travel the length and breadth of the Americas." "Our devil has pale skin and blue eyes." "They are not making babies.... It's a matter of time." "we now have a critical mass." "The explosion is in our population."[695] To accomplish these goals, he founded La Raza Unida, one of the largest and most influential Mexican-American organizations. An example of his intellectual prowess is his claim to "the land that historically has been ours for forty thousand years." In fact, however, the earliest proven sites of *homo sapiens* in the western hemisphere date to only twenty thousand years ago.

Anti-Americanism. Some professors are Marxists who teach anti-Americanism and are generally pro-jihad. Some of these are at Columbia University, Brandeis, University of California/Irvine, University of California/Santa Cruz (whose faculty includes several communists including Angela Davis and whose provost is a Marxist), Kent State, Princeton, University of Oregon, Rutgers, SUNY/Buffalo, CUNY, University of Colorado/Boulder, University of Denver, UCLA, among others.[696] Some consider the collapse of the Soviet Union to be a setback for human progress.[697]

Some of these anti-American professors are famous and their books are read world-wide, especially in the third world.[698] Some argue that America is moving toward fascism.[699] A professor of anthropology at Columbia told thousands of students that "U. S. patriotism is inseparable from imperial warfare and white supremacy."[700] A Navajo professor at the Metropolitan State College in Denver co-authored a book which holds that "progressive" professors are "entitled to use the classroom to foment social rebellion against capitalist, Anglo-Saxon America."[701] A professor of sociology at SUNY/Stony Brook is another Marxist activist who opposed attacking Afghanistan and Iraq, urging the crowd to "hope that America will lose." He has received grants from the National Science Foundation.[702] A professor at the University of Hawaii teaches that "The enemy is the United States of America and everyone who supports it."[703]

One lawyer handling a free-speech defense for a college student said, "I can't wait to get off Penn's campus and get back to the United States of America."[704]

Anti-white. Some professors are avidly and explicitly anti-white and anti-Jewish. One of these is at Rutgers University but has been honored at Columbia and other colleges.[705] Another teaches at Emory University.

A professor at Texas A & M and past president of the American Sociological Association holds that American society is inherently racist and all white people are racists. He agrees with a number of other professors who teach that America should pay Black people $3 trillion dollars as reparations for past slavery.[706]

In 2004, a Black female professor slashed her own tires and painted racist slogans on her own car and cried, "Victim." Mass rallies on campus were held in her support. Even after eye-witnesses identified the perpetrator as none other than the "victim" herself, faculty and students continued to support her. Faith in the ideology outweighed evidence from eye-witnesses. Four years earlier, this same "victim" has been seen inflicting bruises on her own arms and tearing open her blouse in a claim of police brutality when she was arrested for shop-lifting. On another occasion, she posed as a nurse to obtain prescription drugs.[707] She remains on the faculty.

Anti-Semitic. Leonard Jeffries, a professor at CUNY, teaches that "Jews are a race of skunks and animals that stole Africa from the Black Man." A proponent of Afrocentrism, he was appointed to the commission that in 1988 drafted a new curriculum for New York State's K-12 schools. He holds that Blacks are "morally and culturally superior" to white people. Jeffries claimed that when an undergraduate at Lafayette College, he headed a Jewish fraternity. The only problem was Lafayette never had a Jewish fraternity. Jeffries teaches that rich white men codified their bigoted ideals in the Constitution.[708]

One faculty member of the Middle Eastern Culture department at Columbia wrote publicly that the physical bodies of Israeli Jews are in their very structure evil. Another member of that department calls for the destruction of Israel and claims that all Jews are supremacists. He was investigated by the University for screaming at students in class but was allowed to remain on the faculty. He claims, contrary to his writings, that he is pro-Jewish.[709] If the term "*taqiyya*" flashes through your mind at this point, you're not alone.

Transforming religion

Departments of Religion have also been influenced by the Ideology of Submission. Some faculty members are adamant Dhimmists. Some have even developed a strain blending Marxism with Christianity, dubbed "Liberation Theology," whose objective is to show how Marxist-Leninist ideology is really "a secular form of the Christian gospels." It preaches things like "the responsibility of the affluent to reshape the global order into one that is more just, compassionate and peaceful" by addressing "global poverty."[710]

At St. Xavier University in Chicago, a dedicated Marxist professor of history teaches anti-Americanism, informs students that the CIA is a terrorist organization, that the U. S. is racist, etc. He was given an award by the college for excellence in teaching. "Teaching," he holds, "is a moral act. It is NOT a dispassionate, neutral pursuit of 'truth.' It is advocacy and interpretation."[711]

A professor of Islamic Studies at De Paul University, America's largest Catholic college, teaches that Islamic terrorists are merely patriotic (to Islam) activists like the American Independence revolutionaries. She is a consultant to the Ford Foundation's Civil Rights and Muslims in America project.[712]

A professor with a neo-Marxist bent has infiltrated the Quaker Earlham College in Indiana and teaches community activism with a reading list of leftists unsullied by any other viewpoints.[713]

A professor at Penn State and co-director of the race relations project is a specialist in "Liberation Theology." Another Marxist in sheep's clothing is at Villanova and heads a Center for Peace and Justice.[714]

Students majoring in religion are influenced by these professors. Most of these students become ministers, priests, etc. Maybe this explains why the major denominations are losing church-going members, while the fundamentalist Christian churches are growing in numbers.

Transforming Radio, TV and Motion Pictures

Movies at the present time, one film critic proudly wrote, "paint a world where small towns breed monsters, where the family is limping if not crippled, where the unconscious dances giddy circles around good old horse sense."[715] "We have become the *enemy*," Oliver Stone intoned while accepting yet another award for his filmmaking.[716] Hollywood reveals its Dhimmism in the justification it offers for making movies portraying America as a vile place. It claims to be merely "trying to provide an honest view of a violent, corrupt, and demented society."[717] This anti-American view, of course, *is* Dhimmism.

Even teen sex comedies, futuristic thrillers, love stories, and cartoons for kids push this anti-American view. In "An American Tail 2: Fievel Goes West" (1991), a turn-of-the century immigrant mouse complains to his children that "at least in Russia we always had enough to eat." Michael Medved contrasts this with his grandfather's accounts based on personal experience of the difference between Russia and America.[718] Guess which was better.

This change from support of America by Hollywood in the past to its present anti-Americanism has been traced to the years 1965 to 1969, and it was not driven by economic factors. After 1965, "motion picture attendance showed another sudden and disastrous decline ... even more cataclysmic than the introduction of television."[719] Attendance went from 44 million in 1965 to 17.5 million in 1969. Video and cable are not the explanation since they were not introduced until ten years after the movie theatre audience had disappeared.

Why did this happen? The "values of the entertainment industry changed, and audiences fled from the theaters in horror and disgust."[720] By the year 1980, the Oscars for Best Picture had changed. Previously, only box office successes had any chance of being nominated. From 1980 onward, only movies that in one way or another trashed America had any chance of being nominated. In a study of influential TV producers, media analysts found that 66 percent of them held that "TV should promote social reform."[721] By reform, they meant promotion of the Dhimmist ideology.

This anti-American bias has been expressed in a number of different ways. Movies trashing the American military in whole or in part jumped from 23 percent to 80 percent. These newer movies were commercial flops, which "demonstrates the way that Hollywood's deeply held biases can interfere with its commercial self-interest."[722]

While sales of movies to Americans have plummeted, foreign consumption of American movies has increased. "Nearly half of all movie income now comes from abroad, compared with 30 percent in 1980."[723] Consequently, moviemakers are no longer dependent on whether American audiences like their movies or not. Further, these movies contribute to the growing anti-American sentiment around the world.

Also, a comprehensive study of prime-time TV discovered that "big business has become television's favorite villain."[724] While facts show "the destitute and disadvantaged strikingly overrepresented among violent lawbreakers, on prime time" it is more likely to be the wealthy that are the lawbreakers. And the type of crime is preposterous. While it is possible to claim that many business leaders are selfish and corrupt, it strains credibility to believe them to be pimps and murderers.[725]

American police fared no better. Before 1975, nine out of ten shows portrayed American law enforcement as honorable. Since then, half the shows have portrayed it as corrupt.[726]

American history has taken a beating from Hollywood. Movies have focused on, enlarged upon or even *made up* past faults or atrocities that America is supposed to have committed. One prime example is the movie "Revolution" (1985) which even portrayed the patriots who fought for

American Independence as *the bad guys*! When the movie flopped, movie pundits explained their failure by saying that the American people were not interested in American history!⁷²⁷

Besides wallowing in one-sided pictures of America's treatment of American Indians and of interment of Japanese, and besides glorifying the Black Panthers and other groups, movies have had a field day with the Vietnam War. Veterans are invariably portrayed as psychotic. Ghastly atrocities against Vietnamese civilians are commonplace in movies, even though the facts show "that only a tiny minority of our troops ever engaged in such brutalities."⁷²⁸

Western history fares no better. A "documentary" was shown on PBS called "Civilization", which purported to show the rise of Western culture. The purpose was to state as fact the claim that Western culture came from the Middle East. The spokesman in the film stood on top of a hill on one of the Greek Islands in the eastern Aegean and pointed to the Turkish mainland a few miles away, stating in a very authoritative voice that there was where Western culture came from. The big deception was that the western coastline of what is now Turkey was inhabited in ancient times by Greeks. The city-state of Miletos, a thriving Greek seaport at the time, was where Thales lived and worked. It was his writings that started the Greek explosion of knowledge.

Some recent mainstream movies like "Alexander" and "Troy" serve the function of denigrating the Western heroes Alexander and Achilles. Eliminating heroes removes the chance that such heroes will inspire young people to try to make something of themselves. (Remember that *achievement* is opposed by the Dhimmists since it is elitist.) Another movie rewrites the Crusades, making Westerners the villains.

When it comes to portraying terrorists, Islamists, and the like, guess which side Hollywood is on. Even a conservative powerhouse like Arnold Schwarzenegger is not free. A film he was doing about Arab Muslim terrorists was protested by CAIR (an organization with terrorist ties). The villains were changed to Hispanic drug dealers.⁷²⁹

Weekly TV shows portray federal law enforcement's efforts against terrorism as barbaric and racist. California has a weekly radio program called

"Islam today," hosted by a University of California/Berkeley professor who advocates an "*Intifada*" in America. A professor of communications at the University of Texas/Austin advocates Marxism and Critical Race Theory and claims that the United States is the world's number one terrorist state. She opposes tightening airport security and condemns the Pledge of Allegiance.[730]

A professor of humanities at SUNY/Binghamton and director of the Institute for Global Cultural Studies has been a spokesman for Islamic extremist groups and a member of organizations like the American Muslim Council, whose leadership has declared its support for terrorist organizations. In 1986, he hosted a PBS series called The Africans: A Triple Heritage which castigates Europe for slave trading without mentioning the Arab involvement in Black slave trading or the fact that his own ancestors were slave traders until they were forced to stop by the British.[731] Nor does he mention that the Muslims were, during this same period, enslaving white Europeans and selling them in the slave markets of Tripoli, Tunis, Algiers, etc. At least a million white people were enslaved during these three centuries.[732]

Michael Moore is one of the leading Dhimmists in Hollywood, making "documentaries." "He's careless with facts ... [a paradigm example of] the unreliable narrator." In his film attacking gun-owners, he represents getting a gun as immediate and easy, whereas in fact there are background checks and a long waiting period. A cartoon sequence equates the NRA with the KKK. Set in a town where schoolboys went on a shooting spree, the "documentary" insinuates that the presence in the town of a factory that manufactures rockets was a cause. But the rockets are for launching television satellites. He frankly lies about a plaque under a B-52 on display at the Air Force Academy. He demonizes Charlton Heston by taking audio of seven sentences from five different places in two different speeches and splicing them together, and uses video footage from a different speech in which Heston was given an antique musket and picturing it as part of a speech at Columbine.[733] Moore's books and "documentaries" are best sellers and Academy Award winners.

In Fahrenheit 9/11, he claims the U. S. president used the 9/11 attacks as an excuse to wage war. The "documentary" is characterized by distortions, sarcasm, mocking tone, glaring omissions, out of context quotes, etc. One study lists the distortions throughout the film.[734] Nonetheless, the film is praised by academics teaching film, for instance at the University of Rhode Island.[735]

"In Hollywood and in the arts community of New York, it's *de rigueur* to be left-wing."[736] In 2003 after Castro sentenced dissident writers and poets to prison, Hollywood elites signed a "declaration of support" for Cuba, condemning U. S. "harassment against Cuba."[737] The lead character of the Academy Award-winning film "Good Will Hunting," who is described as a genius, demolishes the arguments against Dhimmism offered by a group of college students by quoting various anti-American doctrines of Chomsky.[738]

On a social level, movies and TV have less dramatic effects, but those effects may be just as devastating. "The very nature of film—its ability to draw us in and to move us—makes it vulnerable to the Thought Police" says Tammy Bruce. Hollywood eliminates any ideas for projects that challenge Dhimmism.[739] People learn how to interact with their husbands or wives from TV sitcoms (constant bickering, impatience, etc.) Happy families are regarded by TV producers as boring. Family movies now, as often as not, portray dysfunctional families. Many people are so used to this that dysfunctional families seem normal to them. The hostility expressed is not even noticed. Similarly, the way to treat children (with impatience, condescension, etc.) is taught by TV and movies.

Individuals too are being portrayed in a way different from the past. Consider the image of children. In the Walt Disney movies of the late 1940s, there were good kids and bad kids. Today, the way normal kids are portrayed is essentially the same as the way the bad kids were portrayed in the early Walt Disney movies. In other words, today kids are expected to be brats, and no one sees anything wrong in that.

Similarly, it is almost unheard of in today's movies to see adults behave with integrity and fortitude. The man of character, almost a cliché of the 1940s, is a rarity today. If Gary Cooper or Alan Ladd or even Jimmy Stewart were alive today, they'd have a hard time finding parts. Copycat killers are not the only ones influenced by films. Everyone to some extent models himself/herself on the characters frequently portrayed in movies and TV shows. The power of these media to shape who Americans are should not be underestimated.

A common saying is, "If it didn't happen on TV, it didn't happen." This truism is a sad comment on the state of the information that most people have about the world around them. "The more we allow the media to shape our views and create our world, the more we become a cocooned, isolated society, and the more we will condemn each other with opinions based on stereotypes and fear."[740]

Thanks to spin-off sales, Hollywood's attitudes have even gotten into the nursery schools. Toddlers play with frowning dolls designed to resemble The Terminator. Pull a string and it growls "I'll be back!" The Freddy Krueger dolls have knives for fingernails to honor the scared, cackling, sadistic serial killer. One enterprising firm has even started serial killer trading cards for kids, on the back of which are the killers "box score": the number of victims chalked up, the preferred methods of murder, etc. A mayor of Los Angeles even proclaimed "Freddy Krueger day." Whenever a mass murderer is apprehended, a crowd of agents and producers immediately flock to him to buy the movie rights to his story.[741]

Rap music is another source of inspiration to millions of young people. Most grownups do not take rap seriously because they think it is so ridiculous that no one could be influenced by it. But kids do not *listen* to music. They have it on constantly while they do other things. The music and the words are absorbed subliminally. Material absorbed subliminally is more effective than information attended to. It cannot be thought about or screened. Messages of hate are common among rappers. How popular are they? One person typed "Eminem" into a search engine and got 13 million hits, which is more than most of the famous people in the world. This rapper sells millions upon millions of CDs. Even more frightening is that some mainstream politicians and New York Times columnists take him and others seriously in a positive way.[742] One professor at Penn, who has taught at UNC, Columbia, etc. and has appeared on the Today Show, wrote a book glorifying one gansta rapper as a black Jesus figure. The rapper had been convicted of gang rape, robbery, etc.[743] A member of a prominent rock group said "I hope the Muslims win."[744]

Transforming the News

During the 1970s, many of what were called "alienated youth" majored in journalism. Most got jobs on newspapers. Many stayed in school to get advanced degrees and began to teach in university schools of journalism. As the Ideology of Submission developed, the point of view of their teaching was more and more influenced by Dhimmism. One of these was the sixties activist Todd Gitlin, who teaches at the Columbia University School of Journalism where many of today's top newspaper people are trained and which administers the Pulitzer Prizes.[745] Another teaches journalism at the University of Texas/Austin. He teaches that the victims of 9/11 were "little Eichmanns", opposes protecting U. S. borders and excoriates merit-based hiring and school admissions.[746] Another Marxist teaches at the University of Illinois/Urbana and is a member of the editorial board of Monthly Review, the Communist magazine.[747]

Perhaps the most important of the leftists at Columbia School of Journalism is Victor Navasky, who as chairman of the Columbia Journalism Review sets the standards for American journalists. Surreptitiously, Navasky bankrolled the Review, so that in effect he controls the magazine. He also directs The Nation magazine, the leading left-wing journal in America. He along with Todd Gitlin, Anna Quindlen and others were appointed to a task force to determine "how future journalists should be taught."[748]

The UC/Berkeley Graduate School of Journalism also has a prominent Maoist-Marxist as its Dean. His faculty appointments have included other leftist advocates.[749]

Not only the slant or "spin" of news reports is affected, but the choice of what to include and what to exclude. One clear-cut case is that of Patrick Chavis, a Black man who was admitted to medical school under race preferences. The New York Times Magazine ran a glowing piece on Chavis, telling how he was working in a ghetto as a physician. The Times reporter ignored the fact that Chavis was being investigated by the Long Beach Memorial Hospital and by the IRS and used the "news" piece to trumpet the benefits of "affirmative action." Two years after the piece ran in the Times, Chavis had his license suspended for "inability to perform some of the most basic duties required of a physician." Many of his patients suffered and one of his patients died from Chavis's botched procedures.[750] Chavis, naturally, claimed to be the victim of a racist medical system. But the journalistic malpractice did not end there. None of the media which had trumpeted his case as a glowing example of the success of racial discrimination printed the rest of the story. In other words, Chavis's malpractice didn't happen on TV or in the news: it didn't happen.

Also, the newsroom itself was a target for "affirmative action," and newspapers were required to hire more and more of the members of the designated privileged groups.[751] In 1996, for instance, the Boston Globe had a policy that whites were not even allowed to apply for the paper's internship program. David Wilson, a 23-year-old from Kansas sued the paper and won.[752]

The privileged minorities have also organized their own journalistic promotion societies and in 1999 held a convention of several thousand minority journalists in Seattle.[753]

In the mid 1990s, something drastic happened to the most influential newspaper in the United States. The publisher of the New York Times retired and his son took over. The son, a product of 1960s, was a fervent believer in the Ideology of Dhimmism. "If white men were not complaining, it would be an indication we weren't succeeding," the new publisher is quoted as saying. Since that time, "a chief principle at the Times has been its dedication to cheap partisanship."[754]

One of its projects was to purchase a TV station in Oklahoma City and silence the investigative reporter who was working to expose the Oklahoma City bombing's connection to terrorism. The reporter found funding elsewhere and was able to complete her ten-year research and publish it.[755]

TRANSFORMING BOOKS

Publishers of schoolbooks wait until the school boards of California and Texas decide the restrictions on schoolbooks for the next year, then they do what those school boards want. They cannot afford to publish different schoolbooks for every school district or even every state.

In the past, if any sizeable school district opposed a particular topic or point of view, that topic or point of view did *not* get into the schoolbooks. Now, book publishers such as Houghton-Mifflin and McGraw-Hill hire Islamists as advisers to insure that any information about Islamic activities will not be offensive to Muslims. Also, there are organizations that pre-screen information going into schoolbooks. One is the Women's Educational Equity Act Publishing Center. This outfit promotes Dhimmism and has produced more than 350 publications distributed to hundreds of educational conferences and has "received more than $75 million in federal funds—otherwise known as *your* tax dollars!"[756]

A paradigm example of the books being published is Howard Zinn's A People's History of the United States, otherwise described as a Marxist tract. The book has sold over a million copies despite its lack of footnotes and is used in college classrooms in many universities. A New York Times review called it a "new version of American history." The book has remained in print and selling for over twenty-five years, even though he added a coda admitting that the book was "a biased account" and "a part of the social struggle". It is a long indictment of white people and the capitalist system, in which the answer is the same whatever the question.[757]

Publisher's Weekly, the official trade publication that reviews books every week for booksellers, has now become so heavily Dhimmist that its "reviews" are a joke on Amazon.com.

Even children's books are now being written by Dhimmists. Parents who assume that a book is safe for their small children because it is a children's book need to be forewarned. Children's books also appear by the thousands in *public libraries* across the country, and this section of the libraries is heavily patronized by parents and children. *Parents need to screen the books* before letting their children get hold of them.

Transforming bookstores

To see the effect of Dhimmism on bookstores, one has only to browse one of the book superstores and then browse Amazon.com. Even with all the books in a superstore, very few books critical of Dhimmism are on display and those are usually the most strident of such books, such as Ann Coulter. By contrast, in one or another of the various areas it has penetrated, there are numerous books pushing Dhimmism. At Amazon.com, by contrast, one can find numerous books critical of Dhimmism, most of which are quite level-headed. It requires more searching to find them, but the important thing is that they are there. The existence of these books can be verified by any reader.

Part of the reason is that bookstore managers are intimidated by the Dhimmists and their "activists." Any books that the various Dhimmist organizations oppose strongly enough do not get into the bookstores. For instance, a particular book criticizing U. S. immigration policies made the New York Times bestseller list, but could not be found in bookstores in Los Angeles and other places because the bookstore managers feared a riot by immigrants (legal and illegal) if they displayed the book in their stores.

Bookstore chains CEOs also have their political beliefs. In the past, the ideal of pluralism of opinions influenced bookstore owners. Today, with most bookstores being owned by chains headquartered in New York, books expressing opinions disapproved by the executives of these chains are not present or are grossly underrepresented in most bookstores. The books are not absent entirely. Usually, the *least persuasive* of the books criticizing various aspects of Dhimmism will be visibly displayed in bookstores. Other, more sober and convincing books, will *not be available* in the bookstores. Local bookstore managers report that they have no say in what books to carry in "their" stores or even where to locate those books within the store. These decisions are made in New York. Readers can order books, of course; but if readers do not know the books exist, how can they order them?

Transforming Public Libraries

Public librarians discriminate between the books they choose to admit into their libraries. Nominally, the criterion for inclusion is what the people in the community want. In fact, the librarians don't ask and don't tell. They admit books and movies they agree with or approve of. There is no oversight except for the town library boards, which usually have more to do with funding than with the library's collection.

Today, schools of library science have been influenced by Dhimmism, as have other professional schools. The professors are for the most part Dhimmists, and most of the students are committed to the Ideology by the time they graduate. Books critical of the Ideology do not get into public libraries.

Most people are unaware that librarians purge books as well as acquiring books. Older books, books that are not circulating have to be sold or discarded to make room for newer books, since the amount of space in local libraries is severely limited.

What all of this means is that over the years the public libraries have become more and more hospitable to Dhimmism. Islamic organizations generously donate books to local libraries by the thousands. Every public library in the nation, large and small, is a recipient of the beneficence of these Islamic organizations.

The good news is that in some libraries, readers (library patrons) have online access to Books in Print. In some libraries, readers can even purchase books out of Books in Print, with the library getting a small percentage of the income from the sale. The service is free, but there is a small setup cost. If your library does not have this service, try to persuade the librarian to subscribe to it.

Transforming the Law

As everyone knows, the Supreme Court has been in effect rewriting the Constitution for some time; but recently, it has gone beyond that to what amounts to actually legislating.

"The rights of criminals have been steadily expanded and those of the community contracted."[758] "The same is true of public schools, where the power to ... expel [has been] virtually amputated.... no more the expulsion or segregation of students who make learning next to impossible for others."[759] A public library evicted a "homeless" man who had set up camp in the library and was even shouting and disrupting the library. A court ruled against the library.[760]

Florida released hundreds of murderers, kidnappers, etc. when a court ruled the prison "overcrowded." The Supreme Court upheld the ruling. The discomfort to prisoners of overcrowding was more important than the rights of citizens to be protected from violent criminals.[761] The overcrowding scenario was repeated in Philadelphia with the result that felons after being convicted were immediately released onto the streets.[762]

"Contrary to the plan of the American government, the Supreme Court has usurped the powers of the people and their elected representatives.... The crisis of legitimacy occurs because the political nation has no way of responding. The Founders ... provided no safeguards against its [the Court's] assumption of powers not legitimately its own and its consistent abuse of those powers."[763]

The Founders were well aware of this problem. As soon as the Constitution was finished in 1787, many began agitating for changes or amendments to the document. The Bill of Rights was soon added. Still, in 1798, some Founders such as Jefferson and Madison were worried that no checks and balances had been put on the Supreme Court, and various resolutions were drafted and introduced, but none succeeded. That situation was made worse when the first Chief Justice, John Marshall, claimed the power to decide what was and what was not in the Constitution. Thus, the Court superseded the written Constitution which Jefferson and others had placed their hopes on as a safeguard against the power of government.

The most egregious example of this abuse of power came in 1996, when by direct vote, the people of California expressed their will to remove special privileges for some groups and reinstitute equal treatment regardless of race, religion, etc. A federal District Court blocked enforcement of the law. (Luckily, in this case the appeals court overturned the decision. But the point is that these days it is a matter of luck rather than law when the Constitution is upheld.)

"Today, it is increasingly the *Federal Courts v. American People*, a contest that is escalating, and that the people are losing."[764] How did American law get this way?

The law schools as well as American law have been transformed.[765] Critical Legal Studies is the name given to Dhimmism in the law schools. This ideology holds that the apparent reasoning of law is really a cover for a particular mindset of social and political judgments. "Objectivity and neutrality are merely shams concealing a dominance game."[766] "Rather than relying solely on legal or interdisciplinary authorities, empirical data, or rigorous analysis, legal scholars have begun to offer stories."[767] Dhimmist law professors and judges hold that "The idea of 'freedom of speech' is just another one of those illusions the law uses to rationalize the outcome of cases.... first amendment rulings never have and never will rest on anything more than personal preferences."[768]

One of the means judges have used to get around the laws passed by legislatures and coded in the Constitution is the notion of *intent*. This weasel word has been slippery enough in the past. Now, with Critical Legal Studies, intent has been extended even farther. "the real question is not the legislature's intent but the message carried by a statue—its 'cultural meaning.'"[769] This desire to replace elected representatives with appointed judges and to replace the law with a power struggle may reflect the fact that at present the Dhimmists are the ones with the power.

One professor of law at the University of Pennsylvania holds that law is not a body of rules applicable equally to all citizens but rather is subordinate to one's perceived identity interests.[770] She rejects the distinction between lawful and unlawful behavior and advises African-Americans to break the law.[771]

Derrick Bell, professor of law at New York University, is regarded as the godfather of "Critical Race Theory." He teaches that equality before the law is oppressive to African Americans, whose moral claims are superior to those of whites.[772]

A Columbia University professor of African-American Studies promulgates "a black theory of justice" which maintains that the American criminal justice system is irredeemably racist. He also advocates reparations for

American slavery and claims that the purpose of history is to "reconstruct America's memory about itself."[773]

Another professor of law at Emory University is a former secretary of the Black Panther Party and has no books or academic articles to her credit. According to her, racism and white supremacy are "ingrained" in Americans, who are incapable of treating "Black people in a human fashion." She claims that terrorism is a propaganda invention of the U. S. government.[774]

A professor of law at Georgetown teaches a course which opposes the government's "surveillance standards" of "targeting of foreign nationals," etc. He has defended persons who were found guilty of materially aiding terrorists, condemning the guilty verdicts with claims that it is the Justice Department that is guilty of terrorism. He opposes the Patriot Act for denying entry into the U. S. of aliens for the "pure speech" of endorsing "terrorist activity."[775]

Another professor of law at Georgetown specializes in Critical Race Theory and is the leading architect of university speech codes: codes forbidding any speech that offends the sensitivities of the designated minorities. However, "expressions of hatred, revulsion, and anger directed against member of historically dominant groups by subordinated-group members are not criminalized by the definition of racist hate messages used here."[776]

Predatory litigation. Ours has become an age of "predatory litigation." A woman sued the city of New York because she was hit by a subway train. She was awarded $9 million even though she had been lying on the tracks trying to commit suicide. In another case, after lightning knocked out a Florida prison's TV satellite dish, a prisoner sued the state because it interrupted his TV watching. In a dozen states, medical emergencies cannot be handled because of a shortage of doctors who can no longer afford malpractice insurance. One public-interest organization says, "Our system of justice is now considered a tool for extortion."[777]

Bernardine Dohrn, of Weatherman fame, after years on the FBI's ten most wanted list, is now a professor of family law at Northwestern University Law School. She is also a member of boards and committees of the American Bar Association and the ACLU. Her main focus is arguing against the punishment of criminals, especially violent juvenile offenders.[778]

In 2003, a group of parents sued the California school system for indoctrinating their children into Islam. The U. S. District court ruled that making children adopt Muslim names and clothes, etc. and making them kneel down and pray to Allah was not indoctrination but learning *about* Islam.[779] Praying to God on the other hand is routinely outlawed by the courts (on the grounds of separation of church and state).

Transforming the Government

Some government agencies created with the best of intentions have become fiefdoms unto themselves. The Equal Employment Opportunities Commission (EEOC) has become one of the most notorious, discriminating against "white" people and any others not on the list of preferred groups.

One Black woman who was on the Civil Rights Commission from 1980 to 2004 and head of the Commission for the last decade of those years holds that America is pervasively racist and that race preferences are justified. She has been a university Chancellor and a professor at the University of Maryland and at the University of Pennsylvania.[780]

The National Museum of American History in Washington, D.C. devotes six times more space to the interment of Japanese Americans in World War II than to the entire rest of World War II.[781]

Creating the Department of Education as a branch of the federal government administration was opposed by the American Federation of Teachers (AFT) and by many liberals and educators at the time, including S. I. Hayakawa. Since that time, federal spending on projects related to education has tripled and federal regulations have multiplied exponentially. Almost from the first, the department was populated by advocates for the emerging ideology of Dhimmism.

The DOE has established its own Office of Civil Rights, headed during one recent administration by a woman who was a veteran of the Mexican-American Legal Defense Fund. As a result, the DOE aggressively advances bilingual education in all the nation's public schools and is a watchdog for instances of "sexual harassment"[782] among other functions.

Among the consequences of federal aid has been the desirability of having as many pupils as possible. Some schools near the border actually bus children in from Mexico to beef up their enrollments. Others take a more direct approach. In Los Angeles, one "educator" created "phantom students worth $700,000 in additional funding."[783] In New York City, a principal was fired because hundreds of pupils who had moved or dropped out were still being marked present. Often, even their classes didn't exist![784]

Cover-ups. In 1995, the Oklahoma City federal building was bombed. Even though a number of eyewitnesses had seen Arabic-looking men running or driving away from the scene immediately before the explosion, the government claimed that two white men had committed the crime and that Muslims had nothing to do with it. An indefatigable reporter, through years of investigation has proved otherwise. Iraqi refugees recruited McVeigh and helped him build the truck bomb. There is also evidence that a second bomb was placed in the parking deck under the building, explaining why much debris was blown *out* from the building instead of *into* the building as would have happened if the truck bomb on the street had been the only explosion.[785]

In 1996, TWA Flight 800 was shot down off Long Island. The government again covered up the fact in a prolonged and expensive "investigation" that blamed the crash on a mechanical flaw. Investigative reporters found otherwise. The Navy was on an unpublicized terrorist alert that night because of suspicions that terrorists were going to fly a small plane loaded with explosives into a commercial airplane or other target, as had previously been threatened. A small jet taking off from Boston and packed with explosives was actually looking to do just that. The plane headed toward US Air Flight 217 but veered under it at the last minute and targeted the much larger TWA plane. A Navy ship fired a surface-to-air heat-seeking missile at the plane but hit the TWA plane instead just as the small jet exploded its cargo. The combined explosions downed Flight 800. Government agents were caught in the act of hammering out pieces of the plane to make them conform to the mechanical flaw theory.[786]

Transforming the Foundations

Many foundations, like the Rockefeller, MacArthur and Ford Foundations, are now controlled by Dhimmists and promote the Ideology and the programs of the Ideology. The Ford Foundation is estimated to spend one billion dollars every year. It uses this money, for instance, "to file suits against the detention of captured terrorists" and to oppose the "racial profiling of Arabs and Muslims."[787] University projects in order to receive grants from the Ford Foundation must present detailed specifications that show that the project meets the goals of the Dhimmist ideology. The Ford Foundation fights for open U. S. borders, donating more than $60 million dollars to the cause. It funded the creation of the militant Mexican-American Legal Defense and Education Fund, and has been pushing "the massive expansion of bilingualism in U. S. public schools."[788] In 2003, seventeen congressmen issued a public demand that Ford "cease funding of subversive groups."[789]

Another public-service organization that has done a complete about-face is the American Civil Liberties Union. For years, the ACLU defended individuals who were being stepped on by the government. Now, the ACLU defends *groups*—the right groups, the groups the Dhimmist ideology says should be protected against the vile American white people. Among other helpful activity, the ACLU now opposes profiling of Arabs, sues to stop the Boy Scouts for meeting in a city park (on the grounds that the Boy Scouts are a religious organization), and argues that doctors should not be allowed to tell a wife that her husband has AIDS.[790]

Can America Be Saved?

Historians have always been amazed that the people in a society on the brink of collapse did not see it coming. With hindsight, the signs and indicators seem so obvious. Maybe the people did see, but the human mind is so adept at explaining away unpleasant details that the signs, so obvious later, were given a "spin" that neutralized them. Maybe they did see, but were prevented from stopping the forces that were undermining their society.

For those today that see the indicators of the fall of America, luckily there are a number of feasible remedies that would solve or lead to the solution of most of these problems and avert the destruction of the United States.

Unluckily, none of these remedies will be applied.

If these "nice" and relatively easy solutions are not used, there are no "nice" solutions to the problems presented in this book. In that case, if America is to be saved, it will be difficult, will involve a lot of time and work on the part of a large number of individual citizens, and will be uncertain of outcome.

Perhaps there is some way around the blocks that are up against the "nice" solutions presented in this chapter. Perhaps there is some way to remove the blocks. The reader is invited to think of some.

RE-INTRODUCE PROFILING

Even though all the terrorists of 9/11 were Arabs, let's start with the assumption that not all Arabs are terrorists. If that is so, then the task is to decide which Arabs, if any, *are* and which are *not* terrorists. In order to do that, you have to look at Arabs. The same applies to Muslims. That's what profiling is: examining Arabs and Muslims to determine whether each is or *is not* a terrorist.

Arab and Muslim organizations vehemently object to this practice. This fact in itself is interesting. If they are all innocent, one would think they would not only welcome such examinations but would be demanding them. The fact that they are so panicked by profiling is the best evidence that profiling is needed.

But it was stopped by the U. S. government. This fact is a demonstration of the frightening power that Islamists already have over the United States.

The usual charges of racism, etc. were leveled against the practice and against the government. And as usual, nobody demanded proof that the practice was based on racism. As usual, the *charge* is the proof. Since all the 9/11 hijackers were Arab Muslims, the burden of proof is on Arabs and Muslims to show why no examination should be made to determine which Arabs and Muslims are and are not terrorists. No such proof has been offered. No support for the claim has been offered.

But profiling remains unusable in America. And the same goes for wiretapping and other forms of spying. Individual Islamists and Islamic groups are immune to scrutiny in the United States.

REMOVE RELIGIOUS IMMUNITY FROM ISLAM

In spite of the presumed separation of church and state in the United States, religions have certain privileges. They pay no taxes and their practices are largely immune to government scrutiny.

However, not every group that claims to be a religion is officially recognized as such by the government. This raises interesting questions about what is and what is not a religion. It is not the number of people involved. It is not the content of the beliefs or practices, although if the beliefs are too eccentric, the organization is not "recognized" as a religion. And if the practices are too far from the mainstream, the practice is forbidden by the government.

Even if an organization *is* recognized as a religion, its practices are not immune to government regulation. The most familiar example, of course, was the Mormon practice of polygamy. One man having two wives was not regarded by the government as a private matter of individual rights nor was it deemed within the purview of religion, even though the practice is frequent among men in the official Bible of Christian religions. It would be an interesting enough case even if the practice were not sanctioned by the Bible. But the fact that the practice is in the Bible and is still forbidden by the secular government makes this case very interesting.

What this shows is that it is not unthinkable for the government to tell people what they can and cannot do in the name of religion.

Other than Islam, no other belief system recognized as a religion advocates the killing of those who disagree with the beliefs. Other than Islam, none requires inhumane treatment of women. Whether Islam deserves the name "religion" or not, it needs to be recognized that this is a very different kind of thing from other belief systems that go by the name of "religion."

The time has come to re-examine the immunities usually accorded to religions in general and to Islam in particular. If polygamy can be outlawed by the government, then surely preaching the overthrow of the U. S. government can be outlawed. And storing munitions and plans for terrorist acts in religious buildings can be outlawed.

But we face the same problem as with profiling: how do you know which mosques are preaching sedition, which mosques are storing weapons, which are serving as meeting places for terrorists, and the like? The only way to find out is to look. If mosques are off-limits to government scrutiny, they will always be safe havens for terrorists and apt training facilities for new recruits.

But monitoring mosques for terrorist activity and seditious propaganda is not going to happen. Muslims claim "freedom of religion" as grounds for preventing the government from any surveillance of mosques or spying on Islamists. (It has not escaped notice that there is an irony about a religion that seeks to end freedom of religion demanding freedom of religion for itself.)

DE-MOLE THE GOVERNMENT

The suggestion is straightforward: remove Islamists from the FBI, the CIA, the Department of Homeland Security, from airport security, baggage handling, etc. Stop bringing Islamists to tour government nuclear facilities. Prevent Islamists from studying subjects in American universities like nuclear physics and bio-chemistry that could be used to make nuclear, biological and chemical weapons.

Even Muslims who are "moderate" or nonmilitant do not always stay moderate. The bomber of the London subways was said to be a moderate Muslim and a long-term resident of England who was converted to militant Islam.

Removing moles from the government is not going to happen, first of all, because of the usual protests of racism, etc. which for some unaccountable reason the government takes seriously.

Secondly, there is a need in the FBI and the CIA for people who speak and read Arabic. This was the excuse for hiring Islamists into the FBI in the first place.

The excuse is spurious. First, there are many Israelis who read and speak Arabic fluently. It could be feared that they would funnel information back to Israel, but there may be ways to guard against this.

Second, there are many Christian Arabs in the United States. Many Lebanese have been Christians for generations and are loyal American citizens, and they have no love for the Islamists who have taken over their country and who seek to take over this one.

But politicians want votes and they want campaign contributions from the oil-rich Arabs who are more than happy to "contribute" through their American organizations and PACs. The belief that most Muslims are "moderate" is an unshakable article of faith for American politicians.

Removing Muslims from sensitive government posts and facilities is not going to happen.

A MORATORIUM ON IMMIGRATION

Since the amount and type of immigration is a highly controversial issue, it needs to be discussed and decided by the citizenry. Until this happens, there needs to be an immediate and total moratorium on *all* immigration. Illegal immigration must be stopped completely. Student visas, asylum seeking and all other excuses for immigration must be suspended until the entire citizenry has had a chance to inform itself, discuss the issues and vote on the matter. This would include a temporary freeze on the importing of relatives.

It would be important to send a message to other countries that the practice of anchor babies no longer works. It would also be important to send a message that "asylum seekers" should stay in their own countries and fight to liberate their own governments.

Duration of the moratorium. How long should the moratorium last? Until the immigrants who are already here have *assimilated*. This would provide some incentive for immigrants to assimilate. Immigrants who refuse to assimilate would simply be prolonging the period during which further immigration from their countries is prohibited.

The burden of proof of assimilation would be on the immigrants, and the criterion of proof should be set high. This means that they would have to *invite* the FBI to observe them, examine their textbooks, videotape their sermons, etc. for a period of a year or more. They would have to be willing to serve in the military.

None of this will happen, of course. All of these suggestions violate the Dhimmist principle of so-called "multiculturalism," that every culture is good except ours. Every time even the most modest bills are introduced in the House to limit immigration, the bill is defeated. Of course, the corporations' desire for cheap labor and the politicians' desire for votes help to defeat any efforts to curb immigration, both legal and illegal. In the case of illegal immigration, this refusal on the part of legislators and administrators to enforce the law should be grounds for impeachment. Citizens should loudly call for the impeachment of every Congressman and state legislator who votes against enforcing the immigration laws. City council members who vote to make their cities safe havens for illegal immigrants should be arrested.

IMMIGRATION MUST BE DECIDED *ONLY* BY REFERENDUM

Given the power of corporations over legislators, new laws on immigration must be decided by a direct vote of the people. This has to be done soon, otherwise the immigrants will outnumber the assimilated population, and a vote would simply open the floodgates of immigration further.

DEPORTATION OF ILLEGAL ALIENS

Criminal proceedings are time-consuming and costly. The number of illegal immigrants is increasing faster than courts can process them and the cost of housing them is prohibitive. Those operating the illegal immigrant racket know this and are exploiting it. Hence, illegal immigrants must be deported on sight, as in the past. They are not entitled to the protections of American citizens, nor should American citizens be forced to pay for their housing, legal defense, medical expenses, schooling, food stamps, etc. as is now done.

Illegal immigrants who are repeat offenders must be jailed without bail. Those operating illegal immigrant rackets or otherwise aiding illegal immigrants must be caught and jailed without bail.

All seditious immigrants (Reconquistadores, Jihadists), whether legal or not, must be jailed.

None of this will happen, of course. The government will do again what it has done twice already: "amnesty" for illegal immigrants. In other words, by a few words, illegal immigrants become legal immigrants. This is required by the ideology of Dhimmism. To do otherwise is "racism."

INVASION OF NORTHERN MEXICO

Patrolling the borders adequately, building jails for the one million illegal immigrants per year—all of this costs a great deal of money. And experience has shown that the appropriations will always been inadequate and the enforcement sabotaged by Dhimmist elements within the various levels of government.

Consequently, what I propose is the same that the U. S. has done in other countries: first, reach an agreement with the Mexican government for *a joint military operation* into northern Mexico to wipe out the drug dealers and immigrant racketeers.

Second, the economy of northern Mexico should be developed, roads and factories built, etc. until the region is a thriving part of Mexico and a desirable place to live. At that point, the U. S. military, as usual, should leave the area and turn full control over to the Mexican government.

This would remove the incentive to crash the borders of the United States. Some immigrants already in this country might even sneak back across the border to Mexico to get in on the ground floor of the burgeoning opportunities in northern Mexico.

Anyone who thinks the above plan will happen hasn't been paying attention.

CHECKS ON THE SUPREME COURT

In order to do anything about the abuses of law in America, some kind of checks and balances must be introduced for limiting the unbridled power of the Supreme Court. Americans have disliked presidents and they have been displeased with various Congresses, but they have never hated the Presidency *per se* and they have never hated Congress *per se*. But people hate the Supreme Court, and with good reason. At this point, the Supreme Court is one of the greatest dangers to the survival of the United States of America. The rise and spread of Dhimmism would have been impossible without the Supreme Court's encoding the key programs of the Ideology of Submission into the law of the land.

The Founders were well aware that no checks or balances had been put in the Constitution to protect the nation against the possibility of a runaway Court. They floated various proposals almost immediately after the Constitution was ratified. But since the Court did not abuse its power for the first hundred and sixty years, the issue was forgotten. Now, the problem is urgent. How can checks be introduced for the Supreme Court?

Tenure. Since the Constitution does not specify the number of members of the Supreme Court (it was initially six), or the terms of office, one proposal is to *limit the term of office* to ten years.[791] With this change, the damage wrought by a particular member of the Court would not go on and on.

Conditions for overruling. Another proposal is *a Constitutional amendment* which would provide specific *conditions for overruling* the Supreme Court.[792] One such specific condition would be blatant ignoring of the wording of the Constitution itself or of the laws of Congress. The Founders put great store by the fact that they had spelled out limits on the power of the federal government in a written document, the Constitution. As we now know, these words have ceased to limit the Court.

Impeachment. Another possibility is the *impeachment* process. Justices who show blatant disregard for the wording of the Constitution should be impeached. Attempts at impeaching various Justices have been made in the past, usually without sufficient grounds. The attempts failed. But given the behavior of the Court in recent years, impeachment might very well succeed. One successful impeachment might be all it takes to cause the Court to stop disregarding the Constitution.

Amend the weasel words. Another possibility is to *remove the elastic clauses* in the Constitution that the Supreme Court has used to abrogate power to itself, such as "equal protection" and "general welfare" and replace them with a clear specification of what the government can and cannot do. But recently, the Court has not bothered with such clauses and merely uses the blanket term "unconstitutional" to do whatever it wants to do.

To solve some of the most pressing problems America now has, that derive from or have been made worse by the law, some of the specific legal issues that must be clarified are:

Enforce the Bill of Rights. The two rights most frequently violated in America today are freedom of speech and due process.

The procedures required by due process such as the right to be presumed innocent until proven guilty, the right to a trial by a jury of one's peers, right to call and confront witnesses, etc. are not at issue at this point. What is at issue is how to force universities to follow these procedures. Universities are being taken to court constantly, and so far the courts have ruled against the universities and in favor of due process. But there is always the threat that the Supreme Court will get its hands on one of these cases and repeal the right of due process.

Freedom of speech is slightly less clear. The problem is that Dhimmists, mostly in the universities, are claiming that action is speech.[793] So, shouting down speakers, confiscating newspapers, burning books—all of these are regarded by Dhimmists as speech. Moreover, they are held to take precedence over the mere expression of ideas by the speaker or the newspaper. This is a new departure.

Freedom of speech and press were intended to protect the dissemination of *ideas,* not protect the suppression of ideas. Not even all *verbal* expression was permitted, the standard example being shouting "Fire!" in a crowded auditorium. Also, the mode of expression of an idea is sometimes reasonable grounds for disallowing it. Someone publicly expressing political ideas largely in terms of obscenities or delivering them in a public mall while nude or shouting them over a loudspeaker in a residential neighborhood at three o'clock in the morning could be prosecuted for the mode of expression but not for the ideas themselves, however offensive those ideas might be.

These days even ideas are forbidden on college campuses if they are contrary to the Ideology of Submission. The argument is that these ideas are likely to offend the sensitivities of some groups. Such a position effectively terminates freedom of speech for anyone other than Dhimmists.

Distinguish between free speech and treason. Opposition to particular laws or even to the U. S. government is a protected right, but opposition to the United States *per se* is sedition and should be forbidden and punished. The most appropriate punishment would be deportation. If the U. S. is beyond repair as far as a person is concerned and that person is working and arguing to destroy America, then that person should be somewhere else.

So, arguing that *the government* is evil, racist, imperialist, or whatever is a protected right. Arguing that *America* is evil, racist, imperialist, etc. is treason. (Whether such teaching, even if applied to the government only, should be allowed in public schools and colleges, however, is arguable, since there is a captive audience and the speaker has the power of grading over the audience.)

A case in point is flag burning. First, the act of burning a flag is not speech. Second, the symbolism of the act is opposition to America per se, not opposition to the present government or the current occupant of the White House. Hanging the President in effigy should be allowed. Burning the Presidential shield should not be.

As you might guess, the Supreme Court allows burning the American flag.

Change or clarify the laws on discrimination. Lawsuits based on alleged "racism" must prove more than refusal to provide special treatment or special facilities. These days it is the threat of the lawsuit itself, not the threat of winning the lawsuit or the threat that the condition of discrimination exists that is the weapon. The process is the punishment. Such predatory litigation has made certain groups invincible.

Groups that bring such suits without adequate cause should be heavily fined or otherwise punished, to even up the stakes between these groups and the common weal.

As we have seen, groups such as Islamists are using the weapon of the predatory or punitive lawsuit to be allowed to continue their preparations in secret without any danger of being wiretapped, or having their mosques visited by arms inspectors, etc.

However, getting these laws changed or clarified is unlikely because of the very problem itself. Legislators would be accused of racism. Lawsuits would be brought, injunctions obtained. And the Supreme Court would likely veto the laws as "unconstitutional" even if the laws were to be encoded in an amendment to the Constitution itself.

Reform criminal law and the criminal justice system. Criminals must be treated as responsible adults not as helpless incompetents, and they must be held accountable for their actions. Middle-class Dhimmists have a classist view of lower-class criminals. They think the criminals are dumb. The criminals are not dumb. They know exactly what the criminal law allows, how it is enforced, what happens in court. They know exactly how much they can get away with and why.

But getting laws passed or even Constitutional amendments to say the obvious, that criminals are adults with sufficient intelligence to know what they are doing, would be of no avail. The Supreme Court would likely declare such a Constitutional amendment "unconstitutional." "The rights of criminals have been steadily expanded and those of the community contracted."[794]

Also, laws are needed so that the prisons can no longer be used as recruiting grounds for Islamists and Jihadists. This means that Islamist "chaplains" must be monitored and must be restricted in their activities to Muslims, not given access to the inmate population in general.

This would not be allowed on the grounds of freedom of religion. Such an argument is ridiculous, of course. Recruiting for a violent overthrow of the government and of American society is not a right protected by the Constitution.

At the same time, the right of every American to keep and bear arms (which *is* protected by the Constitution but is being steadily eroded) needs to be re-instated. Such a right was spelled out in the Second Amendment, and the Founders, including Thomas Jefferson, knew exactly what they were doing. The Constitution had already provided for the existence and arming of a militia in Article I, Section 8, so there would have been no need for the Second Amendment if all that amendment provided was a militia. "The militia is the whole people," wrote George Mason, the author of the Bill of Rights. One early Supreme Court justice said, "The right of a citizen to keep and bear arms has justly been considered the palladium of the liberties of the republic, since it offers a strong moral check against the usurpation and arbitrary power of rulers, and will generally, even if these are successful in the first instance, enable the people to resist and triumph over them."[795]

For these very reasons, the Dhimmists are opposed to gun ownership by citizens and the Supreme Court is likely, as usual, to back them. Congress is removing this right gradually, forbidding one type of gun, then another.

Everything Else

The problems of indoctrination cannot be dealt with directly. A misinterpretation of "academic freedom" not only permits but protects using college classrooms and schoolrooms to indoctrinate young Americans into the Ideology of Submission. The "news" and entertainment media reinforce the ideology and are beyond the control and largely beyond the influence of the people.

Only publicity via the Internet and the alternative book publishers can hope to counter the unremitting propaganda of the Dhimmists.

Reclaiming the Individual

America, we have a problem. Assuming that the relatively painless solutions of the previous chapter will not be used, we have a problem.

If America is to be saved, individual Americans must do the work themselves. If Americans do not, the Reconquistadores and the Islamists will extend their hegemony over their various sections of the country, producing a fractured nation. These sections will continue to enlarge in size, and a presence in other segments will be established and will grow.

It is difficult to say what will happen then. A lot of population migration will likely take place, individuals feeling that the only way they have left to vote is with their feet. Certainly, a fractured Congress is a possibility, with a Reconquista Party, an Islamic Party, a Democratic Party, and a Republican party. A new era of feudalism is not inconceivable with gated communities surrounded by high walls and armed guards. Alternatively or following that, a true civil war like the one in Bosnia is a real possibility.

A similar scenario in Europe is likely. Also, who would own controlling shares in the stock of the multinational corporations by that time is an interesting question. And what would they do with their control?

On the other hand, if America is to continue in any kind of recognizable form, the power of the Dhimmists must be confronted and stopped. If that could be done, perhaps some of the "nicer" and "easier" solutions might be put into action. But how are the as-yet unconverted Americans to curb the expanding power of the Dhimmists? The place to start is at home, and the people to start with are the children.

Depriving the Indoctrination Establishment of its Power

There are a number of things parents can do to protect their children from being turned into brain-disabled Dhimmists.

Parental counter-propaganda. Many parents try to counter the propaganda their children hear in public or private school all day. Some have an hour of "lessons" each weekday evening, in which the parents have the child or children present what they were taught in school that day and parents point out which parts are acceptable and which are not, and why. Or how what was presented was biased or slanted in various ways.

With the information in this book, parents will know exactly the dogmas that the school will be trying to instill in the child and can be quite specific in pointing out what is wrong with those dogmas, the dangers of accepting those dogmas, etc.

On a more mundane level, parents can teach their children arithmetic and reading. There are good computer programs in which the child can teach himself/herself these things, starting at age four or five.

It can be argued that parental counter-propaganda would set up an emotional conflict in the child. This is a real concern, especially since the school will be able to martial peer-pressure as well as the "authority" of the teacher year after year to assure the child that they are being told the one and only right way to think.

Some religious groups are able to counter the propaganda of the schools and provide peer support from others in the religion and the "authority" of the religious authorities. But for those who are not religious, it would hardly be acceptable to join a religious group for this express purpose, since for them, this would be protecting their children from one dogma only to have them subjugated by another dogma, in plain terms, jumping from the frying pan into the fire.

But helping the child to see the point of view of the teachers and to see why what they are saying appears to be reasonable to them, even though it isn't, could be beneficial in itself. It could not only (a) immunize the child against the indoctrination but (b) positively help the child by giving the child mental exercise in taking the point of view of the other. If children develop the habits of open-mindedness, it will be very difficult for the education establishment to close those minds and to convince them that there is only one correct way to think.

Assisted home schooling. Instead of fighting the power and influence of the indoctrination establishment, however, you might want to opt out and remove your children from the control of the Dhimmists entirely. The public school establishment fights in every possible way against parents who think of doing this. The thought of parents having other options terrifies school administrators. Their methods to counter the parents include misinformation of parents, intimidation and other threats against the parents.

First, every state now gives you the legal right to home school your child. Don't let school "authorities" tell you otherwise. Also, there are even legal aid organizations to help you fight for your right, if your local school district is particularly fascist-oriented. The Home School Legal Defense Association (www.hslda.org) can help, as can The Rutherford Institute (rutherford.org).

Socialization. One of the scares that the school establishment likes to throw at parents is that home-schooled children don't get socialized, because they are isolated from other children. This is simply a lie. In one study in which trained counselors observed children at play but did not know which were home-schooled and which were public-schooled, no differences were found among the two groups on children on tests of self-concept or assertiveness. Also, videotapes showed that the home-schooled children had *fewer* behavior problems.[796]

The truth is that most child socialization happens *after school.* Like public school children, your child can join local baseball teams, play with other neighborhood kids, join the Boy Scouts, etc.

Most important, there is good socialization and bad socialization. Schools provide the bad kind. Instead of being forced to associate with children you wouldn't want your children associating with, home school kids get to choose their associates and so do you.[797]

If you don't have time to do all the schooling yourself at home or if you're unsure whether you're qualified to do it, there are a number of different forms of assisted home-schooling. All of these schools operate via the Internet.[798]

Correspondence courses. Some of the Internet schools are traditional correspondence schools. They mail course material to the pupil, who studies the material, takes tests, etc. and mails back material.

Online courses. Other schools offer the course material online. Pupils read the material online, take tests online. The teacher reviews the tests, provides comments, etc.

Interactive courses. Other schools are virtual classes. Pupils interact with teachers online, ask questions, take tests, receive feedback, etc.

In all these types of assisted home-schooling, children work at their own pace and thus most can finish school (K through 12) sooner than 12 years. Since these schools are cheaper than private schools (about $1,000 a year compared to $4,000 a year), there are economic advantages as well as social and educational advantages. Not every Internet school provides all twelve grades. Some do and some only offer high school.[799]

Home schooling. Home-schooled children learn more than public or private school children. In one national survey, home-schooled children scored in the 84th percentile for reading, 80th for language, 81st for math, 84th for science and 83rd for social studies.[800] The Tennessee Department of Education conducted its own study of its schools and found to its embarrassment that Tennessee's home-schooled children scored in the 93rd percentile on the Stanford Achievement Test while their public school children scored in the 52nd percentile.[801] So, not only are you saving your children from indoctrination, but you are also giving them a better education.

General information websites. Even if you decide to teach your own children, you are not thrown entirely on your own resources. There are general information websites, such as Education Revolution (EducationRevolution.org), Home School Central (HomeschoolCentral.com), Family Education Network (FamilyEducation.com), American Homeschool Association (American-Home

SchoolAssociation.org), and the pioneer who fought for and started it all, John Holt (holtgws.com).[802]

Teaching materials. There are websites that offer home-schooling teaching materials, such as Core Curriculum of America (core-curriculum.com), Home Schooling books and software (www.startup-page.com), The Resourceful Homeschooler, books and software (ResourcefulHomeschooler.com), The Home School Source, books, materials, lending library (TheHomeSchoolSource.com), etc.[803]

Internet libraries. There are Internet libraries, such as the Internet Public Library Kid Space (ipl.org/kidspace), Inet Library (inetlibrary.com), Awesome Library (AwesomeLibrary.org), and the Library of Congress (www.loc.gov).[804]

College prep. There are college testing preparation and admissions requirements help sites, such as Test Prep (testprep.com), Apply4Admissions (apply4admissions.com), Homeschool Central (HomeschoolCentral.com), Kaplan Test Prep and Admissions (kaptest.com) The Admissions Office (TheAdmissionsOffice.com), the Homeschoolers College Admissions Handbook, etc.[805]

Parents associations. There are even home schooling parents associations, such as the American Homeschool Association (AmericanHomeschoolAssociation.org), Homeschool Help for Parents (HomeschoolHelpForParents.com), Home-schooling Friends (Home-schooling-friends.org), etc.[806]

Books. And of course, there are books.[807] Examples: Samuel L. Blumenfeld, *Homeschooling: A Parent's Guide to Teaching Children*, Replica Books, 1999; Gregg Harris and Sono Harris, *The Home School Organizer*, Noble, 1995; Grace Llewellyn, *Freedom Challenge: African-American Homeschoolers*, Lowry House, 1996; Rebecca Rupp, *The Complete Home Learning Source Book: The Essential Resource Guide for Homeschoolers, Parents, and Educators Covering Every Subject from Arithmetic to Zoology*, Three Rivers Press, 1998.

When you get down to it, teaching your child is not as difficult as you may have thought. Children have insatiable curiosity, which means they are eager to learn. "Input!" is the cry of children. Aversion to information has to be learned from parents. It is not innate. The same is true of boredom. Children have to be taught by adults to be bored. *Boredom is a learned trait*, not the natural condition of humans.

Reading. Children want to know what a sign "says," what a label says. Small children also like to do anything that their parents do with them, if their parents like to do it. It is said that Oriental parents simply sit with their children around the dining room table and read while their children do their homework. The sheer fact that their parents are with them and doing something similar makes the activity rewarding.

Start at the age of two by reading stories to your child, at bedtime or at any other time. At four, let the child look on at the book while you are reading, but don't try to push reading. Move your finger along under the words. Show them the correspondence between the pictures in the book and the sentences. Eventually, they will want to learn to read.

There are computer programs that are structured like games. By simply playing the games, the child learns to read without knowing that he/she is learning something terribly significant and of immense usefulness. Your local library may have copies of this software. If not, buy the best program you can (whether you can afford it or not). The programs are not very expensive.

Playing word games and sentence games with your child also attunes them to words. A game I played with my daughter when she was very young was one I made up, and which I called "sentences." One of us would start a sentence by saying one word. The other then had to add another word to the growing sentence. We continued taking turns. There was no agreement ahead of time about where the sentence was going and what it was going to be about. This is not only a word game but a creativity game. Finding that they can make up any sentence they want is very exciting and liberating for them. It also forces them to think and to explore possibilities. Being partially in control of the process rather than always having it given to them is a new experience for them.

Another game I called "stories." One of us would start with the first sentence of a story. The other would add the second sentence, and so on, alternating. Again, there was no agreement ahead of time on what the story was going to be about or where it was going. We simply made it up as we went along. It was challenging and required ingenuity, since we each had to constantly readjust where the story might go, as the other person threw us a curve. Eventually, the choices grew fewer and we put together the story more rapidly. Again, this is creativity as well as becoming sensitive to words.

Another game was simple: rhymes. One of us would say a word, the other would rhyme it, then the one who started would rhyme it again, etc. This attunes the child to the sound of words.

As with any game, it is essential for the *parent* to *enjoy* it. If the parent enjoys it, the child will enjoy it. If you don't enjoy a game, don't play it with your child. It will make the children dislike not only the game but the subject matter. There are many other ways to teach.

Math. Again, there are board games and computer programs to teach numbers to four-year-olds, to teach arithmetic, even algebra. To teach the concepts of math, there are (or were) games like WffnProof and OnSets. Contrary to popular belief, math is about relations, not about numbers. Contrary to even-more-popular belief, math can be fun.

Writing. Have your child write a letter to grandma or to someone else. If your child has made up a story that she particularly likes, urge her to write it down. These days, there are also software programs that teach very young children how to type.

How to use the mouse will hardly have to be taught. Find a list of Internet sites for children. Type them into your address list one by one and go to each. That will put them on your computer browser's (e.g. Internet Explorer's) pull-down address list. Show your child how to pull down this list using the mouse and how to "click on" any one of them. It won't take long. Then, your child can go to these websites and explore on her own.

Science. If you don't enjoy science, then you probably went to a public or private school. News flash: science is about discovery, not about facts. Get story books on the lives of the great scientists and inventors. These stories should show how the scientist became curious about something, how he went about exploring it, the moment of discovery, and how and why he had to then prove it. Sit down with your children and watch the movie "Madame Curie" (1943). Not only is this a very good movie, but it will convey to your children what science is all about.

The basic principles of mechanics might be a good place to start: how and why levers work. These are simple "machines" and can get children thinking like scientists. Okay, so you may have to learn one or two things yourself in the process, but that's not a bad thing. You may be surprised to learn that science can be fascinating after all.

History. First, show children *what* there was in the past: for example, pictures and documentaries of the monuments of Egypt, the statuary of the Assyrians, the sculpture of the Greeks. Show them some old maps, and how people's image of the world changed through time.

As your child grows older, you can talk about *why* groups of people did what they did. You need particularly to focus on America to counter the negative propaganda of the mass media. It is important that children know what the early English colonists did and why, what principles motivated them, particularly how *self-government* was an essential part of *freedom* for them. *The Politically Incorrect Guide to American History* in the first few chapters can provide you with the gist.

If you've done it right in the first few years, your child will take over and begin to learn on his/her own. You should still sit with your child. If you work from home via a terminal, locate it in the same room with your child. The fact that you are doing your serious, grown-up work while they are doing their work will be a message worth all the words in the world.

The Arts. Children are usually given crayons at an early age. If they have drawing ability, it will show itself early on. Drawing helps people to learn to see.

Children should be sung to from the time they are born. Music should be played around them, also, not the monotonous rhythms and enraged screaming of current pop music, but simple tunes and more complex rhythms. When my daughter was seven days old—yes, days—she was nursing when I happened to put on a recording of Rachmaninoff's Second Piano Concerto. After slow chords in the beginning, the music goes into a pronounced swinging rhythm. When that rhythm started, my daughter altered the tempo of her sucking and immediately got into perfect synch with the rhythm of the music.

As children grow up, encourage them to sing with you. Even if you don't have musical ability yourself, it doesn't mean that your child doesn't. Children should be given the opportunity to learn to play a musical instrument. Unfortunately, music lessons are and have always been designed for children who are trying to become professional performers. Piano lessons teach the reading of music and after that emphasize manual dexterity and an almost paranoid attention to the minutiae of touch. As a result, the few who do become concert pianists hate the music they are playing.

Children should be taught to *play* the piano first, before they are even taught to *read* music. Here's how I taught my five-year-old daughter: I taught her the positions of the five fingers and had her play the notes up and down. I told her that this was simply a muscle exercise and was not playing the piano. After a few minutes, when her fingers were strong enough, I instructed her to play the same five notes, but play them in any order she wanted to. No further guidelines. She started a little hesitantly at first but played some notes. I encouraged her to go on for awhile, then pointed out that she probably had noticed that she liked certain sequences or strings of notes better than others. I suggested that she remember those sequences and ignore the others. When she had enough strings that she liked, she could put those together and make longer strings that she liked. She played again. After awhile, I pointed out that all the notes didn't have to be the same length and illustrated by improvising some dotted-rhythm melodies using the same five notes. Then it was her turn. She readily played some strings of dotted notes and got into it a little more. In this way, one at a time, I introduced the different rhythmic patterns and she made up strings of notes with them.

This way of proceeding did several beneficial things for her. First, she had to *create*, to generate, not merely passively reproduce the notes that someone else had written. Second, she was learning to listen, and to *listen discerningly* or evaluatively. Third, she was developing her own tastes. I didn't tell her which strings were good. She selected them herself. She was also developing the habit of creating in general and learning that she could *make* things herself.

Important! I did *not* tell her that she was writing music, even though that's what she was doing. I also did not tell her there was anything at all unusual about what she was doing. The result was that in less than an hour, she was making up melodies and thinking nothing about it. Some of the melodies were good. I then left her and told her she could go on *playing* for as long as she wanted to. She did. A few days later, I wrote down some of her melodies. They were quite good.

But whether or no, the point is she was enjoying it and she was playing the piano, not merely reading music. Learning to read music can come later. If you employ an outside piano teacher, try to find one who believes that playing should be fun and who is *not* into training concert pianists.

Result. All in all, you have a better than good chance of not only depriving the Dhimmists of the chance to indoctrinate your child but of giving your child a good and an enjoyable education. If you foster rather than thwart their predisposition to enjoy learning, they will go on learning for the rest of their lives.

DEPRIVING THE MAINSTREAM NEWS MEDIA OF ITS POWER

The good news is you are no longer at the mercy of the mainstream news media to find out what's going on in America. You no longer have to read The New York Times. Not only does it no longer print "all the news that's fit to print", it is arguable whether it prints any of it. You don't have to read Newsweek or watch the evening news or the "news magazine" programs.

The Internet. There are Internet websites and "blogs". Many are conservative sites, like WorldNetDaily.com, FrontPageMag.com, News-Max.com. But some are moderate: www.themoderatevoice.com. Some are even liberal, like www.tammybruce.com, and the like. Many of these websites link to other like-minded sites, so you can branch from one to the other. You'd be surprised what you'll find. Other sites are more special interest like jihadwatch.org, campus-watch.org, danielpipes.org, www.incorrect.com, www.pcidiots.com, pcwatch.blogspot.com, etc.

Caveat. The Dhimmists also have many, many websites and in true Dhimmist fashion, they typically try to cover the identity of these sites by pretending to be nonpartisan or liberal or whatever. But with the information in this book, you should be able to recognize these sites for what they are. Dhimmists, like all True Believers,[808] can't help pushing their dogmas and their agendas.

Independent publications. Thanks to POD publishing, New York no longer controls what America reads. As many readers are discovering every day, there is a wealth of information that most Americans don't know about and don't even dream exists. It is not to be found at the book superstores (although it can be ordered from them). It is to be found at the Internet bookstores.

Since you are reading this book, you have already found some of these books. Let your friends know. The good news is: Americans no longer have to read books published by publishers controlled by Dhimmists.

Cable news. Some of the cable TV networks also have news shows that depart from the strict Dhimmist dogmas.

AM talk radio. Alternative views are sometimes available on AM talk radio. Naturally, the Dhimmists are actively engaged in trying to silence these commentators who do not tow the Dhimmist party line.

DEPRIVING DHIMMIST ENTERTAINMENT OF ITS POWER

American people are no longer at the mercy of whatever is on TV on a given night or of whatever movies are being shown in the local theaters. Thanks to videotapes and DVDs, you can *pull the plug* on television without missing a thing. You can choose from the best movies ever made and also from nonfiction or documentary films. You don't even need a local store to carry them. They are available for order on the Internet. Amazon.com, for example, carries 50,000 movies and documentaries. The Internet Movie Data Base (imdb.com) provides free access to information on even more movies, both foreign and domestic.

Even recent years have produced some good family-friendly movies, and many are available on video and DVD, such as "The Secret Garden" (1975), "A Christmas Carol" (1984), "Anne of Green Gables," and

"Heidi" (2005). (The dates associated with these movies are important, since other versions of the movies exist and are less good.) There is also a wealth of movies from the golden years like the films of Shirley Temple or of Deanna Durbin, the Frank Capra films or the Dickens movies of the late 1940s, such as "Oliver Twist" (1948), "Great Expectations" (1946), "Nicholas Nickleby" (1947), and "Pickwick Papers" (1952).

Some families have revived the traditional family custom of reading aloud. Novels like *David Copperfield* and *Anne of Green Gables* can be read a chapter at a time over a number of months. This will show children that books provide a different and more thorough form of entertainment that does not duplicate the movies. It also instills a positive attitude toward reading. This hour of reading aloud need not substitute for other forms of entertainment. There will still be time for a movie or other activities each evening.

Some families enjoy a family entertainment night with children performing in ways they enjoy: some playing a musical instrument, others singing a song, some performing a dance, others doing a standup comedy routine or performing a skit. *Children love to perform*, especially if their parents approve and enjoy watching them.

In this way, the passive entertainment of movies and reading is varied with the active entertainment of performing. Children need both.

FIGHTING THE INDOCTRINATION ESTABLISHMENT

Those who want a more active and more social involvement in countering the indoctrination establishment could get together with others and hold a teach-in at the local library or church auxiliary, alerting people to what is going on in America.

They could also write and print pamphlets or alternative reading lists or lists of websites and hand them out at PTA meetings at local schools or on campus after classes on specific subjects. Some students might be willing to help in distributing material.

Reclaiming the Economy

There are many economic problems, large and small, and there are a plethora of proposals for dealing with them. But the economic problem that most threatens the independence, and indeed the continuance, of the United States is the problem of the economic power wielded by Saudi Arabia. This power, as we saw in the second chapter, extends into the internal affairs of our nation and involves everything from building mosques and Islamic schools to influence over politicians and administrators so that even law enforcement cannot do what is necessary to combat as serious a problem as terrorism, let alone all the other types of jihad that are being used to undermine our nation.

This economic power is created by the oil usage of Americans. The only ways to reclaim the economic independence of the U. S. are either to produce more oil or to decrease oil consumption.

Oil Exploration

Some "experts" don't hold out much hope for this option. Striking more oil could help, they say, but not produce enough to substantially affect our net dependency on foreign oil. The counterargument to this is that "every little bit helps." Besides, it's difficult to know before discovering it, how much oil will be discovered.

Recently, a promising find was made deep in the Gulf of Mexico. Early signs even indicated that it could represent more oil than the Middle East. The Democrats in Congress immediately moved to halt further exploration in the area on the grounds that it would endanger the marine life in the Gulf of Mexico.

With friends like these, America doesn't need Jihadists or Reconquistadores.

TELECOMMUTING

Two-thirds of America's oil is consumed by transportation. Sixty percent of that is used by cars, minivans, SUVs and pickup trucks.[809] The overwhelming majority of that use is devoted to commuting to jobs. And virtually all of the involuntary use of consumer transportation is controlled by the necessity of getting to and from a job.

Many jobs these days are done at an office using a telephone and a computer. Both these facilities are available in every home. So, technologically there is no reason why those jobs cannot be done at home. This would save the nation an enormous quantity of gasoline each day.

Business managers are opposed to their employees working at home because managers are fond of having meetings, which largely waste everybody's time but make the managers feel that they are doing something useful. However, even meetings can be done online by means of video hookups or by teleconferencing using telephones alone.

Working from home would also save most people an unbelievable amount of time. Around every large city in the nation, the roads at rush hour are clogged with cars. The larger the city, the longer the lines of cars. And "rush hour" now stretches from 6 A.M. to 10 A.M. and from 3 P.M. to 7 P.M. with a mini rush hour from noon to 2:30 P.M. And "rush hour" is getting longer all the time. People spend up to two hours getting to work and two hours getting home. This is three or four hours every day out of a person's life. So, not only is oil being wasted but lives are being wasted by the simple process of getting to work.

Also, workers would not start the workday fatigued and irritable, as they do now.

What we have is a situation in which all the advantages are on one side (the side of telecommuting) and there are no disadvantages on the other side. You might think this would be a no-brainer. Businesses should institute telecommuting as fast as possible.

This will not happen.

Why not? Because managers like to feel in control. Even though no manager goes around and looks over the partitions to see if their employees are working, the fact that the workers are physically there in their cubicles makes the managers feel that work is being done. If the people were not in the building, managers feel insecure.

The fact is, of course, that these "workers" are not in fact working a great deal of the time. They are on the phone talking to friends or relatives. They are playing solitaire on their computers, or surfing the web, or shopping on the web. They are reading magazines or chatting with the workers on the other side of the partition.

There are two clear reasons why the excuses of managers can safely be said to be based on irrational factors. One is that there is software that can keep track of the activity of any given computer on a network. The amount of connect time, the amount of keystroke activity, the files accessed, how often, for how long, etc. Virtually everything a person does can be monitored and reported to a manager.

The other factor is that many workers are judged based on the *results* they produce. They have tasks to perform and are required to complete those tasks in approximately two-thirds of the amount of time required to do the task. How soon they finish and how good a job they do are factors used as the basis to determine amount of raises, promotions and job retention. Obviously, these same criteria would apply if the person were working from home.

There is thus no excuse for requiring these workers to commute to a particular building. Businesses would also save on office space and the expenses of upkeep on that space. The traffic accidents, injury and loss of life during commuting go without saying.

In spite of all these advantages, telecommuting is not happening and can safely be expected to continue not to happen.

ONLINE SHOPPING

As people demanded more and more choice in their shopping, stores tended to congregate into shopping malls, and these places tended to be located farther and farther from where people lived. The neighborhood store and even going to town to shop are a thing of the past. This requires more driving, more time and more oil consumption.

Now, with the Internet, online shopping not only requires zero oil consumption but zero driving time. And the choices are fabulous. It is a win-win-win situation.

As more people learn to use this method, a savings in oil consumption will result. Also, fleets of delivery trucks, such as UPS, have switched to electric motors, thus saving on noise, air pollution and oil consumption.

LOCAL PRODUCTION

In the producer market, goods are often shipped thousands of miles to areas to be sold. In many cases, those areas once produced those same items themselves. For instance, apples are shipped three thousand miles from Washington state to Massachusetts, an apple growing state (and birthplace of Johnny Appleseed), driving the local orchards out of business. In virtually every state, where people used to buy produce from local farmers, they are purchasing fruits and vegetables that are trucked in from hundreds or thousands of miles away.

This not only wastes fuel but requires that the fruit be picked while it is still green, otherwise it would be rotten by the time it gets to market. Producers have also used breeding methods to breed a tougher fruit so that it will not get bruised from all the shipping and handling.

In the case of some industries, the argument of economies of scale is used to justify this driving of local entrepreneurs out of business. Even where this argument is sound, the economies of scale are purchased at a price of the dis-economies of using oil and increasing the oil dependency of the U. S. on foreign governments.

Whether it would be possible to rejuvenate local industries again is unclear. Perhaps a surtax on businesses that increases with the distance which they ship their goods would force these businesses to at least pay for their contribution to our nation's oil dependency.

JOB RE-MATCHING

As any commuter in an urban area will have noticed, not only are there endless streams of cars heading *into* the city in the mornings but there are also at the same time endless streams of cars heading *out of* the city to get to work. And it hasn't escaped the notice of many that this resembles something that might have been devised by the Keystone Cops.

Many of these commuters have similar job skills and are heading to similar jobs. The problem is that job slots are only advertised when they become unoccupied. If all jobs (whether occupied or not) could be listed in a central database along with their job requirements, and all workers (whether employed or not) could be listed in a database along with their job skills, a simple computer program could match these two lists and furnish businesses with lists of possible workers near them and furnish workers with lists of possible jobs near them. It would then be up to the individual decisions of businesses and workers whether they were interested. If so, they could notify each other of interest in case the job slot became unoccupied.

This re-matching would cut down on commuting time and the gasoline consumption involved.

Business managers would complain about the time needed to "train" the new employees in their jobs. But there are also advantages to businesses. Employees would not be exhausted and irritable by the time they got to work and should do a better job as a result. There might also be less job-switching, since workers wouldn't be continually jockeying for jobs closer to home.

POPULATION

All of the above problems are driven by population, and population expansion is driven almost solely by immigration. The population of Americans is nearly stable. It is the Arabs and the Hispanics that are primarily fueling population expansion. If population continues to expand, the savings in oil consumption from all of the above methods would be wiped out in time by the population expansion.

Immigration from third-world nations needs to be stopped.

HYBRID CARS

Hybrid cars are just beginning to come on the market. These cars operate part of the time on gasoline and part of the time on batteries which are recharged during the time the car is running on gasoline. This results in reductions in gasoline consumption.

Auto manufacturers, of course, ever on the lookout for the main chance, charge more for these cars, so that the cost to the consumer at this point is the same as buying that much more gasoline over the lifetime of the car. However, there is still some saving in oil consumption; and this amount will increase, provided use of these vehicles becomes more widespread.

NUCLEAR AND OTHER FORMS OF ENERGY

Whenever there is a discussion of energy consumption, the talk immediately jumps to wind power, solar power, hydrogen fuel cells and other possibilities. And in every case, this option is said to be without drawbacks and to be just around the corner.

The problem is that the corner seems to recede as we approach it. More sober discussions admit that the solution to the remaining technological problems of these "alternative" sources of energy is still some years away and that, even then, the energy produced will only compensate for a small percentage of the oil consumption of Americans.

Also wind and solar power require large amounts of land surface, and land surface is needed to house the ever-expanding population. Population, again, is driven by immigration. Thus, favoring unlimited immigration and favoring wind and solar power are incompatible with each other. Yet, those for favor the one almost invariably favor the other. Again, inconsistent thinking is being taught by Dhimmists in America's schools and colleges.

Nuclear power plants have disadvantages, including the problem of disposing of nuclear waste and their vulnerability to terrorist attacks from small airplanes and the devastation that would be produced if even one is hit. Also, Ralph Nader argues that a single phone call from a terrorist claiming to have placed a bomb in one of the plants, without disclosing which plant, would require shutting down all of the plants and making an inspection, with enormous disruption to thousands of homes and businesses that depend on the electricity from each plant.

Reclaiming the Government

To be forced to choose between a pro-Islamic Republican administration and a give-them-all-they-want Democrat administration is not democracy. In the last however-many elections, the American people have been forced to vote for the lesser of two evils. This is hardly self-government.

CREATE DEMOCRACY

There are two ways to establish government by the people and for the people.

One is for the people to take over one of the two Parties. This was almost done in the 2004 election by using the Internet.[810] Even in that case, however, the TV studios and the big money contributors co-opted the candidate once he had become the front runner. (In the 2004 case, this candidate later self-destructed anyway.)

The other way is to establish a third "moderate" Party to create the possibility of a "no" vote, so that people can demand some concessions from the two major Parties. The option of establishing a third party is no longer taken seriously, because attempts at establishing third parties have always failed in the past. But up to now, these third parties were usually special-issue parties that appealed to a small number of voters. A general interest party would be different. Also, some studies claim to show that most voters are "independents" or "moderates." If this is so, and if the third party were explicitly targeted at centrists or moderates, the third party would have a realistic chance of success. Also, some conditions are different now. First, the Internet makes communication among voters possible. Second, the level of dissatisfaction now is much higher. Third, the stakes are much higher.

Some observers have conjectured that the big money contributors have, in recent years, tried to rig elections by contributing money to the weakest of the opposing Party's candidates in the primaries, insuring that the weakest candidate will actually get the nomination of the opposing Party. Whether this is true, nobody knows, but it would explain the appalling nominees in some of the elections in the last thirty years. And it would be a powerful strategy, so there are incentives for doing it.

If this is happening, then the more promising candidates in either Party have *less* chance of getting the nomination. If some of them begin to figure this out and realize that they are *never* going to get nominated by their Party, they may be open to running on a third Party ticket, if a serious Moderate Party could be set up.

With a couple of strong candidates, perhaps one from each of the major Parties, a third Party could have a chance.

BREAK THE CONTROL OF CAMPAIGN CONTRIBUTORS

People have been trying to do this for years. Congress passes laws but is always careful to leave loopholes in those laws that allow the big money people to continue to buy influence.

One possibility that might have broken their influence was the line-item veto. Why? Because the way influence pays off is by "pork-barreling." Congressmen tack onto a bill a provision for funding this and that, where this and that will benefit a campaign contributor. They are unable *not* to do this, because they would lose funding and lose their next election. The line-item veto would have allowed the President to veto all those pork barrel add-ons but still let the bill that benefits the common good become law. Now, the only way to stop the pork-barrel items is to veto the whole bill and have Congress re-submit. But the re-submitted bill would also contain pork-barrel items. The line-item veto would have made the buying of Congressmen pointless and thus have greatly decreased the power of money people over Congress. The law was passed by the House and the Senate and signed by the President and vetoed by the Supreme Court.

Even with a line-item veto, campaign contributors would still try to buy the Presidential candidates, but it would be more difficult; and in the President's second term, the influence would be less effective, since there would be no coming election in which the President would need campaign contributions.

CAMPAIGN AGAINST ANY POLITICIAN WHO OPPOSES THE SECOND AMENDMENT

There are organizations already set up to support and fund candidates who *oppose* the Second Amendment. They have been very effective. They keep score on how many of "their" candidates won and how many lost Congressional elections.

The power of these organizations needs to be countered by citizen organizations to support candidates who *support* the Constitution. The websites of the anti-gun organizations need to be visited to see which candidates they are pushing. Those candidates must be opposed, not just at the ballot box but in the campaigns. Citizens need to get the word out that a candidate is opposed to the Second Amendment and thus probably "flexible" on the rest of the Constitution as well.

CAMPAIGN AGAINST ANY JUDGE WHO SUBVERTS OR IGNORES THE CONSTITUTION

Some judges are appointed, not elected. Nonetheless, as much publicity as possible needs to be given to judges who subvert the Constitution. At present, although judges operate publicly, no one knows what they are doing. This must change. Anti-American judges need to be given all the publicity that citizens can muster.

Also, citizens must pressure their Congressmen to impeach any judge or justice who attempts to re-write the Constitution or to thwart the will of Congress by overruling a law passed by Congress. One successful impeachment would probably be all it would take to bring the Supreme Court back into line. The Constitution is designed to be changed by the Amendment process, which has a number of checks built into the process to protect against usurpation of power by any branch of the federal government.

Supreme Court rewriting of the Constitution has become epidemic during the last forty years. And for the first hundred and fifty years, it was almost unheard of because the Justices were men of integrity. Given the Ideology of Submission, the integrity of the individual members of the Court can no longer be relied on as a check against unconstitutional judicial activity.

SUPPORT OR FIELD CANDIDATES WHO OPPOSE JIHAD AND IMMIGRATION

There are many candidates for Congress and even some for the Senate who favor more immigration, less enforcement of immigration laws, etc. With immigration come jihadists. These candidates must be defeated at the polls.

They cannot be defeated if no one is running against them. There is a great deal of public support at the present time for opposing immigration and opposing terrorists. Candidates could do very well running on such a platform. Candidates running on implicitly pro-terrorist, pro-immigration platforms must be forced to state publicly where they stand on the issues of terrorism and immigration, and their stance or their *lack of stance* against these problems must be publicized as widely as possible. Also, incumbents could have their voting records made public.

Obviously, these are possibilities that can only be engaged in at the present time. In the next few years, the ballot box will cease to be an option, since the Reconquistadores and the Islamists will be a majority in more and more Congressional districts.

If All Else Fails

To find out what is going to happen to the United States, we might look at other nations in which "minority" groups became majorities, gained positions in government and eventually took over the country. Among all the news that's not fit to print you might find, if you're lucky, the stories of what happened to the various African nations when aggrieved groups took control.

One of the first things they did, after the European governments left, was to disarm the white people who lived in those nations. The white people who didn't leave were the ones who couldn't leave. Everything they owned was in their houses and their land, and once the European government left, the value of their land was zero. They couldn't afford to move even if they could have found jobs in England or Belgium or Portugal or France. After their guns were confiscated, evictions, mass executions, rapes and arsons followed.

In the Congo, a film crew (the same people who made the celebrated documentary "Mondo Cane") happened to be in a town when a local elementary school was surrounded by soldiers and all the white children and teachers were forced to stay inside while the building was burned to the ground, burning all the children alive.[811] They were able to film the aftermath of some of the evictions, rapes, mass murders, etc. Even these were only a few of the incidents in that nation's emergence into "democracy"—an event celebrated in the Western world.

In Rhodesia, when it attained its independence and emerged into "democracy," white farmers and their families were massacred. A total media blackout covered up these atrocities, but a few books are now beginning to appear.[812] An American, who fought there as a mercenary soldier, has also reported it. He predicts the same for the United States.[813]

White people in South Africa were already living in walled communities when South Africa emerged into "democracy". Another total media blackout greeted this happy event. No mentioned of what happened to the white people has broken the media silence in America since that time.

When the state of Lebanon was created in the late 1940s, there were an equal number of Muslim Arabs and Christian Arabs. The parliament was therefore divided equally between Muslim seats and Christian seats. The Muslims increased their population faster than the Christians until they were a substantial majority. The Muslims then changed their demand from "equal representation for Muslims" to "one man, one vote." The tolerant and multicultural Christians of Lebanon did not see what was coming. The result in the 1970s was civil war, which the Islamists won. Their treatment of the Christians was hardly a model of tolerance and multiculturalism.[814]

In Bosnia, gangs of Muslims butchered entire villages of non-Muslims, and gangs of non-Muslims butchered entire villages of Muslims.[815]

These historical examples are not isolated incidents but are the norm. A recent collection of essays provides an extensive list of cases of peoples that have allowed Islam to become dominant in their societies or cities.[816]

Slavery. Another little-known but publicly available fact is that, even though slavery is outlawed by Muslim law, the practice still continues in lands occupied by Muslims.[817] You can witness this for yourself in a documentary film.[818] This film also makes it clear repeatedly that this practice is hardly race-neutral. Light-skinned people bring a much higher price than Black Africans.

The practice of Muslims enslaving white Europeans is not a novelty. It was rampant in the Mediterranean until the nineteenth century with an estimated one million Europeans sold into slavery. In the nineteenth century, the European powers fought back. France took over Algeria and Morocco, and Britain took over Egypt. That ended both piracy and white slave trading in the Mediterranean, although the practice continued in sub-Saharan Africa and Arabia. Several books have recently appeared detailing this practice.[819]

White slavery and sex slavery are also on the increase in the United States itself at the present time.[820] According to a 1999 report by the CIA, between 45,000 and 50,000 women and children are trafficked as slaves into the U. S. from Asia, Europe, Latin America, India and Africa every year.[821] A recent movie called Human Trafficking (2005) dramatizes the practice. Some claim that the trade has surpassed the drug trade in the amount of money involved. How extensive the Islamic involvement in this lucrative trade is, no one knows; or if they do, they are not telling.

What all this shows is that some sober thought should be given by Americans at the present time to their situation while there is still time for humane solutions. Waiting for the demographic proportions to get worse will only make the resolutions worse.

It's up to you

However, if the rest of America continues to slumber before their sit-coms and their spectator sports, what are you, as an individual, going to do when the Jihadists and/or the Reconquistadores make their move?

One option that Americans are already choosing is moving into a walled-off or "gated" community. This should offer a measure of safety, but it is a temporary measure. If the minorities who have become majorities vote themselves into office, the police and the military will be under their control. Jobs will be lost. Schools will be unsafe. The walls of the community will be useless.

Ironically, Islamists are already doing this themselves in Europe. They have taken over sections of cities or suburbs and more or less sealed them off. They are demanding self-government for those sections. But the self-government they have in mind is not just deciding conditions that affect them locally. They demand that their sections be governed by Sharia law. Englishmen are now waking up to the sound of the call to prayers over loud speakers in the Muslim sections.

Another option that too many Americans are already choosing is relocating to a "safe" state such as Wyoming or Idaho. Abandoning sections of America to the Reconquistadores or to the Islamists, though, is only the beginning of problems, not the solution. States throughout the union have already been "colonized" and the colonies are growing. Given the birthrate and the nonstop flow of immigrants, it is merely a matter of time—a short time—before the "safe" states are no longer safe.

So, the question is: what do you do then?

Self-defense. The thought of owning a gun, much less using one, is distasteful to Americans of the younger generation. This too is part of the Ideology of Submission: one should not defend oneself. One should submit. But in the not too distant past, guns were a respected part of American life. Much of the reason that the would-be criminals tended to leave other people alone in those days is that those other people, more often than not, were armed. It is safer to pick on a sitting duck than to risk the uncertain outcome of a gunfight.

Another sobering piece of information is the fact that in all cases of mass extermination of one group of people by another, the genocide has been preceded by gun confiscation. In 1911, Turkey established "gun control" and confiscated the weapons of the Armenians. From 1915 to 1917, an estimated one and a half million Armenians in Turkey were exterminated.

Germany established gun control in 1938 and proceeded to eliminate millions of Jews, Poles, Communists and other undesirables.

In the 1990s, Rwanda established gun control and proceeded to exterminate nearly one million Tutsis.

The United States has adopted a gradual approach, outlawing first one type of gun, then another; first automatic rifles and pistols, then semiautomatic. Look for total gun control legislation in the near future. The guns *already* outlawed are the ones citizens would need when and if the Jihadists make their move.

(Unfortunately, it is necessary to point out the obvious, that Jihadists and Reconquistadores do not buy their guns at the local gun shop. They wouldn't if they could. Their weapons are smuggled into the country. Gun control has no effect on them.)

CITIZEN PREPAREDNESS

There are now books on how to be prepared for terrorist attacks and other such disasters.[822] Even the Department of Homeland Security is putting out manuals on citizen preparedness: how to be prepared for chemical weapons attacks, how to be prepared for nuclear weapons attacks, how to be prepared for biological weapons attacks, etc. These are available on the Internet. By and large, the focus of these books and manuals is on single-hit type attacks like the World Trade Center.

If the Reconquistadores or the Jihadists attempt to establish continuing control over "their" section of the country by votes or by a guerrilla-style insurgency, the disaster will be ongoing, not a single-hit. Which section of this divided America will you be living in? Which section would you *like* to be living in? And what can you do about it *then*?

Now is the time to answer that last question by reflecting on the reality of what life would be like under Sharia law[823] or under a government controlled by La Raza ("for our race everything, for others nothing"). It may not be as "inclusive" or as "diverse" as you may think. Given the dominance of the Ideology of Submission, it is likely that, even in such an emergency, large numbers of Americans will quietly sink into dhimmitude, and for you and your family it will be too late. You will have no choice but to live under the Reconquistadores or under the Islamists.

The time to wake up is now. The bottom line is that when America is no longer the home of the brave, it will cease to be the land of the free.

Endnotes

1. Jayna Davis, *The Third Terrorist: The Middle East Connection to the Oklahoma City Bombing*, WND Books, 2004, p. 16.
2. Jack Cashill and James Sanders, *First Strike: TWA Flight 800 and the Attack on America*, WND Books, p. 3.
3. www.legacy.com
4. Leonard A. Cole, *The Anthrax Letters*, National Academy of Science, 2003.
5. Irshad Manji, *The Trouble with Islam*, St. Martin's Press, 2005, p. 42, 43.
6. Cf. Gregory M. Davis, *Religion of Peace?*, World Ahead Publishing, 2006.
7. Daniel Pipes, "Jihad and the professors," in Robert Spencer, ed., *The Myth of Islamic Tolerance: How Islamic Law Treats Non-Muslims*, Prometheus Books, 2005, p. 523.
8. ibid. p. 524.
9. ibid. p. 523.
10. Robert Spencer, "The myth of Islamic tolerance" in Robert Spencer, ed., *The Myth of Islamic Tolerance: How Islamic Law Treats Non-Muslims*, Prometheus Books, 2005, p. 30.
11. Robert Spencer, "The myth of Islamic tolerance" in Robert Spencer, ed., *The Myth of Islamic Tolerance: How Islamic Law Treats Non-Muslims*, Prometheus Books, 2005, p. 31.
12. Kenneth R. Timmerman, *Preachers of Hate*, Crown, 2003, p. 292.
13. Steven Emerson, *American Jihad*, Free Press, pb edition, 2003, p. 205

14. Timmerman, *op. cit.*, p. 291.
15. Daniel J. Flynn, *Why the Left Hates America*, Prima, 2002, p. 16.
16. Bat Ye'or, "Eurabia," in Robert Spencer, ed., *The Myth of Islamic Tolerance: How Islamic Law Treats Non-Muslims*, Prometheus Books, 2005, p. 292.
17. Quran, 5:55
18. Quran 4:76, 4:74
19. Quran, 44, 51–54
20. Quran, 25: 15–16
21. Quran 4:74
22. Bat Ye'or, "Past is prologue: the challenge of Islamism today," in Robert Spencer, ed., *The Myth of Islamic Tolerance: How Islamic Law Treats Non-Muslims*, Prometheus Books, 2005, p. 162.
23. Ibn Warraq, "The genesis of a myth" in Robert Spencer, ed., *The Myth of Islamic Tolerance: How Islamic Law Treats Non-Muslims*, Prometheus Books, 2005, p. 13.
24. Robert Spencer, "The myth of Islamic tolerance" in Robert Spencer, ed., *The Myth of Islamic Tolerance: How Islamic Law Treats Non-Muslims*, Prometheus Books, 2005, pp. 34–36.
25. Robert Spencer, "The myth of Islamic tolerance" in Robert Spencer, ed., *The Myth of Islamic Tolerance: How Islamic Law Treats Non-Muslims*, Prometheus Books, 2005, p. 32.
26. Robert Spencer, "The myth of Islamic tolerance" in Robert Spencer, ed., *The Myth of Islamic Tolerance: How Islamic Law Treats Non-Muslims*, Prometheus Books, 2005, p. 32.
27. Cf. Steven Emerson, *American Jihad*, Free Press, pb edition, 2003.
28. Steven Emerson, *American Jihad*, Free Press, pb edition, 2003, p. 169.

29. Mark Durie, "The dhimmitude of the west" in Robert Spencer, ed., *The Myth of Islamic Tolerance: How Islamic Law Treats Non-Muslims*, Prometheus Books, 2005, p. 279

30. Giles Milton, *White Gold: The extraordinary story of Thomas Pellow and Islam's one million white slaves*, Farrar, Straus & Giroux, 2004.

31. Bat Ye'or, "Historical amnesia," in Robert Spencer, ed., *The Myth of Islamic Tolerance: How Islamic Law Treats Non-Muslims*, Prometheus Books, 2005, pp. 108–109.

32. Bat Ye'or, "Israel, Christianity and Islam: the challenge of the future," in Robert Spencer, ed., *The Myth of Islamic Tolerance: How Islamic Law Treats Non-Muslims*, Prometheus Books, 2005, p. 570.

33. Michael D. Evans and Jerome R. Corsi, *Showdown with Nuclear Iran: Radical Islam's Messianic Mission to Destroy Israel and Cripple the United States*, Nelson, 2006.

34. See the website www.jihadwatch.org

35. Quran 9:29

36. Bat Ye'or, "Eurabia," in Robert Spencer, ed., *The Myth of Islamic Tolerance: How Islamic Law Treats Non-Muslims*, Prometheus Books, 2005, p. 289.

37. Jack Cashill and James Sanders, *First Strike: TWA Flight 800 and the Attack on America*, WND Books, 2003.

38. Paul Sperry, *Infiltration*, Nelson, 2005.

39. Sperry, op. cit., p. 216–223.

40. Sperry, op. cit., p. 266–273. Sperry names names and provides the details.

41. Robert Spencer, "The Islamic disinformation lobby: American Muslim groups' politically motivated distortions of Islam," in Robert Spencer, ed., *The Myth of Islamic Tolerance: How Islamic Law Treats Non-Muslims*, Prometheus Books, 2005, p. 526.

42. Bat Ye'or, "Historical amnesia," in Robert Spencer, ed., *The Myth of Islamic Tolerance: How Islamic Law Treats Non-Muslims*, Prometheus Books, 2005, p. 108.
43. Sperry, op. cit. p. 246–261.
44. Emerson, op. cit. pp. 203–240.
45. Sperry, op. cit. p. 247.
46. Sperry, op. cit. p. 247.
47. Sperry, ibid.
48. Bat Ye'or, "Historical anmesia," in Robert Spencer, ed., *The Myth of Islamic Tolerance: How Islamic Law Treats Non-Muslims*, Prometheus Books, 2005, p. 108.
49. Sperry, op. cit. pp. 266–273.
50. Sperry, op. cit. p. 273.
51. David G. Littman, "Islamism grows stronger at the United Nations," in Robert Spencer, ed., *The Myth of Islamic Tolerance: How Islamic Law Treats Non-Muslims*, Prometheus Books, 2005, pp. 308–315.
52. Bat Ye'or, "Historical anmesia," in Robert Spencer, ed., *The Myth of Islamic Tolerance: How Islamic Law Treats Non-Muslims*, Prometheus Books, 2005, p. 108.
53. Sperry, op. cit., p. 233–237, p. 244.
54. Sperry, op. cit. p. 235.
55. David Selbourne, *The Losing Battle with Islam*, Prometheus Books, 2005.
56. Steven Emerson, *American Jihad*, Free Press, pb edition, 2003, p. 160.
57. Emerson, op. cit., pp. 174–175.
58. According to a survey sponsored by CAIR, a Muslim PR organization.

59. Steven Emerson, *op cit.,* pp. 12–13.
60. Paul Sperry, *Infiltration*, Nelson, 2005, p. 104.
61. Harvey Kushner, *Holy War on the Home Front*, Sentinel, 2004, p. 57.
62. Kushner, *op. cit.,* p. 58.
63. Kushner, *op. cit.,* p. 59.
64. Emerson, *op. cit.* pp. 197–203.
65. Sperry, *op. cit.* pp. 64–65.
66. Kushner, *op. cit.* p. 6–7.
67. Sperry, *op. cit.* p. 295.
68. Sperry, *op. cit.* p. 312.
69. Sperry, *op. cit.* p. 316.
70. Sperry, *op. cit.* p. 318
71. Sperry, *op. cit.* p. 317.
72. Sperry, *op. cit.* p. 326.
73. Sperry, *op. cit.* p. 139.
74. Sperry, *op. cit.* p. 172.
75. Sperry, *op. cit.* p. 157.
76. Sperry, *op. cit.* p. 160
77. Sperry, *op. cit.* p. 172–173.
78. Sperry, *op. cit.* p. 173.
79. Sperry, *op. cit.* p. 185–190.
80. Sperry, *op. cit.* p. pp. 236 ff.
81. Sperry, *op. cit.* p. 219.
82. Sperry, *op. cit.* p. 221.
83. Sperry, *op. cit.* p. 222.

84. Sperry, *op. cit.* p. 295, 297.
85. Sperry, *op. cit.* p. 300.
86. Sperry, *op. cit.* p. 305.
87. Sperry, *op. cit.* p. 306.
88. Sperry, op. cit. p. 244.
89. Robert Spencer, "The myth of Islamic tolerance," in Robert Spencer, ed., *The Myth of Islamic Tolerance: How Islamic Law Treats Non-Muslims*, Prometheus Books, 2005, p. 37.
90. Bat Ye'or, "Beyond Munich: the spirit of Eurabia," in Robert Spencer, ed., *The Myth of Islamic Tolerance: How Islamic Law Treats Non-Muslims*, Prometheus Books, 2005, p. 287.
91. Bat Ye'or, "Islam, taboo, and dialogue," in Robert Spencer, ed., *The Myth of Islamic Tolerance: How Islamic Law Treats Non-Muslims*, Prometheus Books, 2005, p. 567.
92. William McGowan, *Coloring the News: How Political Correctness Has Corrupted American Journalism*, Encounter Press, 2002, p. 260.
93. McGowan, *op. cit.*, p. 260.
94. McGowan, *op. cit.*, p. 261.
95. McGowan, *op. cit.*, p. 261.
96. McGowan, *op. cit.*, p. 262.
97. McGowan, *op. cit.*, pp. 256–258.
98. McGowan, *op. cit.*, p. 251.
99. McGowan, *op. cit.*, pp. 251–252.
100. Mark Durie, "What is happening in Indonesia?" in Robert Spencer, ed., *The Myth of Islamic Tolerance: How Islamic Law Treats Non-Muslims*, Prometheus Books, 2005, pp. 264–265.
101. Serge Trifkovic, *Defeating Jihad*, Regina Orthodox Press, 2006, pp. 267–293.

102. Jonathan Alter, *Newsweek*, December 21, 2005.
103. Trifkovic, op. cit. pp. 273–274.
104. Trifkovic, op. cit. p. 279.
105. Trifkovic, op. cit. p. 281.
106. Trifkovic, op. cit. p. 288.
107. Trifkovic, op. cit. p. 289.
108. Trifkovic, op. cit. p. 290.
109. Trifkovic, op. cit. p. 290.
110. William Montgomery Watt, *The Majesty That Was Islam: The Islamic World 661–1100*, Sidgwick & Jackson Publishers, 1974, p. 257.
111. Bat Ye'or, "Beyond Munich: the spirit of Eurabia," in Robert Spencer, ed., *The Myth of Islamic Tolerance: How Islamic Law Treats Non-Muslims*, Prometheus Books, 2005, p. 288.
112. Bat Ye'or, quoted in Robert Spencer, "The myth of Islamic tolerance," in Robert Spencer, ed., *The Myth of Islamic Tolerance: How Islamic Law Treats Non-Muslims*, Prometheus Books, 2005, p. 31.
113. Bat Ye'or, *Islam and Dhimmitude: Where Civilization Collide*, Fairleigh Dickinson University Press, 2002, pp. 103–104.
114. Mark Durie, "The dhimmitude of the west" in Robert Spencer, ed., *The Myth of Islamic Tolerance: How Islamic Law Treats Non-Muslims*, Prometheus Books, 2005, p. 279.
115. Bruce Bauer, *While Europe Slept*, Doulbleday, 2006.
116. Ibn Warraq, "The genesis of a myth" in Robert Spencer, ed., *The Myth of Islamic Tolerance: How Islamic Law Treats Non-Muslims*, Prometheus Books, 2005, p. 15.
117. Robert Spencer, "The myth of Islamic tolerance," in Robert Spencer, ed., *The Myth of Islamic Tolerance: How Islamic Law Treats Non-Muslims*, Prometheus Books, 2005, p. 49.

118. Ibn Warraq, "The genesis of a myth" in Robert Spencer, ed., *The Myth of Islamic Tolerance: How Islamic Law Treats Non-Muslims*, Prometheus Books, 2005, p. 14.

119. Samuel Shahid, "Rights of non-Muslims in an Islamic state," in Robert Spencer, ed., *The Myth of Islamic Tolerance: How Islamic Law Treats Non-Muslims*, Prometheus Books, 2005, p. 59.

120. Cf. Toyin Falola and Ann Genova, *The Politics of the Global Oil Industry*, Praeger, 2005.

121. Ali M Ansari, *Confronting Iran: The Failure of American Foreign Policy and the Next Great Crisis in the Middle East*, Perseus, 2006.

122. Robert Baer, *Sleeping with the Devil*, Crown, 2003, pp. 86–87.

123. Michael T. Klare, *Blood and Oil: The Dangers and Consequences of America's Growing Dependency on Imported Petroleum*, Henry Holt, pb ed., 2005, p. 57.

124. Baer, *op. cit.*, p. 60.

125. Baer, *op. cit.*, p. 60.

126. Baer, *op. cit.*, p. 43–44.

127. Bruce Bawer, *While Europe Slept*, Doubleday, 2005.

128. Bat Ye'or, "Eurabia: the road to Munich", in Robert Spencer, ed., *The Myth of Islamic Tolerance: How Islamic Law Treats Non-Muslims*, Prometheus Books, 2005, p. 290.

129. Baer, *op. cit.*, p. 44.

130. Baer, *op. cit.*, p. 59.

131. Baer, *op. cit.*, p. 60.

132. Baer, *op. cit.*, p. 44.

133. Baer, *op. cit.*, p. 45.

134. Baer, *op. cit.*, p. 156.

135. Baer, *op. cit.*, p. 35.

136. Baer, *op. cit.*, p. 36.
137. Baer, *op. cit.*, p. 89.
138. Baer, *op. cit.*, p. 66–67.
139. Baer, *op. cit.*, p. 207.
140. Baer, *op. cit.*, p. 22.
141. Baer, *op. cit.*, p. 20.
142. Baer, *op. cit.*, p. 20.
143. Baer, *op. cit.*, p. 32.
144. Baer, *op. cit.*, p. 20.
145. Baer, *op. cit.*, p. 19.
146. Baer, *op. cit.*, p. 8.
147. Baer, *op. cit.*, p. 146.
148. Baer, *op. cit.*, p. 181.
149. Baer, *op. cit.*, pp. 146–147.
150. Baer, *op. cit.*, p. 168.
151. Baer, *op. cit.*, p. 35.
152. Robert Baer, *Sleeping with the Devil*, Crown, 2003, p. 207. cf. also, Matthew R. Simmons, *Twilight in the Desert*, Wiley, 2005.
153. Baer, *op. cit.*, p. 45.
154. Baer, *op. cit.*, p. 183.
155. Baer, *op. cit.*, p. 180.
156. Baer, *op. cit.*, p. 184.
157. Baer, *op. cit.*, p. 201.
158. Baer, *op. cit.*, p. 203.
159. Quoted in Baer, *op. cit.*, p. 209.

160. Michael T. Klare, *Blood and Oil: The Dangers and Consequences of America's Growing Dependency on Imported Petroleum*, Henry Holt, pb ed., 2005, p. 31.

161. Klare, *op. cit.*, p. 44–45.

162. Baer, *op. cit.*, p. xxviii.

163. Richard Heinberg, *The Party's Over: Oil, War and the Fate of Industrial Societies*, New Society Publishers, 2nd rev. ed., 2005.

164. Jon E. Dougherty, *Illegals: the Imminent Threat Posed by our Unsecured U.S.-Mexico Border*, WND Books, 2004, pp. 18–22.

165. Dougherty, *op. cit.*, pp. 48–51.

166. Hayworth, *Whatever It Takes: Illegal Immigration, Border Security, and the War on Terror*, Regnery, 2006, p. 13.

167. Hayworth, *op. cit.*, p. 13.

168. Hayworth, *op. cit.*, p. 33.

169. Hayworth, *op. cit.*, p. 3.

170. Horowitz, *The Professors*, Regnery, 2005, pp. 204–205.

171. Horowitz, *op. cit.*, pp. 202–205.

172. Hayworth, *op. cit.*, p. 32.

173. *New York Times*, October 4, 1993, p. 3; October 27, 1993, p. 6.

174. Fredrick C. Cuny, "Killing Chechnya," *New York Review of Books*, April 6, 1995, p. 14.

175. *New Jersey Star Ledger*, May 14, 1996, p. 8.

176. *Newsweek*, July 24, 1995.

177. "Gangstas in the Ranks," *Newsweek*, July 24, 1995, p. 48.

178. J. D. Hayworth, *Whatever It Takes: Illegal Immigration, Border Security, and the War on Terror*, Regnery, 2006, pp. 100–105.

179. Donald L. Barlett and James B. Steele, "Who Left the Door Open?", *Time Magazine*, September 20, 2004.

180. Hayworth, *op. cit.*, p. 2.
181. Darlene L. Fitzgerald and Peter S. Ferrara, *Bordergate: The story the government doesn't want you to read*, iUniverse, 2006.
182. Hayworth, *op. cit.*, p. 96.
183. Hayworth, *op. cit.*, p. 181.
184. Hayworth, *op. cit.*, p. 33.
185. Hayworth, *op. cit.*, p. 34.
186. Hayworth, *op. cit.*, p. 37–40,
187. Michael Powell, "New Tack Against Illegal Immigrants: Trespassing Charges," *Washington Post*, June 10, 2005.
188. Dan Walters, "New issues rekindle California's angst over illegal immigration," *Sacramento Bee*, July 20, 2005.
189. William McGowan, *Coloring the News: How Political Correctness Has Corrupted American Journalism.*, p. 192.
190. Hayworth, *op. cit.*, p. 187.
191. Virginia Deane Abernethy, PhD., on newsmax.com
192. Jon E. Dougherty, *Illegals: the Imminent Threat Posed by our Unsecured U.S.-Mexico Border*, WND Books, 2004, p. 84.
193. George J. Borjas, *Heaven's Door: Immigration Policy and the American Economy*, Princeton University Press, 2001.
194. Frosty Wooldrige, *Immigration's Unarmed Invasion*, Authorhouse, 2004, p. 2.
195. Hayworth, *op. cit.*, p. 29.
196. Peter Brimelow, *Alien Nation: Common Sense About America's Immigration Disaster*, Harper, 1996.
197. Virginia Deane Abernethy, PhD., newsmax.com
198. Hayworth, *op. cit.*, p. 189.
199. Hayworth, *op. cit.*, p. 19.

200. Hayworth, *op. cit.*, p. 19, 185.

201. Hayworth, *op. cit.*, p. 20.

202. Hayworth, *op. cit.*, p. 25.

203. George Borjas, "Increasing the Supply of Labor through Immigration: Measuring the impact on native-born workers," Center for Immigration Studies, May 2004.

204. Virginia Deane Abernethy, PhD., newsmax.com

205. Hayworth, *op. cit.*, p. 59.

206. Hayworth, *op. cit.*, p. 113.

207. Hayworth, *op. cit.*, p. 34.

208. Hayworth, *op. cit.*, p. 130.

209. Government Accountability Office, "Information on Criminal Aliens Incarcerated in Federal and State Prisons and Local Jails," March 29, 2005.

210. Government Accountability Office, "Information on Certain Illegal Aliens Arrested in the United States," April 2005.

211. Heather MacDonald, "The Illegal Alien Crime Wave," *City Journal*, Winter 2004.

212. Michelle Malkin, *Invasion: How America Still Welcomes Terrorists, Criminals, and Other Foreign Menaces to our Shores,*" Regnery, 2002, pp. 113–115.

213. Jeff Wilson, " 'Where's Mommy?' Child of Slain Policewoman Asks at Her Funeral," Associated Press, 15, February, 1991.

214. Michelle Malkin, *Invasion: How America Still Welcomes Terrorists, Criminals, and Other Foreign Menaces to our Shores,*" Regnery, 2002, pp. 117–119.

215. Stephanie K. Moran, "Timbrook's Family Talks of Their Loss," *Winchester Star*, 27, January 2001.

216. Jon E. Dougherty, *Illegals: The Imminent Threat Posed by Our Unsecured U.S.-Mexico Border*, Nelson, 2004.
217. Hayworth, *op. cit.*, p. 33.
218. Tom Tancredo, *In Mortal Danger: The Battle for America's Border and Security*, WND Books, 2006.
219. Madeleine Cosman, "Illegal Aliens and American Medicine", *Journal of American Physicians and Surgeons*, vol. 10, no. 1, Spring 2005.
220. Hayworth, ibid.
221. testimony before the Senate Select Committee on Intelligence, February 16, 2005.
222. Hayworth, *op. cit.*, p. 6.
223. Stewart Bell, *Cold Terror: How Canada Nurtures and Exports Terror Around the World*, Wiley, 2005.
224. Hayworth, *op. cit.*, p. 8.
225. Hayworth, *op. cit.*, p. 7.
226. Hayworth, *op. cit.*, pp. 8–9.
227. Hayworth, *op. cit.*, p. 9.
228. Hayworth, *op. cit.*, p. 10.
229. www.ImmigrationsHumanCost.org
230. www.ImmigrationsHumanCost.org
231. www.ImmigrationsHumanCost.org
232. www.ImmigrationsHumanCost.org
233. www.ImmigrationsHumanCost.org
234. www.ImmigrationsHumanCost.org
235. www.ImmigrationsHumanCost.org
236. www.ImmigrationsHumanCost.org
237. www.ImmigrationsHumanCost.org

238. www.ImmigrationsHumanCost.org
239. www.ImmigrationsHumanCost.org
240. www.ImmigrationsHumanCost.org
241. www.ImmigrationsHumanCost.org
242. www.ImmigrationsHumanCost.org
243. www.ImmigrationsHumanCost.org
244. www.ImmigrationsHumanCost.org
245. www.ImmigrationsHumanCost.org
246. www.ImmigrationsHumanCost.org
247. www.ImmigrationsHumanCost.org
248. www.ImmigrationsHumanCost.org
249. www.ImmigrationsHumanCost.org
250. www.ImmigrationsHumanCost.org
251. www.ImmigrationsHumanCost.org
252. www.ImmigrationsHumanCost.org
253. Hayworth, *op. cit.*, p. 61.
254. "Stonewall Simpson," *Wall Street Journal*, October 12, 1990.
255. Sarah Vowell, "Lock and Load," *New York Times*, July 23, 2005.
256. H. G. Reza, "Minor Offenders in Orange County Taken to Border Patrol," *Los Angeles Times*, February 12, 2001.
257. Peter Wallsten and Nicole Gaouette, "Immigration Rising on Bush's To-Do List," *Los Angeles Times*, July 24, 2005.
258. Dean E. Murphy, "Imagining Life Without Illegal Immigrants," *New York Times*, January 11, 2004.
259. Eduardo Porter, "Illegal Immigrants Are Bolstering Social Security with Billions," *New York Times*, April 5, 2005.

260. Hayworth, *op. cit.*, p. 74–77; compare Lloyd Grove, "Reliable Source," *Washington Post*, Februrary 15, 2002.
261. *Arizona Republic*, November 10, 2003.
262. *Arizona Republic*, October 17, 2005.
263. "Minutemess Patrol," *Arizona Republic*, March 9, 2005.
264. *Arizona Republic*, November 18, 2005.
265. William McGowan, *Coloring the News: How Political Correctness Has Corrupted American Journalism.*, pp. 183–185.
266. McGowan, *op. cit.*, p.. 186–187.
267. McGowan, *op. cit.*, p. 187.
268. Hayworth, *op. cit.*, p. 184
269. Hayworth, *op. cit.*, p. 184.
270. Hayworth, *op. cit.*, p. 181–182.
271. Hayworth, *op. cit.*, p. 125.
272. Hayworth, *op. cit.*, p. 125.
273. Hayworth, *op. cit.*, p. 27.
274. Hayworth, *op. cit.*, p. 124.
275. Hayworth, *op. cit.*, p. 124.
276. Hayworth, *op. cit.*, p. 106.
277. Hayworth, *op. cit.*, p. 123.
278. James G. Gimpel and James R. Edwards, *The Congressional Politics of Immigration Reform*, Longman, 1998.
279. J. D. Hayworth, *Whatever It Takes: Illegal Immigration, Border Security, and the War on Terror*, Regnery, 2006, p. 178.
280. Onell R. Soto and Leslie Berestein, "Border agent said to also be smuggler," *San Diego Union-Tribune*, August 5, 2005.

281. Jim Gilchrist and Jerome Corsi, *Minutemen: The Battle to Secure America's Borders*, World Ahead Publishing, 2006.
282. Paxton Quigley, *Stayin' Alive: Armed and Female in an Unsafe World*, Merril, 2005, p. 8.
283. Quigley, *op. cit.*, pp. 13–17.
284. Quigley, *op. cit.*, pp. 33–34.
285. Richard Stevens, *Dial 911 and Die*, Jews for the Preservation of Firearms Ownership, Inc., 1999.
286. Quigley, *op. cit.*, p. 47.
287. Aaron Zelman and Richard W. Stevens, *Death by "Gun Control": The Human Cost of Victim Disarmament*, Mazel Freedom Press, 2001, pp. 9–23..
288. Zelman and Stevens, *op. cit.*, p. 16.
289. Zelman and Stevens, *op. cit.*, p. 17.
290. Quigley, *op. cit.*, p. xvii.
291. Richard Poe, *The Seven Myths of Gun Control*, Prima Lifestyles, 2001.
292. Gary Kleck and Don B. Kates, *Armed: New Perspectives on Gun Control*, Prometheus Books, 2001.
293. John R. Lott, *The Bias Against Guns: Why Everything You've Heard About Gun Control is Wrong*, Regnery, 2003.
294. See www.liberty-belles.org, an organization of women gun-owners.
295. Zelman and Stevens, *op. cit.*, p. 250.
296. Tammy Bruce, *The New American Revolution*, William Morrow, 2005, p. 133.
297. Waters, *op. cit.*, p. 77.
298. Tammy Bruce, *op. cit.*, p. 134.

299. Paxton Quigley, *Stayin' Alive: Armed and Female in an Unsafe World*, Merril Press, 2005, p. xvii.
300. Charles Krauthammer, *Washington Post*, 16 April, 1996.
301. "Mr. Cuomo's Good Start on Guns," *New York Times*, 21 December, 1993, editorial, A26.
302. Tammy Bruce, *The New American Revolution*, William Morrow, 2005, p. 137.
303. Aaron S. Zelman and Richard W. Stevens, *Death by "Gun Control": The Human Cost of Victim Disarmament*, Mazel Freedom Press, 2001.
304. Paxton Quigley, *Stayin' Alive: Armed and Female in an Unsafe World*, Merril, 2005.
305. Senator Larry D. Craig, quoted in Robert A. Waters, *Guns Save Lives: True Stories of Americans Defending Their Lives With Firearms*, Loompanics Unlimited, 2002, p. vii.
306. Robert A. Waters, *Guns Save Lives: True Stories of Americans Defending Their Lives With Firearms*, Loompanics Unlimited, 2002, p. xiv.
307. Waters, *op. cit.*, pp. ix-x.
308. Waters, *op. cit.*, p. xi.
309. Waters, *op. cit.*, p. xiii.
310. John R. Lott, *The Bias Against Guns: Why Everything You've Heard About Gun Control is Wrong*, Regnery, 2003.
311. Quigley, *op. cit.*, p. xviii.
312. Quigley, *op. cit.*, pp. 1–4.
313. Quigley, *op. cit.*, p. 7.
314. Quigley, *op. cit.*, p. 9.
315. Quigley, *op. cit.*, p. 10.
316. Quigley, *op. cit.*, pp. 39–40.

317. Quigley, *op. cit.*, p. 77.
318. Quigley, *op. cit.*, p. 82.
319. Quigley, *op. cit.*, pp. 84–86.
320. Robert A. Waters, *The Best Defense: True Stories of Intended Victims Who Defended Themselves with a Firearm*, Cumberland House, 1998.
321. Robert A. Waters, *Guns Save Lives: True Stories of Americans Defending Their Lives with Firearms*, Loompanics, 2002.
322. Waters, *op. cit.*, p. 165.
323. Waters, *op. cit.*, p. 165.
324. Waters, *op. cit.*, p. 166.
325. Waters, *op. cit.*, p. 166.
326. Waters, *op. cit.*, pp. 56–59.
327. Waters, *op. cit.*, pp. 25–35.
328. Waters, *op. cit.*, pp. 80–81.
329. Waters, *op. cit.*, p. 101.
330. Waters, *op. cit.*, p. 102.
331. Waters, *op. cit.*, pp. 135–137.
332. Waters, *op. cit.*, pp. 138–141.
333. Waters, *op. cit.*, pp. 141–143.
334. Robert Spencer, "The myth of Islamic tolerance," in Robert Spencer, ed., *The Myth of Islamic Tolerance: How Islamic Law Treats Non-Muslims*, Prometheus Books, 2005, p. 49.
335. Aaron Zelman and Richard W. Stevens, *Death by "Gun Control": The Human Cost of Victim Disarmament*, Mazel Freedom Press, 2001, p. 3; 75–122.
336. Zelman and Stevens, *op. cit.*, pp. 133–148.
337. Zelman and Stevens, *op. cit.*, pp. 159–182.

338. Zelman and Stevens, *op. cit.*, pp. 149–158.
339. Zelman and Stevens, *op. cit.*, pp. 123–132.
340. Zelman and Stevens, *op. cit.*, pp. 47–62.
341. Zelman and Stevens, *op. cit.*, pp. 63–74.
342. www.adversity.net
343. William McGowan, *Coloring the News: How Political Correctness Has Corrupted American Journalism*, Encounter Books, 2002, p. 144.
344. Martin L. Gross, *The End of Sanity*, Avon, 1997, p. 230.
345. Linda Matthews, "When Being Best isn't Good Enough: Why Yapang Au Won't Be Going to Berkeley," *Los Angeles Times Magazine*, July 19, 1987, pp. 23–28.
346. www.adversity.net
347. www.adversity.net
348. www.adversity.net
349. www.adversity.net
350. www.adversity.net
351. www.adversity.net
352. www.adversity.net
353. www.adversity.net
354. www.adversity.net
355. www.adversity.net
356. www.adversity.net
357. www.adversity.net
358. www.adversity.net
359. www.adversity.net

360. Terry Eastland, *Ending Affirmative Action: The Case for Colorblind Justice*, Basic Books, 1997, pp. 4–5.
361. Eastland, *op. cit.*, pp. 3–4.
362. Frederick R. Lynch, *Invisible Victims*, Praeger, 1989.
363. Thomas Sowell, *Inside American Education: The Decline, The Deception, The Dogmas*, Free Press, 1993, pp. 132–173.
364. Terry Eastland, *Ending Affirmative Action: The Case for Colorblind Justice*, Basic Books, 1997, p. 87.
365. Fred M Hechinger, "On Campus, the Political Pendulum Swings Again," *New York Times*, September 22, 1987, p. C5.
366. Christina Salvin, "Takaki on Target," *City of a Hill*, January 25, 1990, p. 11.
367. Constance Casey and Renee Koury, "The Walls of Ivy," *San Jose Mercury News, West*, magazine section, February 17, 1991, p. 12.
368. Shelby Steele, "The Recoloring of Campus Life," *Harper's Magazine*, Februrary 1989, p. 47.
369. Lisa Birnbach with Annette Geldzahler, *Lisa Birnbach's New and Improved College Book*, Prentice-Hall, 1990, p. 283.
370. Thomas Sowell, *Inside American Education: The Decline, The Deception, The Dogmas*, Free Press, 1993, pp. 133.
371. Sowell, *op. cit.* p. 135.
372. Clyde W. Summers, "Preferential Admissions: An Unreal Solution to a Real problem," *University of Toledo Law Review*, Spring, 1970, p. 381.
373. David Riesman, *On Higher Education: The Academic Enterprise in an Era of Rising Student Consumerism*, Jossey-Bass, 1980, pp. 80–81.
374. Macklin Fleming and Louis Pollak, "An Exchange of Letters: The Black Quota at Yale Law School," *The Public Interest*, Spring, 1970, p. 44.

375. Macklin Fleming and Louis Pollak, *loc. cit.* p. 46.
376. Terry Eastland, *Ending Affirmative Action: The Case for Colorblind Justice*, Basic Books, 1997, p. 86.
377. Sowell, op. cit., p. 140.
378. Sowell, op. cit., p. 145.
379. Bernard D. David, *Storm Over Biology: Essays on Science, Sentiment and Public Policy*, Prometheus Books, 1986, p. 169.
380. Gross, *op. cit.*, p. 247.
381. Sowell, op. cit., p. 135.
382. See also, J. McWhorter, *Losing the Race: Self-Sabotage in Black America*, HarperCollins, 2001.
383. Thomas Sowell, "Colleges are skipping over competent Blacks to admit authentic ghetto types," *New York Times Magazine*, December 13, 1970, p. 49.
384. Roy Wilkins, "The Case Against Separatism: Black Jim Crow," in Bayard Rustin, *Black Studies: Myths and Realities*, A. Philip Randolph Fund, 1969, pp. 38, 39.
385. Eric Hoffer, *The True Believer*, Harper Perennial, 2004. Originally published in 1951.
386. John McWhorter, *Losing the Race: Self-Sabotage in Black America*, HarperCollins, 2001
387. Frederick Lynch, *Invisible Victims: White Males and the Crisis of Affirmative Action*, Prager, 1991.
388. William McGowan, *Coloring the News: How Political Correctness Has Corrupted American Journalism*, Encounter Press, 2002, p. 146.
389. Paul Craig Roberts and Lawrence M. Stratton, *The New Color Line: How Quotas and Privilege Destroy Democracy*, Regnery, 1995, p. 82.
390. McGowan, *op. cit.*, p. 146.
391. McGowan, *op. cit.*, p. 147.

392. McGowan, *op. cit.*, p. 161.
393. McGowan, *op. cit.*, p. 160.
394. McGowan, *op. cit.*, pp. 160–161.
395. McGowan, *op. cit.*, p. 161.
396. McGowan, *op. cit.*, p. 164.
397. McGowan, *op. cit.*, p. 165.
398. McGowan, *op. cit.*, pp. 165–166.
399. McGowan, *op. cit.*, p. 166.
400. McGowan, *op. cit.*, p. 167.
401. McGowan, *op. cit.*, pp. 167–168.
402. William McGowan, *Coloring the News: How Political Correctness Has Corrupted American Journalism*, Encounter Press, 2002, p. 258.
403. McGowan, *op. cit.*, p. 167.
404. Terry Eastland, *Ending Affirmative Action: The Case for Colorblind Justice*, Basic Books, 1997, p. 150.
405. Gross, *op. cit.*, p. 230.
406. Eastland, *op. cit.*, p. 184.
407. William Julius Wilson, *The Truly Disadvantaged*, University of Chicago Press, 1978, pp. 18–19.
408. Gross, *op. cit.*, p. 235.
409. William McGowan, *Coloring the News*, Encounter Books, 2002, pp. 196–197.
410. Thomas Sowell, *Inside American Education, the Decline, The Deceptions, The Dogmas*, Free Press, 1993, pp. 70–71.
411. Quoted in D'Souza, *The End of Racism: Principles for a Multiracial Society*, Free Press, 1995, p. 344.
412. Patrick J. Buchanan, *The Death of the West*, St. Martin's Press, 2002, pp. 130–131.

413. Alan C. Kors and Harvey A. Silvergate, *The Shadow University: The Betrayal of Liberty on America's Campuses*, Free Press, 1998, p. 213.
414. Daniel J. Flynn, *Why the Left Hates America*, Prima Forum, 2002, pp. 147–183.
415. Peter Wood, *Diversity: the Invention of a Concept*, Encounter Books, 2004.
416. Martin L. Gross, *The End of Sanity: Social and Cultural Madness in America*, Avon, 1997, p. 161.
417. Rosalie Pedalino Porter, *Forked Tongue: The Politics of Bilingual Education*, Basic Books, 1990, pp. 33, 123–124, 186.
418. Gross, *op. cit.*, pp. 167–168.
419. Gross, *op. cit.*, pp. 169–170.
420. Gross, *op. cit.*, p. 172.
421. Gross, *op. cit.*, p. 123.
422. William McGowan, *Coloring the News: How Political Correctness Has Corrupted American Journalism*, Encounter Press, 2002, p. 188.
423. McGowan, *op. cit.*, p. 189.
424. McGowan, *op. cit.*, p. 189.
425. McGowan, *op. cit.*, p. 190.
426. McGowan, *op. cit.*, pp. 191–192.
427. McGowan, *op. cit.*, p. 193.
428. McGowan, *op. cit.*, pp. 196–197.
429. Oriana Fallaci, *The Force of Reason*, Rizzoli, 2006.
430. Cf. Brian Barry, *Culture and Equality: An Egalitarian Critique of Multiculturalism*, Harvard University Press, 2002.
431. Daniel J. Flynn, *Why the Left Hates America*, Prima, p 23.
432. Flynn, *op. cit.* p. 25.
433. Flynn, *op. cit.* p. 30.

434. Daniel A. Farber and Suzanna Sherry, *Beyond All Reason: The Radical Assault on Truth in American Law*, Oxford University Press, 1997, p. 119.

435. Quoted in George Roche, *The Fall of the Ivory Tower*, Regnery, 1994, p. 200.

436. Quoted in D'Souza, *What's So Great About America*, Regnery, 2002, p. 38.

437. Quoted in Buchanan, *The Death of the West*, p. 161.

438. Daniel J. Flynn, *Why the Left Hates America*, Prima, p. 17.

439. Joshua Greene, "Forget the Media and See the Truth," *Daily Athenaeum*, September 13, 2001, p. 4.

440. Flynn, *op. cit.* p. 18.

441. Flynn, *op. cit.* p. 18.

442. Flynn, *op. cit.* p. 18.

443. Flynn, *op. cit.* pp. 18–19.

444. Flynn, *op. cit.* p. 19.

445. Flynn, *op. cit.* p. 20.

446. Peter Beinart, "Talk Show," *New Republic*, October 22, 2001, p. 6.

447. Flynn, *op. cit.* p. 21–22.

448. Lisa Mann, "America is not a nation of innocents," *Old Gold and Black*, September 13, 2001, p. 10.

449. Flynn, *op. cit.* p. 23.

450. Flynn, *op. cit.* p. 22.

451. Flynn, *op. cit.* p. 26–28.

452. Flynn, *op. cit.* p. 29.

453. Flynn, *op. cit.* p. 30.

454. Flynn, *op. cit.* p. 31.

455. Martin L. Gross, *The End of Sanity*, Avon, p. 130.
456. Gross, *op. cit.*, p. 123.
457. Robert Patterson, *Reckless Disregard*, Regnery, 2004, p. 104.
458. Patterson, *op. cit.*, p. 104.
459. Patterson, *op. cit.*, p. 104.
460. Patterson, *op. cit.*, p. 105.
461. Patterson, *op. cit.*, p. 106.
462. Patterson, *op. cit.*, p. 107.
463. Patterson, *op. cit.*, p. 108.
464. Patterson, *op. cit.*, p. 108.
465. Bat Ye'or, "Islam, taboo, and dialogue," in Robert Spencer, ed., *The Myth of Islamic Tolerance: How Islamic Law Treats Non-Muslims*, Prometheus Books, 2005, p. 566.
466. Alison Jagger, *Feminist Politics and Human Nature*, Rowman and Littlefield, 1983, p. 44.
467. Marilyn Friedman, "Does Sommers Like Women? More on Liberalism, Gender Hierarchy, and Scarlett O'Hara," *Journal of Social Philosophy*, vol. 21, no. 2, Fall-Winter 1990, p. 83.
468. Harry Stein, *How I Accidentally Joined the Vast Right-wing Conspiracy (and found inner peace)*, HarperCollins, 2000, p. 2.
469. Alan C. Kors and Harvey A. Silvergate, *The Shadow University: The Betrayal of Liberty on America's Campuses*, Free Press, 1998, p. 227.
470. Eric Hoffer, *The True Believer*, Harper Perennial, 2004. Originally published in 1951.
471. Thomas Sowell, *Education in America*, Free Press, 1993, p. 84.
472. Christina Hoff Sommers, *Who Stole Feminism? How Women Have Betrayed Women*, Simon and Schuster, 1995.
473. Sommers, op. cit., pp. 64–65.

474. Alan C. Kors and Harvey A. Silvergate, *The Shadow University: The Betrayal of Liberty on America's Campuses*, Free Press, 1998, pp. 222–223.
475. Tammy Bruce, *The New Thought Police*, Crown, 2001, p. 111.
476. Kors and Silvergate, *op. cit.*, p. 211.
477. Heather MacDonald, *Wall Street Journal*, September 29, 1992.
478. Mary Maples Dunn, "College Response to Bias Incidents," AcaMEDIA, December 19, 1992.
479. Martin L. Gross, *The End of Sanity*, Avon, 1997, p. 130.
480. Kors and Silvergate, *op. cit.*, p. 227.
481. Abraham M. Miller, "Inside the Sensitivity Session," *The Intercollegiate Review*, Fall, 1992; Walter Williams, "Gestapo Tactics Used to Crush Campus Dissent," *Cincinnati Enquirer*, Feb. 21, 1993; Lloyd Billingsley, "Sensitivity Police Brutality," *Heterodoxy*, September, 1992; Nicholas and James Damask, "Inside Room 101: Anatomy of a Sensitivity Training Cover-up," *The World & I*, November; 1994.
482. Kors and Silvergte, *op. cit.*, p. 153.
483. Kors and Silvergte, *op. cit.*, p. 156.
484. Kors and Silvergte, *op. cit.*, p. 156.
485. Kors and Silvergte, *op. cit.*, p. 158.
486. Tammy Bruce, *The New Thought Police*, Crown, 2001, p. 28.
487. Donald Alexander Downs, *Restoring Free Speech and Liberty on Campus*, Cambridge University Press, 2005, pp. 50 ff.
488. Nat Hentoff, *Free Speech for Me but not for Thee*, Harper, 1992.
489. Alan C. Kors and Harvey A. Silvergate, *The Shadow University: The Betrayal of Liberty on America's Campuses*, Free Press, 1998, pp. 114–115.
490. Downs, *op. cit.*, p. 56.
491. Downs, *op. cit.*, p. 59.

492. Andrew Zappala, "Free Speech Violations: A Sampling," *Campus*, Fall 1990, p. 6.
493. Kors and Silvergate, *op. cit.*, p. 120.
494. Downs, *op. cit.*, p. 63.
495. Alan C. Kors and Harvey A. Silvergate, *The Shadow University: The Betrayal of Liberty on America's Campuses*, Free Press, 1998, p. 128.
496. Sommers, *op. cit.* pp. 107.
497. Tammy Bruce, *The New Thought Police*, Crown, 2001, p. 214.
498. Sommers, *op. cit.* p. 111.
499. Alan C. Kors and Harvey A. Silvergate, *The Shadow University: The Betrayal of Liberty on America's Campuses*, Free Press, 1998, p. 132.
500. Kors and Silvergte, *op. cit.*, p. 145.
501. Kors and Silvergte, *op. cit.*, p. 149.
502. Kors and Silvergte, *op. cit.*, p. 152.
503. Kors and Silvergte, *op. cit.*, p. 149.
504. Kors and Silvergte, *op. cit.*, p. 150–152.
505. Kors and Silvergte, *op. cit.*, p. 152.
506. Kors and Silvergte, *op. cit.*, p. 154.
507. Kors and Silvergte, *op. cit.*, p. 156.
508. Kors and Silvergte, *op. cit.*, pp. 159–160.
509. Sommers, *op. cit.* pp. 107.
510. Sommers, *op. cit.* p. 113.
511. Sommers, *op. cit.* pp. 113–114.
512. Mason Weaver, *It's OK to Leave the Plantation*, Reeder Publications, 1998.
513. Alan C. Kors and Harvey A. Silvergate, *The Shadow University: The Betrayal of Liberty on America's Campuses*, Free Press, 1998, p. 6.

514. Thomas Sowell, *Inside American Education*, Free Press, 1993, p. 177.
515. Sowell, *op. cit.*, p. 177.
516. Thomas Sowell, *Inside American Education*, Free Press, 1993, p. 176.
517. Sowell, *op. cit.*, p. 176.
518. Daniel J. Flynn, *Why the Left Hates America*, Prima, 2002, p. 6.
519. Flynn, *op. cit.*, p. 6.
520. Flynn, *op. cit.*, p. 7.
521. Flynn, *op. cit.*, p. 8.
522. Alan Charles Kors and Harvey A. Silvergate, *The Shadow University: The Betrayal of Liberty on America's Campuses*, Free Press, 1998.
523. Sommers, *op. cit.* pp. 114–115.
524. Kors and Silvergate, *op. cit.*, p. 278.
525. Kors and Silvergate, *op. cit.*, p. 298.
526. Kors and Silvergate, *op. cit.*, p. 296
527. Kors and Silvergate, *op. cit.*, pp. 296—300.
528. Kors and Silvergate, *op. cit.*, pp. 300–302.
529. Kors and Silvergate, *op. cit.*, pp. 300–302.
530. Kors and Silvergate, *op. cit.*, pp. 305–306.
531. James T. Evans, *EduCrisis!*, West Eagle Publishing, 1999, p. 2.
532. Christina Hoff Sommers, *Who Stole Feminism? How Women Have Betrayed Women*, Simon and Schuster, 1995, pp. 50–73.
533. Sommers, *op. cit.*, p. 54.
534. Sommers, *op. cit.* pp. 52–53.

535. Allan Bloom, *The Closing of the American Mind: How Higher Education Has Betrayed Democracy and Impoverished the Souls of Today's Students*, Simon and Schuster, 1987, p. 249.

536. Alan Sokol, *Fashionable Nonsense: Postmodern Intellectuals' Abuse of Science*, Picador, 1999.

537. Sommers, *op. cit.*, p. 50.

538. Stanley Fish, *Doing What Comes Naturally*, Duke University Press, 1989, p. 176.

539. Robert R. Detlefsen, *The New Republic*, April 10, 1989.

540. Daniel A. Faber and Suzanna Sherry, *Beyond All Reason: The Radical Assault on Truth in American Law*, Oxford University Press, 1997.

541. Gerda Lerner, *The Creation of Patriarchy*, Oxford University Press, 1986, p. 224.

542. George Levine, *et. al.*, *Speaking for the Humanities*, American Council of Learned Societies, occasional paper no. 7, 1989.

543. Sommers, *op. cit.*, p. 76.

544. Sommers, *op. cit.*, p. 63.

545. Linda Alcoff and Elizabeth Potter, *Feminist Epistemologies*, Routledge, 1993.

546. Sandra Harding, *The Science Question in Feminism*, Cornell University Press, 1986, p. 113.

547. Sommers, *op. cit.*, p. 83.

548. Thomas S. Kuhn, *The Structure of Scientific Revolutions*, 2nd ed., University of Chicago Press, 1970, p. 206.

549. Willis Harman, *Global Mind Change*, Berrett-Koehler Publishers, 2nd ed., 2004.

550. John McWhorter, *Losing the Race: Self-Sabotage in Black America*, HarperCollins, 2000, p. 223.

551. Mary Field Belenky, Blythe McVicker Clinchy, Nancy Rule Goldberger, and Jill Martuck Tarule, *Women's Ways of Knowing*, Basic Books, 1986, p. 104.

552. Sommers, *op. cit.*, p. 67.

553. William McGowan, *Coloring the News: How Political Correctness Has Corrupted American Journalism*, Encounter Press, 2002, p. 167.

554. Sommers, *op. cit.*, p. 71.

555. Virginia Held, "Feminism and Epistemology: Recent Work on the Connection between Gender and Knowledge," *Philosophy and Public Affairs*, 14, no. 3, p. 299.

556. Cf. Linda Alcoff and Elizabeth Potter, eds., *Feminist Epistemologies*, Routledge, 1993.

557. Sommers, *op. cit.*, p. 69.

558. Sommers, *op. cit.*, p. 62.

559. David O. Sacks and Peter A. Theil, *The Diversity Myth: "Multiculturalism" and the Politics of Intolerance at Stanford*, The Independent Institute, 1995, pp. xx, 2–6.

560. Sommers, *op. cit.*, p. 98.

561. Sommers, *op. cit.*, pp. 51–52.

562. Caryn McTighe Musil, *The Courage to Question: Women's Studies and Student Learning*, Association of American Colleges, 1992.

563. Noretta Koetge, ed., *A House Built on Sand: Exposing Postmodernist Myths About Science*, Oxford University Press, 2nd ed., 2000.

564. See Mark Kelman, *A Guide to Critical Legal Studies*, Harvard, 1998, pp. 4–5.

565. Donald Alexander Downs, *Restoring Free Speech and Liberty on Campus*, Cambridge University Press, 2005, p. 48

566. Sommers, *op. cit.*, p. 82.

567. Sommers, *op. cit.*, p. 109.

568. Sommers, *op. cit.*, p. 107.
569. Roger Scuton, Angela Ellis-Jones, and Dennis O'Keefe, *Education and Indoctrination*, Sherwood Press, 1985.
570. Sommers, *op. cit.*, p. 94.
571. Dale M. Bauer, "The Other 'F' Word: The Feminist in the Classroom," *College English*, 52, no. 4 (April 1990), p. 385.
572. Sommers, *op. cit.*, p. 65.
573. Stanley Fish, *Is there a text in this class? The Authority of Interpretive Communities*, Harvard University Press, 1980, p. 16.
574. Stanley Fish, *Doing What Comes Naturally*, Duke University Press, 1989, p. 10.
575. Stanley Fish, *Doing What Comes Naturally*, Duke University Press, 1989, p. 340.
576. Stanley Fish, *Doing What Comes Naturally*, Duke University Press, 1989, p. 4.
577. Barbara Herrnstein Smith, *Contingencies of Value*, Harvard University Press, 1988, pp. 112–113.
578. Jamie Whyte, *Crimes Against Logic*, McGraw-Hill, 2004.
579. Sommers, *op. cit.* p. 71.
580. See Thomas Nagel, *The Last Word*, Oxford University Press, 1997 and John M. Ellis, *Against Deconstruction*, Princeton University Press, 1989.
581. Stanley Fish, *Doing What Comes Naturally*, Duke University Press, 1989, p. 4.
582. Donald Alexander Downs, *Restoring Free Speech and Liberty on Campus*, Cambridge University Press, 2005, p. 52.
583. Downs, *op. cit.* p. 48.
584. Ihab Hassan, "POSTmodernISM," in *Paracriticisms: Seven Speculations of Our Time*, Univ. of Illinois Press, 1975.

585. Joel Turtell, *Public Schools, Public Menace*, Liberty Books, 2005, pp. 78, 80.

586. Turtell, *op. cit.* p. 76.

587. Berit Kjos, *Brave New Schools*, Harvest Books, 1995, p. 87.

588. Kjos, *op. cit.*, pp. 89–92.

589. Thomas Sowell, "Indoctrinating the Children", *Forbes*, February 1, 1993, p. 65.

590. Kjos, *op. cit.*, p. 55.

591. Marlin Maddoux, *Public Education Against America: the Hidden Agenda*, Whitaker House, 2006, p. 121.

592. Maddoux, *op. cit.* pp. 120–123.

593. Alison Hornstein, "The Questions We Should Be Asking," *Newsweek*, December 17, 2001, p. 14.

594. Joel Turtell, *Public Schools, Public Menace*, Liberty Books, 2005, pp. 56–60.

595. Thomas Sowell, *Inside American Education: The Decline, The Deception, The Dogmas*, Free Press, 1993, p. 3.

596. Sowell, *op. cit.*, p. 1.

597. Sowell, *op. cit.*, p. 4.

598. Diane Ravitch, *The Schools We Deserve: Reflections on the Educational Crisis of Our Time*, Basic Books, 1985, p. 8.

599. Karen DeWitt, "Verbal Scores Hit New Low in Scholastic Aptitude Tests," *New York Times*, August 27, 1991, pp. 1ff.

600. James T. Evans, *EduCrisis!*, West Eagle Publishing, 1999, pp. 1, 3–4.

601. Sommers, *op. cit.* pp. 61–62.

602. Diane Ravitch and Chester E. Finn, Jr., *What do Our 17-year-olds Know?*, Harper, 1987, pp. 53, 62.

603. Evans, *op. cit.*, p. 2.
604. Evans, *op. cit.*, p. 10.
605. Evans, *op. cit.*, p. 11.
606. *The New York Times*, January 30, 1998.
607. Evans, *op. cit.*, p. 25.
608. Charles J. Sykes, *Dumbing Down Our Kids*, St. Martin's Press, 1996.
609. Milton R. Rokeach, *The Open and Closed Mind*, Basic Books, 1960.
610. Tammy Bruce, *The New Thought Police*, Crown, 2001, pp. 211–212.
611. Milton Rokeach, *The Three Christs of Ypsilanti*, Knopf, 1964.
612. Eric Hoffer, *The True Believer*, Harper Perennial, 2004. Originally published in 1951.
613. Marlin Maddoux, *Public Education Against America: the Hidden Agenda*, Whitaker House, 2006, pp. 19–30.
614. Eric Hoffer, *The True Believer*, Harper Perennial, 2004. Originally published in 1951.
615. Leon Festinger, *When Prophecy Fails*, HarperCollins, 1964.
616. James T. Stephens, *EduCrisis!*, West Eagle Publishing, 1999, p. 165.
617. Rita Kramer, *Ed School Follies: The Miseducation of America's Teachers*, Free Press, 1991.
618. Stephens, *op. cit.*, pp. 165–166.
619. David Horowitz, *The Professors*, Regnery, 2006, pp. 296–299.
620. Stephens, *op. cit.*, pp. 177–178.
621. Horowitz, *op. cit.*, p. 32.
622. Horowitz, *op. cit.*, p. 64.

623. Joel Turtell, *Public Schools, Public Menace*, Liberty Books, 2005, pp. 86, 89, 93.
624. Turtell, *op. cit.*, p. 89
625. James T. Stephens, *EduCrisis!*, West Eagle Publishing, 1999, p. 134.
626. Stephens, *op. cit.*, p. 99.
627. Stephens, *op. cit.*, p. 135.
628. *Newsweek*, August 7, 1995.
629. Turtell, *op. cit.*, p. 90.
630. Turtell, *op. cit.*, p. 92.
631. Stephens, *op. cit.*, p. 162.
632. Turtell, *op. cit.*, pp. 97–98.
633. Turtell, *op. cit.*, pp. 98–99.
634. B. K. Eakman, "EDUCATION: Bushwacking Johnny," *Chronicles Magazine*, September 2002.
635. Marlin Maddoux, *Public Education Against America: the Hidden Agenda*, Whitaker House, 2006, p. 135.
636. Turtell, *op. cit.*, pp. 127–159.
637. Peter R. Breggin, *Talking Back to Ritalin: What Doctors Aren't Telling You about Stimulants and ADHD*, Perseus, rev. ed., 2001, p. 128.
638. Breggin, *op. cit.* pp. 13–14.
639. Breggin, *op. cit.* p. 24.
640. Breggin, *op. cit.* p. 7.
641. Turtell, *op. cit.*, pp. 138–139.
642. Turtell, *op. cit.*, p. 139.
643. Turtell, *op. cit.*, pp. 145, 147.

644. Turtell, *op. cit.*, p. 134.
645. Breggin, *op. cit.* pp. 217–128, 249. cf. also, Breggin, *Toxic Psychiatry*, 1991.
646. Turtell, *op. cit.*, p. 43.
647. Turtell, *op. cit.*, p. 41.
648. Turtell, *op. cit.*, p. 41.
649. Cited in Turtell, *op. cit.*, p. 43.
650. Charles J. Sykes, *Dumbing Down Our Kids*, St. Martin's, 1995, p. 171.
651. Bernard Goldberg, *100 People Who Are Screwing Up America*, HarperCollins, 2005, pp. 182–186.
652. Aaron Zelman and Richard W. Stevens, *Death by "Gun Control": The Human Cost of Victim Disarmament*, Mazel Freedom Press, 2001, pp. 15–16.
653. Zelman and Stevens, *op. cit.*, p. 16.
654. Turtell, *op. cit.*, p. 107.
655. Joel Turtell, *Public Schools, Public Menace*, Liberty Books, 2005, p. 84.
656. Sykes, *op. cit.*, pp. 157–158.
657. Sommers, *op. cit.*, pp. 51–52.
658. Horowitz, *op. cit.*, pp. 197–201.
659. Christina Hoff Sommers, *Who Stole Feminism?*, Simon & Schuster, 1995, chapter 3.
660. Richard Long, "All that is solid melts into air," paper presented at a conference on academic freedom, University of Wisconsin, February 2002, p. 3.
661. Donald Alexander Downs, *Restoring Free Speech and Liberty on Campus*, Cambridge University Press, 2005, p. 31.

662. cf. Mary Leftkowitz, *Not Out of Africa*, Basic Books, 1996, pp. 164–167.
663. Downs, *op. cit.*, 2005, p. 44.
664. Elisabeth Lasch-Quinn, *Race Experts: How Racial Etiquette, Sensitivity Training and New Age Therapy Hijacked the Civil Rights Revolution*, Norton, 2001, p. 81.
665. Downs, *op. cit.*, p. 47.
666. Mary Lefkowitz, *Not Out of Africa: How Afrocentrism Became an Excuse to Teach Myth As History*, Basic Books, 1996.
667. Lefkowitz, *op. cit.*, p. 156.
668. Lefkowitz, *op. cit.*, p. 157.
669. Sommers, *op. cit.*, pp. 58.
670. Horowitz, *op. cit.*, pp. 358–364.
671. Sally Shuttleworth, "Critical Commentary" to George Eliot's *The Mill on the Floss*, Rutledge, 1991, p. 490.
672. Shuttleworth, *loc. cit.*, p. 491.
673. Shuttleworth, *loc. cit.*, pp. 499–500.
674. Shuttleworth, *loc. cit.*, p. 502.
675. Shuttleworth, *loc. cit.*, p. 508.
676. Horowitz, *op. cit.*, pp. 71–73.
677. Horowitz, *op. cit.*, p. 120.
678. Horowitz, *op. cit.*, p. 230.
679. Horowitz, *op. cit.*, p. 24.
680. Horowitz, *op. cit.*, pp. 40–43.
681. Horowitz, *op. cit.*, pp. 329–332.
682. Horowitz, *op. cit.*, p. 53.
683. Horowitz, *op. cit.*, pp. 100–102.

684. Horowitz, *op. cit.*, pp. 110–114.
685. Horowitz, *op. cit.*, p. 150.
686. Horowitz, *op. cit.*, pp. 152–153.
687. David Horowitz, *The Professors*, Regnery, 2006, p. 306.
688. Horowitz, *op. cit.*, pp. 115–119.
689. Horowitz, *op. cit.*, pp. 190–191.
690. Horowitz, *op. cit.*, pp. 241–244.
691. Horowitz, *op. cit.*
692. Horowitz, *op. cit.*, pp. 300–303.
693. Horowitz, *op. cit.*, pp. 288–291.
694. Horowitz, *op. cit.*, pp. 202–205.
695. Horowitz, *op. cit.*, pp. 204–205.
696. Horowitz, *The Professors*, Regnery, 2006.
697. Horowitz, *op. cit.*, p. 180.
698. Horowitz, *op. cit.*, pp. 84–88.
699. Horowitz, *op. cit.*, pp. 160–161.
700. Horowitz, *op. cit.*, p. 123.
701. Horowitz, *op. cit.*, pp. 284–287.
702. Horowitz, *op. cit.*, pp. 319–322.
703. Horowitz, *op. cit.*, pp. 342–344.
704. Bernard Goldberg, *100 People Who Are Screwing Up America*, HarperCollins, 2005, p. 80.
705. Horowitz, *op. cit.*, pp. 35–37.
706. Horowitz, *op. cit.*, pp. 120,168.
707. Bernard Goldberg, *100 People Who Are Screwing Up America*, HarperCollins, 2005, pp. 69–72.

708. Horowitz, *op. cit.*, pp. 234–237.
709. Horowitz, *op. cit.*, pp. 271–276.
710. David Horowitz, *The Professors*, Regnery, 2006, pp. 339–340.
711. Horowitz, *op. cit.*, p. 245
712. Horowitz, *op. cit.*, pp. 262–265.
713. Horowitz, *op. cit.*, pp. 215–218.
714. Horowitz, *op. cit.*, pp. 339–341.
715. John Powers, "Bleak Chic," *American Film*, March 1987, p. 48.
716. Michael Medved, *Hollywood vs. America*, HarperCollins, 1992, p. 217.
717. Medved, *op. cit.*, p. 216.
718. Medved, *op. cit.*, p. 223.
719. Medved, *op. cit.*, p. 277.
720. Medved, *op. cit.*, pp. 277–279.
721. Linda S. Lichter, S. Robert Lichter, and Stanley Rothman, "Hollywood and America: The Odd Couple," *Public Opinion*, December/January 1983, p. 58.
722. Medved, *op. cit.*, p. 218.
723. Medved, *op. cit.*, p. 233.
724. S. Robert Lichter, Linda S. Lichter, and Stanley Rothman, *Watching America: What Television Tells Us About Our Lives*, Prentice-Hall, 1991, pp. 131–132, 203–204.
725. Medved, *op. cit.*, p. 221.
726. Medved, *op. cit.*, p. 222.
727. Medved, *op. cit.*, pp. 226–227.
728. Medved, *op. cit.*, pp. 227–231.

729. cf. Ernest Giglio, *Here's Looking At You: Hollywood, Film and Politics*, Peter Lang, 2nd ed. 2005.
730. Horowitz, *op. cit.*, pp. 92–95.
731. Horowitz, *op. cit.*, pp. 281–283.
732. Giles Milton, *White Gold: The Extraordinary Story of Thomas Pellow and Islam's One Million White Slaves*, Farrar, Straus & Girous, 2004.
733. Laura A. Ingraham, *Shut Up and Sing*, Regnery, 2003, p. 105.
734. This detailed study is Aaron I. Reichel, *Fahrenheit 9–12*, iUniverse, 2004.
735. Horowitz, *op. cit.*, pp. 345–347.
736. Laura A. Ingraham, *Shut Up and Sing*, Regnery, 2003, p. 87.
737. Ingraham, *op. cit.*, p. 97.
738. Horowitz, *op. cit.*, p. 85.
739. Tammy Bruce, *The New Thought Police*, Crown, 2001, pp. 203, 199.
740. Tammy Bruce, *The New Thought Police*, Crown, 2001, p. 29.
741. Medved, *op. cit.*, pp. 210–212.
742. Bernard Goldberg, 100 People Who Are Screwing Up America, HarperCollins, 2005, pp. 136–140.
743. Horowitz, *op. cit*, pp. 132–133.
744. Laura A. Ingraham, *Shut Up and Sing*, Regnery, 2003, p. 79.
745. Horowitz, *op. cit.*, pp. 194–196.
746. Horowitz, *op. cit.*, pp. 238–240.
747. Horowitz, *op. cit.*, pp. 260–262.
748. Horowitz, *op. cit.*, pp. 292–295.
749. Horowitz, *op. cit.*, pp. 315–318.

750. William McGowan, *Coloring the News: How Political Correctness Has Corrupted American Journalism*, Encounter Books, 2003, pp. 1–5.
751. McGowan, *op. cit.*, pp. 9–22.
752. McGowan, *op. cit.*, p. 23.
753. McGowan, *op. cit.*, p. 5.
754. Bernard Goldberg, *100 People Who Are Screwing Up America*, HarperCollins, 2005, pp. 296–300.
755. Jayna Davis, *The Third Terrorist: The Middle East Connection to the Oklahoma City Bombing*, WND Books, 2004.
756. Goldberg, *op. cit.* pp. 11–118.
757. Horowitz, *op. cit.*, pp. 358–364.
758. Robert H. Bork, *Slouching Toward Gomorrah*, Regan Books, 2003, p. 104.
759. Bork, *op. cit.*, p. 104.
760. Martin L. Gross, *The End of Sanity*, Avon, 1997, p. 286.
761. Gross, *op. cit.*, pp. 288–289.
762. Gross, *op. cit.*, pp. 289–290.
763. Bork, *op. cit.*, p. 109.
764. Martin L. Gross, *The End of Sanity*, Avon, 1997, p. 286.
765. Daniel Farber & Suzanna Sherry, *Beyond All Reason: The Radical Assault on Truth in American Law*, Oxford University Press, 1997.
766. Farber & Sherry, *op. cit.* p. 37.
767. Farber & Sherry, *op. cit.* p. 39.
768. Farber & Sherry, *op. cit.* p. 43.
769. Farber & Sherry, *op. cit.* p. 46.
770. David Horowitz, *The Professors*, Regnery, 2006, pp. 26–27.

771. Horowitz, op. cit., p. 27.
772. Horowitz, *op. cit,* p. 56.
773. Horowitz, *op. cit.*, pp. 266–270.
774. Horowitz, *op. cit.*, pp. 89–91.
775. Horowitz, *op. cit.*, pp. 96–99.
776. Horowitz, *op. cit.*, pp. 277–280.
777. Bernard Goldberg, *100 People Who Are Screwing Up America*, HarperCollins, 2005, pp. 29–34.
778. Horowitz, *op. cit,* pp. 125–127.
779. Marlin Maddoux, *Public Education Against America: the Hidden Agenda*, Whitaker House, 2006, p. 29.
780. Horowitz, *op. cit.*, pp. 66–70.
781. Bernard Goldberg, *101 People Who Are Screwing Up America*, HarperCollins, 2005, p. 37.
782. James T. Stephens, *EduCrisis!*, West Eagle Publishing, 1999, p. 98.
783. James T. Stephens, *EduCrisis!*, West Eagle Publishing, 1999, p. 101.
784. *Wall Street Journal*, April 8, 1998.
785. Jayna Davis, *The Third Terrorist: The Middle East Connection to the Oklahoma City Bombing*, WND Books, 2004.
786. Jack Cashill and James Sanders, *First Strike: TWA Flight 800 and the Attack on America*, WND Books, 2003.
787. Bernard Goldberg, *100 People Who Are Screwing Up America*, HarperCollins, 2005, p. 181.
788. Goldberg, *op. cit.*, pp. 181–182.
789. Goldberg, *op. cit.*, p. 181.
790. Goldberg, *op. cit.*, pp. 286–189.
791. Martin L. Gross, *The End of Sanity*, Avon, 1997, p. 303.

792. Gross, *op. cit.*, p. 304. And Robert H. Bork, *Slouching Towards Gomorrah*, Regan Books, 2003, p. 319.
793. Bork, *op. cit.*, pp. 99–102.
794. Bork, *op. cit.*, p. 104.
795. Thomas E. Woods, Jr., *The Politically Incorrect Guide to American History*, Regnery, 2004, pp. 22–24.
796. Joel Turtell, *Public Schools, Public Menace*, Liberty Books, 2005, p. 286.
797. Turtell, op. cit., p. 285.
798. Turtell, op. cit., p. 270.
799. For a list, see Turtell, op. cit., pp. 334–338.
800. Christopher J. Klicka, *The Right Choice: Home Schooling*, Noble Publishing, 1995, p. 132.
801. Klicka, *op. cit.*, p. 237.
802. Turtell, op. cit., pp. 332–333.
803. Turtell, op. cit., pp. 338–341.
804. Turtell, op. cit., p. 341.
805. Turtell, op. cit., pp, 343–344.
806. Turtell, op. cit., pp. 341–343.
807. Turtell, op. cit., pp. 327–332.
808. Eric Hoffer, *The True Believer*, Harper Perennial, 2004. Originally published in 1951.
809. Michael T. Klare, *Blood and Oil: The Dangers and Consequences of America's Growing Dependency on Imported Petroleum*, Henry Holt, 2004, p. 193.
810. Joe Trippi, *The Revolution Will Not Be Televised: Democracy, the Internet, and the Overthrow of Everything*, Regan Books, 2004.
811. This is found in the documentary "Africa Addio" (1966).

812. See Martin Meredith, *Our Votes, Our Guns*, Public Affairs Press, 2003; Geoff Hill, *Battle For Zimbabwe*, Struik, 2005; Ian D. Smith, *Bitter Harvest*, John Blake Publishers, 2001.

813. Thomas W. Chittum, *Civil War Two: The Coming Breakup Of America*, American Eagle Publications, 1996.

814. Brigitte Gabriel, *Because They Hate: A Survivor of Islamic Terror Warns America*, St. Martin's Press, 2006.

815. Thomas W. Chittum, *Civil War II: The Coming Breakup of America*, American Eagle Publications, 1996, pp. 56–57, 62–63.

816. Robert Spencer, ed., *The Myth of Islamic Tolerance: How Islamic Law Treats Non-Muslims*, Prometheus Books, 2005.

817. Bernard Lewis, *Race and Slavery in the Middle East*, Oxford University Press, 1992.

818. "Slave Trade in the World Today".

819. Giles Milton, *White Gold: TheExtraordinaryStory of Thomas Pellow and Islam's One Million White Slaves*, Farrar, Straus and Giroux, 2005. See also Robert C. Davis, *Christian Slaves, Muslim Masters, White Slavery in the Mediterranean 1500–1800*, Palgrave Macmillan, 2004.

820. See www.HumanTrafficking.org

821. Jon E. Dougherty, *Illegals: the Imminent Threat Posed by our Unsecured U.S.-Mexico Border*, WND Books, 2004, p. 57.

822. Joseph A. Ruffini, *When Terror Comes to Main Street: A Citizen's Guide to Terror Awareness, Preparedness, and Prevention*. Archangel Group, 2006. See also, Armando Bevelacaqua and Richard Stilp, *A Citizen's Guide to Terrorism Preparedness*, Thomson Delmar, 2002.

823. Robert Spencer, ed., *The Myth of Islamic Tolerance: How Islamic Law Treats Non-Muslims*, Prometheus Books, 2005.

978-0-595-43524-1
0-595-43524-6

Made in the USA
Lexington, KY
01 May 2013